LEAVING DUBLIN

Leaving Dublin

Writing My Way from Ireland to Canada

Brian Brennan

RMB
Victoria Vancouver Calgary

Rocky Mountain Books
www.rmbooks.com

Library and Archives Canada Cataloguing in Publication

Brennan, Brian, 1943-
Leaving Dublin : writing my way from Ireland to Canada / Brian Brennan.

Issued also in electronic format.
ISBN 978-1-926855-74-5

1. Brennan, Brian, 1943-. 2. Journalists—Canada—Biography. 3. Authors,
Canadian (English)—20th century—Biography. 4. Irish Canadians—Biography.
5. Dublin (Ireland)—Biography. 6. Journalism—Canada. I. Title.

PN4913.B73A3 2011   070.92   C2011-903315-1

Cover photos: *News* ... © Richard Goerg
and *Old Music Sheet* © James Bowyer

Printed in Canada

This book was produced using FSC®-certified, acid-free paper,
processed chlorine free and printed with vegetable-based inks.

The author gratefully acknowledges the support of the Canada Council for the
Arts through the Alberta Creative Development Initiative Program.

Rocky Mountain Books acknowledges the financial support for its publishing
program from the Government of Canada through the Canada Book Fund (CBF)
and the Canada Council for the Arts, and from the province of British Columbia
through the British Columbia Arts Council and the Book Publishing Tax Credit.

 Canadian Heritage Patrimoine canadien Canada Council for the Arts Conseil des Arts du Canada BRITISH COLUMBIA ARTS COUNCIL

Dedicated to the memory of my parents

And it's no, nay, never, no nay never no more
Will I play the wild rover, no never no more.

– old Irish folk song

Contents

An Intermezzo with My Family

Coda

Overture

THE JOURNEY SO FAR

This is a book about a guy (me) who lived in Ireland with his parents until he was 23, came to Canada for a bit of *craic* (the popular Irish word for fun), tried his hand at different things (including playing piano in bars and reading news on the radio), and eventually found his calling as a newspaper reporter, as a chronicler of the passing parade.

Along the way, I met some very good people. I always felt that if I ever wrote an autobiography, I would pay tribute to them. This book is my attempt to do that. The subtext is a thank-you note to those who gave me love, friendship, inspiration, amusement, encouragement or even a kick in the pants whenever I needed it most.

I use the word "tribute" because, at this point in my life, it has a special resonance for me. In 1992, as you will soon read, I started writing an obituary column for the *Calgary Herald* that quickly garnered more positive reader reaction than anything else I had written during my previous 24 years as a journalist. It was called *Tribute: People Who Made a Difference*, and, for the most part, it was about people whose names had never appeared in a newspaper before.

Why did I write about unknowns? Because I thought everyone had a story to tell, and if I discovered that story, I wanted to tell it. While fondly remembered grandmothers, retired railway workers, nurses, teachers and community volunteers might have seemed irrelevant to the news-hardened editors who filled the front page with stories about the shenanigans of politicians, crooks and millionaire athletes, there was nothing irrelevant about them as far as their families and friends were concerned.

It turned out it wasn't just the families and friends who enjoyed reading about the people I wrote about in the column. Everyone I met seemed to enjoy reading about them. In essence, I was practising community weekly journalism in the pages of a big-city daily, where by the conventional standards of newspapering, my subjects had no right to be. Yet, during the seven years I wrote the column, I felt I was producing something just as compelling as the stories about gang shootings and NHL playoff games that appeared in the rest of the *Herald*.

I don't claim any special credit for making *Tribute* as popular as it was. I was merely the facilitator. The stories were already there; it was simply a matter of gathering and telling them. I am grateful for the success of the column because it paved the way for a series of books about individuals from Canada's past that I wrote after leaving the *Herald*. *Tribute* also provided me with the impetus to write this book, to tell my own story in conjunction with the stories of those who have made a difference in my life.

My stories begin in Dublin, where I had a childhood that was mostly happy, peaceful and untroubled. It had none of the poverty, misery, alcoholism or philandering that seem *de rigueur* for Irish memoirs nowadays. My youth was *Angela's Ashes* without the rain; the sunny side of the growing-up-in-Ireland experience.

That said, I cannot paint a picture of cloudless nostalgia for you, because mine was a childhood full of longing. Longing to have a smaller nose, bigger muscles and the ability to be as good at hurling and football as my more athletic classmates. Longing to feel appreciated by my father. Eventually, longing to escape. Escape to what or to where? I hadn't figured that out yet, but as I got older I felt a growing need to find *something better, someplace else.*

In 1966 I took that big step into the unknown. At age 23, I quit my job in the Irish civil service and headed for Canada. Was this to be the *something better, someplace else* for me? Indeed it was. Canada, I quickly discovered, truly was the fabled land of opportunity. There were few barriers. Once the Canadian immigration authorities opened the doors, I was home free.

In Canada, I was able to parlay my love of piano playing into a steady gig as a professional musician. I was able to use my Irish love of talking to charm my way into a job as a radio announcer. I was able to use my love of writing and storytelling to find a job as a newspaper reporter. In each of these instances all I had to do was knock on someone's door, ask for work and the job was mine.

In Ireland, things were different. There were fewer opportunities and more red tape. If you wanted to work as a professional musician, you had to join the musicians' union and satisfy a union board of examiners you could play any popular song on demand. If you wanted to work in radio, you had to earn broadcasting school certification. If you wanted to work as a print journalist, you had to prove you were proficient in shorthand and typing, and be accepted into the National Union of Journalists.

Besides, Ireland was taking me in a different direction. My destiny there was controlled by my parents, who wanted me to be a civil servant: "The best job you'll ever find in this country." In Canada, I was able to start over, to become the master of my own destiny. I came on a mission of adventure, with hope in my heart and a safety net in my back pocket. If my money ran out before I found work in Canada, I knew I still had the civil service job awaiting me back home.

I never went back home, of course, except to visit. My travels took me from Dublin to Cork, Vancouver, Toronto, Dawson City, Smithers, Prince George and, finally, Calgary. Two keyboards have been my constant travelling companions. On one I type, on the other I noodle. "Make the words sing," a *Herald* editor told me once. "Make the music speak to me," said my piano teacher in Dublin. Thus have the strands of my life intertwined. Thus have the stories unfolded.

B.B.
Calgary, 2011

Learning My

Scales in Ireland

PIANO LESSONS

My mother was pregnant again. The year was 1950. It had been five years since my younger brother Michael was born, and now my mother was eager to have a little girl in the family.

"We're going to need a car," said my father. He was getting tired of riding his three-speed Raleigh to work every day.

"We don't need a car, Jack," said my mother. "Why would we need a car? Dublin has the best bus system in the world." Nobody else on our street had a car. My mother had never driven, so a car didn't figure highly on her list of priorities.

"We could take the children to the seaside on Sundays."

"We don't need a car," my mother said. "What we need is a piano."

"Why do we need a piano, Maud?" My father was getting exasperated.

"If we're going to have a baby girl, we should have a piano for her to play."

"We don't know if it's going to be a baby girl," my father said, raising his voice. "What if it's a boy?"

"Brian has great musical talent," said my mother, employing one of her charming non sequiturs. "Remember, he used to rock his cot in time to the music on the radio when he was a baby. He has great rhythm." She didn't really know this about me, but she was determined to get that piano.

They struck a deal. If the new baby was a boy, my father could buy a car. If it was a girl, he would buy a piano.

"And it will have to be a new piano," my mother warned. "Old pianos have woodworm."

I heard this conversation without understanding a word of it. At six and a half, I didn't know anything about pregnancy. All I knew was that your mammy went to the hospital one day, stayed for a night or two and came home with a new baby. I imagined the hospital to be like a big pet shop, with babies instead of puppies and kittens.

My sister, Mary, was born in August 1950, and my father delivered on his promise. Within a week of her arrival, a shiny-new, mahogany, Danemann upright piano arrived at our front door. It was a very impressive-looking instrument. It took up an entire wall and one-quarter of the floor space in our small living room. My mother was delighted.

She promptly enrolled me in piano lessons at the downtown Municipal School of Music. Very strange the lessons seemed to me. I sat in a class with a dozen other six-year-olds, each of us banging away on a dummy piano keyboard. No musical sounds issued forth, just the clack-clack-clack of the plastic keys. Dr. O'Reilly showed us where middle C was located, how to identify the sharps and flats, and how to cup our hands correctly over the keys.

Dr. O'Reilly was the principal of the school. He took all the first-year students for himself, hoping no doubt to single out those who would become the concert pianists of tomorrow. If you got to stay in his class for a second, third and fourth year, you undoubtedly were destined for musical greatness.

The group lessons ended after a few weeks and were followed by individual instruction where we finally got to play real pianos. We followed the syllabus of the Associated Board, which meant we had to learn theory and sight-reading as well as the prescribed scales, arpeggios and exam pieces. I took the 15A bus downtown each week for the lesson and practised at home for half an hour every evening before supper.

I didn't much like the scales and arpeggios. Nor did I like the selected exam pieces, because these faux-classical tunes were all foreign to me. You never heard any of this music played on the radio. Nor did the melodies bear any resemblance to those my father sang on Saturday nights when my mother instructed him to keep watch over me at bath time. While ensuring that I washed myself, he sang the songs and I learned the words. "I'm an old cowhand from the Rio Grande." "'Twas on the Isle of Capri that I found her."

If the exam pieces had featured melodies like those my father sang, I would have been more eager to practise. I also would have rushed to the piano after school if the pieces had included some of the songs – "Mockin' Bird Hill," "Buttons and Bows," "Lavender Blue, Dilly Dilly" – that my mother's sisters, Sheila and Joan, taught me to sing when they babysat at our house. As it was, I only practised the mandatory scales and set pieces to please my mother. She was so keen to have a pianist in the house that I didn't want to disappoint her. But I did like to express myself creatively at the piano. If I had been an ice skater, I would have preferred the free skate to the compulsory figures.

I scored 93 per cent on the grade 1 examination. My mother was overjoyed. "I told you that Brian had great musical talent," she said to my father. What my parents didn't know was that every kid in the first-year class scored 90 per cent or higher. The examiners knew that pianos bought on the instalment plan would be immediately sent back to the music stores if the parents thought their children were lacking in musical talent. As a result, the examiners marked the first-year students as generously as they could. The tuition fees paid their salaries, after all.

I don't know how my father felt about my piano playing. I don't recall him saying anything to me about my score on the grade 1 exam. I suspect he would have been happier if my talents had been more of the sporting kind. He had been a keen athlete as a young man, playing field hockey interprovincially and excelling at rugby and tennis. He encouraged me to play rugby as soon as my feet were big enough to fit into a pair of studded boots. But I was awkward and uncoordinated and, as my classmates would say, kicked and threw a ball "like a *girl*." My younger brother Michael was the athlete in the family, with an ability to excel at different team sports that I could only envy. I, notwithstanding my dislike of the curriculum requirements, was much more comfortable at the piano than I was on the rugby field.

I continued on in Dr. O'Reilly's class for the second year.

The grade 2 pieces were no more appealing to me than the first-year ones had been, so I offered a proposition to my mother: I would practise my scales and pieces for 20 minutes every evening if I could "fool around" for the remaining 10. By this I meant I would spend the last part of every practice being creative, working out the chords and melodies to such popular songs as "Tennessee Waltz" and "How Much Is that Doggie in the Window?" This seemed like a reasonable arrangement to my mother, but she warned that she would only allow it to continue if I did well on the grade 2 exam.

It was around this time that I realized my mother was tone deaf. "Are you practising your pieces?" she asked one evening when I was trying to figure out the chords to "Mockin' Bird Hill."

"Yes, Mammy, I am."

"Cross your heart and hope to die?" If you crossed your heart and died after you told a lie, you would go straight to hell.

"Cross my heart," I said, crossing the fingers of my left hand behind my back to remove the curse.

"Cross your heart and hope to die?"

"Cross my heart and hope to die," I said resignedly. I wondered if I could get to confession to tell the priest before God had me burning in hellfire for all eternity.

"You better be practising your pieces, because your father and I don't want to be wasting money on all those piano lessons."

"Yes, Mammy."

It bothered me that I had to lie about it, but now I was home free. I could play pop songs to my heart's content, and my mother would never know the difference. As long as I played a few scales and arpeggios at the beginning, I could spend the rest of the practice working on my non-classical repertoire. I had visions of taking over the spot on the radio occupied by Charlie Kunz, then the most popular pianist in the British Isles. One of his tunes was called "Clap Hands, Here Comes Charlie." When I got my own program, the song would be called "Clap Hands, Here Comes *Brian*."

I didn't do particularly well in the grade 2 exam. No surprise there; I had been fooling around when I should have been woodshedding. "The pieces were *really* hard, Mammy. You know I practised and practised."

"Yes, child, I know you did your best." She nodded sympathetically. "You'll do better next year, won't you?" She was determined not to send the piano back just yet.

By this time, Dr. O'Reilly had clearly decided I would never become a concert pianist. Far from being a budding prodigy, I was little more than a plodder. He turned me over to an underling – a female piano teacher who wore a big hat and smeary lipstick and who left smudges of red nail-polish trailing across the pages of my music book like streaks of fresh blood. Her teaching method was to rap me on the knuckles with a wooden ruler whenever I hit a wrong note. If I asked her to demonstrate how a tricky passage should be played, she refused. "Play it yourself, that's why your parents are sending you to piano lessons." Dr. O'Reilly had been much more helpful. He could sight-read on demand and often showed me the way when I was struggling. Mrs. Big Hat was no help at all. I soon became convinced she didn't actually know how to play the piano.

I blew my opportunity for a shot at musical glory during my fourth—and, as it turned out, last—year at the Municipal. Mrs. Big Hat chose me to be one of the featured live performers on a Radio Éireann afternoon program called *Children at the Microphone*. She said I would receive 15 shillings for my performance. That was about the equivalent of seven months' pocket money, a *brilliant* return for just five minutes of performing. I practised for weeks— a sonatina by Kuhlau—convinced myself I had the piece down pat and then suffered the indignity of seeing my fingers turn to spaghetti when the red light came on in the studio. The money, however, allowed me to forget the disaster. I used it to buy a battery-operated plastic slide projector.

My tone-deaf mother, bless her heart, had nothing but praise for my performance. I think my father was pleased too, though I can't recall him actually saying anything. I spent the evening amusing my brother Michael, happily projecting comic-strip images of Dan Dare, Pilot of the Future, onto the dining-room wall.

The radio engagement was one of three public performances I gave that year. The others were similarly disastrous. Self-consciousness and nervousness took over whenever I tried to do in public what I did effortlessly in practice. The annual recital at the Municipal School amounted to little more than an exercise in public humiliation for me. I watched with envy and dismay as the other pianists confidently breezed through their pieces. *How can they be so good and I so awful?* The same thing happened at the Feis Ceoil music festival. I was pitted against a group of fellow competitors who could all play like junior Paderewskis. "Technique needs work," the adjudicator wrote on my evaluation form.

My mother removed me from the Municipal, where she could see I was growing increasingly unhappy, and sent me to study with a neighbourhood music teacher named Mrs. McQuaid. After hearing me play one of the easier pieces from the grade 4 syllabus, Mrs. McQuaid declared that I was a "brilliant" pianist. I knew she was exaggerating, of course, but it was a nice boost to the morale after a year of being rapped on the knuckles.

Mrs. McQuaid was like a professional sports coach, encouraging and demanding. "Make the music speak to me," she said. She pushed me to perform challenging pieces that she felt sure I could master. I didn't share her confidence, but I worked hard to please her. Within a couple of months, I could play Chopin's "Minute Waltz" without hitting a wrong note.

In what turned out to be an exercise in poor judgment on her part, Mrs. McQuaid then pushed me into performing as a singer and actor. When my school hired her as a freelance director to stage a production of Gilbert and Sullivan's *The Pirates of Penzance* for the annual Christmas show, Mrs. McQuaid gave me the best comedy part in the opera: the role of the patter-singing Major-General Stanley. But I couldn't handle the tongue-tripping demands of the lyrics, much less develop an effective comic persona for the character. After I had struggled through a few rehearsals, she took me out of my misery by offering me the less challenging role of the Pirate King's lieutenant, Samuel. It was an honourable withdrawal for both of us.

My piano playing grew from strength to strength under Mrs. McQuaid's tutelage. When I turned 14, my mother decided I should put my talents to practical use. She called Father Rogers aside after Mass and said he should consider me for the position of organist at Mount Merrion Church. "His teacher says he's a brilliant pianist, you know."

Father Rogers said he would be happy to let me try out for the position. The regular organist at Mount Merrion, Philip Browne, was leaving to complete his university studies in England. He invited me to play a piece on the church instrument, which was actually a bellows-driven harmonium – not the conventional church organ with pipes, foot pedals and multiple keyboards. It looked like an upright piano, and I tried to play it like a piano, stumbling clumsily through the first few bars of the "Minute Waltz" before my fingers failed me. Browne smiled and explained that staccato playing didn't work very well on the harmonium because of the absence of a sustain pedal. He explained to me that I would have to practise the technique of holding one finger on the keyboard at all times, like an Olympic race walker keeping one foot in contact with the ground.

It didn't take me long to learn the proper technique. Father Rogers offered me the organist's job, and my mother offered a novena to St. Cecilia, the patron saint of music. The job didn't come with a salary attached, but it did bring other benefits. I became the envy of classmates at my boys-only secondary school when I told them the choir consisted of a dozen 13-year-old schoolgirls and that at least four were in love with me. I had the letters and the Valentine cards to prove it. On Sundays, the girls performed with their fathers and older brothers singing "Kyrie eleison" and "Ave verum corpus" at High Mass. On weeknights, during Benediction services, I had them all to myself.

One of the four gave me a lock of her long red hair and agreed to let me take her home from the evening devotions on the crossbar of my bicycle. We never so much as kissed. We were both painfully shy. It was the first flowering of romance, with all the joy and pain and longing. We kept in touch for a while by letter, two years later, after my father received a promotion and moved our family to Cork. But the correspondence ended abruptly after she wrote that I was a "goose" for thinking I might be in love with her. She was probably right. What did a 16-year-old virgin boy know about love?

Playing the church harmonium helped build my confidence after the nerve-racking experience of playing at recitals and festivals where the other players put me to shame. Without the competition, I blossomed. I didn't attain the level of a young Mozart, but I did manage to work up respectable renditions of the keyboard accompaniments to such liturgical favourites as the "Hallelujah Chorus" and "Jesu, Joy of Man's Desiring."

By the time I got to Cork in 1960, I had developed my level of playing to the point where I was good enough to be chosen as the band pianist for my secondary school's production of *The Mikado*. Every other musician in the band was a parent or adult sibling of a youngster in the cast. I was the only student. I felt pretty special. The days of feeling inadequate were behind me. I expected that when I got to university, a year later, I would be paying for my studies with the money I earned playing piano in the pubs.

With a teaching certificate from the London College of Music – which I earned when I was just 16 years old – I could probably have cobbled together a living in the music business, teaching during the day and playing piano in the pubs at night. But I had no appetite for teaching – I viewed the certificate as more of a performance qualification than an education licence – and the best I could expect from the pub playing was a few pounds for each gig. That's how it was for even the most successful entertainers in Ireland during the 1960s. Most of them worked during the day as bus conductors, shop assistants or car-park attendants because there wasn't enough money in performing to sustain them.

As it turned out, I didn't attend university full time after graduating from secondary school in 1961. With the encouragement of my father, who could not afford the university fees, I joined the civil service in Dublin and found a nice balance between working for the Revenue Commissioners as a customs and excise officer, taking evening classes at University College Dublin, and playing music in the pubs. But even with the odds stacked against me, I longed to be in show business full time. I entered talent contests and won a competition that brought me two good opportunities for exposure: a guest television appearance on Gay Byrne's widely watched *Late Late Show* and a featured role in a variety show at Dublin's Olympia Theatre. This, however, was back in the days before victories in nationally televised talent shows resulted in big money, worldwide publicity on YouTube and instant fame. My little starlight soon flickered out, and I was back to wondering if I would ever be able to give up my day job to live my dream.

BOYS WILL BE BOYS

I was in the fifth grade at Oatlands College primary school and I wanted to become a Christian Brother. A recruiter for the religious fraternity came to the school and told us how worthwhile it would be for us to give the gift of education and the love of God to little children. He convinced me I should sign up. I went home and told my mother. "You can tell your father about it when he gets home," she said.

My father was always home on Friday night. That's when my mother went to the Mount Merrion church hall to play bridge and he stayed home to look after me and my younger siblings, Michael, Mary and John. We never saw him on Monday to Thursday nights because he was usually working overtime. He needed the extra cash because he was the only breadwinner, and his regular salary as a tax officer with the Revenue Commissioners didn't cover all the expenses involved in supporting a wife and four children.

"So you want to be a Christian Brother," he said. "Why do you want to be a Christian Brother?"

"Because the Brother came to the school and told us about it. I think I have a vocation."

"What if it hadn't been a Brother who came to your school? What if it had been a general in the army who came and told you how exciting it would be to be shooting guns and driving tanks? Would you then want to join the army?"

"I don't know. Maybe."

"You should think about this for a while, son. If you really want to become a Brother, you should make the decision when you're older. You're only 11. You still have plenty of time to think about these things."

"But the Brother said we would go to a special boarding school, for training."

"You would go to a special school in the army as well. Why don't we talk about this again next week, maybe. You'll probably have forgotten all about it by then."

Needless to say, my father was right. I quickly forgot about the recruiter, and the Christian Brothers lost a potential postulant.

My father didn't have much time for the Christian Brothers. When he was in his 70s, he often mentioned a particularly ignorant Brother who had taken the strap to him as a child for allegedly writing obscenities in a girl's autograph book. The "obscenities" turned out to be a quotation from Byron's "She Walks in Beauty." *All that's best of dark and bright / Meet in her aspect and her eyes.* My father could quote the poem in its entirety. He could quote many poems in their entirety. *In Xanadu did Kubla Khan / A stately pleasure dome decree.* He inherited his love of poetry from his paternal grandmother, a schoolteacher who gave him his first English lessons and encouraged him to increase his vocabulary by learning a new word every week. At age 14, my father was the only boy in his class with a subscription to *John O'London's Weekly*, a popular literary periodical. He was also the only boy who read poetry for pleasure.

When I was in my 20s and working full time as a newspaper reporter, my father confided that he wished he too could have spent his life in a literary setting, reading and writing for a living. His ideal job, had he been able to afford college, would have been that of professor of English at a small university somewhere in England. "But I had to make a living, Brian," he said. "I didn't have the money for university. Once I got a job in the civil service, I was stuck."

He satisfied his literary aspirations by producing a monthly newsletter for the tax officers' staff association, and by writing in his journal short reviews of the hardcover books he received every month from the Readers' Union Book Club. He signed the reviews as Patrick J. Brennan, the formal name he put on his cheques and official correspondence. To friends and family he was Jack Brennan. He wrote the reviews primarily as a reminder of what the books were about, because the ochre-coloured Readers' Union dust jackets didn't provide any information. I'm inclined to believe he wrote the reviews with the intention that only he should read them afterwards. My mother would not have been interested. Her taste in literature extended only to the mysteries of Ellery Queen and Agatha Christie. She borrowed great heaps of their titles from the library every week, not because she had a particular love of reading, but because she needed them as sleeping pills. One hour of Ellery Queen before she went to bed and Mammy would sleep like a baby until Daddy got up for his early-morning shave.

I did get to sneak the occasional illicit peek at my father's reviews because he sometimes forgot to take his journal upstairs and left it on the sitting-room bookcase next to the book he was reviewing. Or did he leave the journal there intentionally? I think perhaps not. The books were written for adults, and my father would not have wanted his children to be reading his reviews. So it was with a sense of guilty pleasure that I occasionally tasted this forbidden fruit. I would never have been tempted to take a sip from the half-empty bottle of Paddy Old Irish Whiskey that sat on our sideboard next to the glass soda siphon, ready for pouring when company arrived. But I couldn't resist the temptation to read what my father was writing in his journal.

I recall that the reviews were an absorbing mixture of trenchant commentary and common-sense observation. In his review of Hemingway's *A Farewell to Arms*, for example, Dad wrote that the "small talk between the lovers is daft." I could just see my father bristling as he wrote those words. No need for convoluted sentence structure here. If Hemingway's chat didn't ring true to the ears of Jack Brennan, an Irishman who knew a thing or two about casual conversation, then he wanted to record that fact in his journal – the repository of his written beliefs and opinions.

Writing book reviews must have been a great source of release for my father, because he loved to vent. When he held court at the dinner table on Saturday and Sunday evenings he often got rid of pent-up anger by expounding on the failings of the government, or railing against Gay Byrne ("it doesn't take any talent to talk on the radio"), or denouncing farm subsidies, or deploring the proliferation of what he called "jungle music" on Radio Éireann.

Where did the anger come from? *Why are you so mad, Daddy?* As kids we never asked that question because our role was to be seen and not heard. I suspect now it may have had something to do with the frustrations of his job. While his colleagues were being promoted, Dad stayed where he was, at the same entry-level grade of clerical officer that he had attained when he first joined the civil service at age 17. He rode his bicycle to work and listened to the radio when his colleagues were buying cars and gramophones.

The promotions didn't start coming to him until he was into his 50s. When he asked why they had taken so long, a senior colleague told him it had to do with the time he had spent serving as general secretary of the tax officers' association – the in-house staff union. "They always thought you were a bit of a Red, Brennan." By odd coincidence, the publisher of the *Prince George Citizen* said exactly the same thing about me many years later, after I had left the paper to come to Calgary. When told I was the one who had redrafted the newsroom contract to bring it more into line with the contracts at the *Vancouver Sun* and the New Westminster *Columbian*, *Citizen* publisher John Evans said, "I always thought Brennan was a bit of a Red." Like father, like son.

The Irish civil service was the biggest employer in the

country. It provided work for thousands of young men and women, including both of my parents and several of their siblings, who flocked into the capital city of Dublin from the rural towns and villages. My father, who came from the garrison town of Naas, County Kildare, joined the service in 1934 when the British government was still in the process of handing over administration to the new Irish government. Dad told me he chose to work for the Irish service rather than the British because the Irish government offered higher salaries. Before he gave me this explanation, I used to tell myself that Dad had probably chosen the Irish civil service for nationalistic reasons. But my father was a pragmatist, not a nationalist. If the British civil service had offered more money, Jack Brennan would have taken the boat over to London and spent the rest of his life there.

He met my mother at a civil service staff picnic in 1942, when both were working for the Revenue Commissioners. She was a 27-year-old farmer's daughter from Ballyvourney, County Cork. He was 25. He didn't know about the age difference then. My mother never revealed her age. I only know her birth date now because I did some genealogical sleuthing after her death in 1977 at age 62. As children, whenever we asked her how old she was, my mother always coyly replied, "Over twenty-one."

Why the secrecy? Because, I believe, the women of my mother's generation, especially the rural women, had a profound fear of growing old and eventually being considered useless. My mother used to tell me about men she had known in West Cork – bachelor farmers in their 40s and 50s – who packed their mothers off to old folks' homes as soon as they found wives to replace them as housekeepers. They didn't marry for love; they married for the catering. Age, infirmity and a diminishing of housekeeping skills made their mothers liabilities. If the women could no longer cook and clean, they had to be moved to places where others could look after them. A man, by contrast, could grow old and frail, continue to live at home with his children, and never have to worry about being tossed out for lack of self-sufficiency. But a woman had to maintain her cooking and cleaning skills or face eviction from her own home.

Under the circumstances, it's perhaps not surprising that my mother kept her age so secret that she didn't reveal it to Jack even after they were married. If she didn't tell her age, it seems, she would stay forever young. At the time of her death from cancer in 1977, Dad still didn't know how old she was, so he put no date of birth on her tombstone. *Didn't he look for a birth certificate?* He guessed she might have been a few years older than him, but it seems they never actually discussed the subject.

At the time they met, Dad said, "I had more interest in sports than in girls." Maud, however, seems to have turned his head. Although she attended the staff outing with another man, she gave Jack the impression she would not object to a phone call from him. He called her a few days later, and she agreed to go out with him.

They married in Cork in September 1942 and made their first home in a small cold-water flat at 46 Grosvenor Square in the Dublin neighbourhood of Rathmines. I don't remember anything about that flat, which was my home too for the first couple of years after I was born. I have a better memory of our second home, a rented, three-bedroom, two-storey row house at 3 Grosvenor Villas, Rathgar. There were five other houses on that street, a short cul-de-sac that ran between the Ashbrook Lawn Tennis Club and the large backyard of a three-storey mansion on Grosvenor Road. I was surprised and delighted recently to see a "street view" of the location on Google Maps. It looks exactly as I remember it.

The children of the well-heeled families who lived on Grosvenor Road referred dismissively to our little street as "the lane," while we responded, equally dismissively, that we had free spectator access to a summertime neighbourhood sport that they could never enjoy: tennis. From our front bedroom windows, we could spend the long evenings after bedtime watching the tennis players in their immaculately laundered whites, serving, volleying and smashing under the court floodlights. We could also play soccer on our street, which the Grosvenor Road kids were unable to do because of the traffic. All we had to do was pile our coats and sweaters onto the road and designate them as goals. We could then kick ball from morning until night without ever having to worry about a passing cyclist, much less a motorist, interrupting our game.

The most unforgettable sounds I remember from Grosvenor Villas, aside from the nightly *whap* of racket against tennis ball, are of air-raid sirens and bombs. A Second World War curfew in Britain prevented German pilots from seeing London at night, so they often overflew the target and bombed neutral Southern Ireland instead. The Dublin Municipal Corporation never bothered to repair the damage done to the city; it just put hoardings around the rubble. Years afterwards, when filmmakers were looking for a location that looked like Berlin after the Allies' bombing campaign, Dublin was their preferred choice.

Our house was quite tiny, with linoleum on the floors, postage-stamp yards front and back, and no access to the outside rear except through the house. Whenever we had a coal delivery, my mother had to put down newspapers to protect her polished floors from the heavy boots of the grimy men with sacks. (The Irish don't subscribe to the Canadian custom of shedding footwear at the front door.) Coal was our only heating fuel. With no central heating in the house, we burned coal in the kitchen and dining room fireplaces to stay warm. We kept a winter's supply of it in a storage bin outside at the back and brought in scuttles of it daily to feed the fires. When coal was rationed during the Second World War, we lived like igloo dwellers. The fires remained unlit, and we wore coats, mittens and leggings in the house. Chilblains on the toes, brought on by sleeping in damp cold beds, were a recurring problem.

As well as the coal deliveries, we had regular shipments of milk and bread. The milk came in glass bottles, six at a time. You put out the empty bottles on the doorstep at night and woke up in the morning to find the full ones sitting next to that day's *Irish Independent*. The bread, from the Johnston Mooney & O'Brien Bakery, came later in the morning, in a battery-run van that hummed through the neighbourhood like a swarm of bees. I still remember the words of the radio jingle: *"Johnston, uh uh, Mooney and O'Bri-en make the best bread, uh uh, bread you can rely on."* The van carried only white bread. My mother baked brown soda bread, but none of us ever wanted to eat it because the crumbling slices caught in our throats.

We bought the rest of our groceries from the shops on the nearby Rathgar Road: butter and eggs from the Monument Creameries; round steak, mutton and lamb chops from the victuallers; potatoes, turnips, carrots and cabbage from the greengrocer. That was one of my daily errands, or "messages" as we called them in Dublin: to take my mother's list of grocery items to the shops, write down what each item cost and bring home the correct change.

Breakfast consisted of porridge and milk until we discovered the sugary delights of Kellogg's Cornflakes and Rice Krispies. We never had the mixed-grill Irish breakfast of tourist brochure fame. The standard midday meal, the main meal of the day, was a tasteless combination of stewed mutton or round steak, boiled potatoes, pearl barley – which we children referred to scornfully as "the slippy things" – carrots and mushy turnips. At least, the dinner always seemed tasteless to me because I was born without a sense of smell and can only differentiate between sweet and sour, between sugary and salty. If it wasn't stew, it was broiled lamb chops and cabbage, or bangers (pork sausages) and mash (potatoes). On meatless Fridays, so designated by the Catholic Church, we had boiled plaice (flatfish), which to me was the most tasteless meal of all – like communion wafers with bones. My mother, bless her heart, had no imagination when it came to finding an alternative to meat.

She did much better, according to my palate, in the evenings when she put away the pressure cooker, took out the pan and served up a delightfully greasy and salty combination of fried eggs, sausages, black (blood) pudding and tomatoes. Flavour before nutrition – that's been my motto ever since. If my mother made scones, she would put raisins in them, and we would eat them for dessert with jam and butter. Or we might have semolina, a kind of sweet, watery pudding with a dollop of jam on top. Other favourite desserts included meringues, apple tart, bread pudding, rice pudding and (in the summer) jelly with custard.

The menu always changed for special occasions. On Christmas Day, the potatoes were peeled and roasted instead of boiled, and served with the turkey and stuffing. Christmas dessert consisted of plum pudding and fruitcake with icing. My father had a little ritual that he did every year with the plum pudding. He would pour a tablespoon of Paddy Old Irish Whiskey over it, light a match, watch the blue flame envelop the pudding and declare, "Good whiskey!" Shrove Tuesday brought pancakes, both sweet and savoury. On Halloween, the big treat from Johnston Mooney & O'Brien was barm brack, a kind of currant loaf with a cheap, gold-coloured metal ring cooked into the dough. Whoever found the ring, so tradition decreed, would be the first of the children to marry. It was a fate the four of us regarded as worse than death.

We never had to bring lunches to school, because my mother was always at home to do the cooking. Nor did we ever go out as a family to a restaurant, although I did get to eat out by myself once a week when I went downtown for my piano lesson. When the lesson was over, I went for my evening meal to a small, four-table café behind Clerys department store on O'Connell Street. It had only one dish on the menu – usually, an uninspired "meat and two veg" offering – and the food was only slightly better than the tasteless fare that came out of my mother's pressure cooker.

My mother was a reluctant homemaker. She had been forced to give up her civil service job after marriage because of a discriminatory government regulation – since revoked – forbidding married females to hold state jobs. A married woman's place, according to the antediluvian Irish labour laws that remained on the books until the 1970s, was in the home looking after the domestic needs of husband and children.

Sociologists have often characterized Ireland as a matriarchal society, possibly because the female poets of Celtic times were the aristocrats of ancient Gaelic society, and because the romantic writers of the 19th century used to refer to it as "Mother Ireland." However, there was no evidence of this matriarchal dominance in the Ireland of the 1950s. If women had any real power or influence, my mother would have resumed her career as a civil servant after her children reached school age. As it turned out, she eventually re-entered the work force as a substitute elementary school teacher in her mid-50s. But that was hardly a sign that Ireland had grown more progressive in the meantime. The Catholic Church was still a dominating force, and the men who treated women as second-class citizens (though they loved their wives and mothers) were still the leaders of government and industry.

When my daughter Nicole spent a year in Ireland in the early 1990s – getting in touch with her Irish roots, as the genealogy aficionados used to call it –she found that most of her Irish contemporaries, females in their early twenties, were focused more on finding husbands than finding good jobs. Like Canadian girls in the 1950s, they were raised to believe that the ultimate destiny for a young woman was to marry and marry well.

Did my mother marry well? In the eyes of her parents, siblings and friends, she probably did. Jack had a steady job in the civil service, with good opportunities for future advancement. He didn't have a drinking problem – his only indulgence was a heavy smoking habit, 40 cigarettes a day, which he didn't kick until he was in his late 40s – and he worked hard to provide for his family. He put all four children through secondary school at a time when post-elementary education in Ireland was an expensive drain on a middle-class family's resources, and he covered all our medical and dental bills at a time when there was no national health service or private health insurance system available.

Yet, I got the sense there was not much warmth in my parents' marriage. It may have been due to the atmosphere of self-restraint that prevailed in Holy Catholic Ireland in those days, but I don't recall them ever hugging or kissing, holding hands or exchanging terms of endearment. Nor did they do things together outside the home. My mother had her bridge night once a week, and my father went to the movies by himself. Later on, he took up golf and became a member of the Bray Golf Club, half an hour's drive from our house, in County Wicklow. But he never invited my mother or us children to accompany him to the club, even though it welcomed spouses and kids.

My Uncle Andy Desmond, by contrast, had his entire family involved in golf. His wife, Sheila, my mother's younger sister, played golf with him, as did their four children as soon as they were old enough to pick up a putter. Through golf, Andy told them, a person learned about patience, teamwork, competitive drive and other attributes that helped one overcome life's challenges. The Desmonds' backyard was a three-hole putting green, and Corballis Golf Club was their home away from home. My father, for whatever reason, chose to keep golf as his own special preserve. Perhaps he just needed to get away.

As I look back on it, my parents' was an oddly formal kind of relationship. At home they addressed one another as Maud and Jack, but when talking to outsiders she always referred to him as "my husband" and he to her as "Mrs. Brennan." I recall that when I was about 11 I accompanied my father to the Stillorgan branch of the EBS Building Society, where he was applying for a loan to cover the expense of putting carpet in the living room. The loans officer asked about collateral, specifically about the assets belonging to my mother. "Mrs. Brennan has no assets," said my father with barely concealed indignation. "She's my wife." In his mind, Maud was little more than a chattel, a kept woman in the Victorian sense.

I don't think my mother thought of herself as a chattel, however. More likely, she would have viewed herself as an equal partner in the firm of Brennan & Brennan. She managed the household budget while he earned the daily bread. She made the key spending decisions for such big-ticket items as piano, house or car. Imbued with a desire for social and cultural advancement – hence the bridge games for her and the piano lessons for her children – she seemed to believe that in some manner she had *graduated* from rural West Cork and moved on to a place where better things were possible. Her goal, therefore, was to attain a measure of middle-class respectability for herself and her family in suburban Dublin.

For my mother and father, the key to future success for us children was a good education. Their parents and grandparents had passed this message down to them. Education should be the most important thing in your life, my parents were told. My father's mother, like his paternal grandmother, was a schoolteacher, so he had the benefits of home-schooling long before he started regular school. My mother too was a beneficiary of home-schooling. Her paternal grandmother, Mary Twomey, was a folklorist and traditional storyteller who lived on the farm with her son, Michael (Michilín) – my maternal grandfather – and recommended books for her grandchildren to read. She then asked questions to see how well they retained what they had read. My mother's task, at age nine, was to tell her grandmother how much she could remember of Dickens's *A Tale of Two Cities*.

Michilín regretted the fact that his formal education had to end at age 12 because there was no high school in Ballyvourney and he was needed at home to work on the farm. But he continued to educate himself by reading the encyclopedia and studying farm journals. "Education can never be taken away from you," he told his children. "It is easier to work with the pen than with the spade."

My own education began at age six when my parents sent me to St. Anne's, a small private elementary institution in Terenure, a neighbourhood located about 20 minutes' walk from our house in Rathgar. The school was quartered in a three-storey Edwardian house. It had a large gloomy backyard with spooky overhanging branches where the students could play at being ghosts and goblins during recess. It was operated by four single women: Miss Cassie, Miss Frances, Miss MacDonald and her older sister, known as "old Miss MacDonald." From them I quickly learned to read. At age seven my standard party piece was to read aloud sections of the newspaper for friends of my mother who dropped in for afternoon tea. I never acquired the same proficiency in mathematics, however. Arithmetic always caused a mental block for me. It still does.

I have fond memories of St. Anne's. The classes were small and the teachers were like doting maiden aunts. Corporal punishment – common in other Irish schools in those days – was non-existent. For three years I never felt the sting of cane or strap. Neither did my brother Michael, who started at the school two years after I did. That changed when I transferred to St. Mary's College, Rathmines, at age nine. This was a private, Dotheboys Hall–type, boys-only institution where dirty fingernails and untied shoelaces were grounds for a trip to the dean's office and what used to be sadistically termed "six of the best."

The Holy Ghost Fathers – a teaching and missionary order now more commonly known as the Spiritans – ran St. Mary's in the first instance as a laboratory for experiments with the cane. Their secondary mission – like that of the Christian Brothers – was to convince the more impressionable boys that they had vocations for the priesthood. The Fathers taught religion three times a day, offered Mass every morning in the school chapel and heard our confessions once a week.

I never had much to confess. It was always the same old litany of lies, disobedience and being mean to my younger siblings. One week, I decided to become a little more adventurous with my sin revelations. I perused the list of prohibited acts in the catechism and told the priest – without knowing what I was actually confessing – that I had committed adultery half a dozen times. I was nine at the time. The priest stifled a gasp, said I had perpetrated a grievous mortal sin and gave me two dozen rosaries for my penance. I suspect his mother had neglected to tell him the facts of life before he embraced his vow of chastity.

On Friday afternoons, the priests at St. Mary's commanded the boys to attend the devotional service of Benediction and take turns at being altar servers. I served just once. A minor accident with the thurible gave the priest reason to banish me to the back pews and cane me afterwards.

I, as the tallest altar boy, had been given the job of standing behind the priest, swinging the smoking thurible back and forth on its chains, and opening and closing the container whenever the priest turned around to add more incense to the embers. Everything ran smoothly until I somehow managed to snag the tail of the priest's outer vestment in the container while I was trying to close it. Unaware of the problem, the priest knelt, facing away from me, with head bowed, praying on the altar steps. I watched with a mixture of horror and fascination as the garment began to smoulder. Giggling boys in the front row gave me away. The priest turned around, frantically pulled his vestment out of the burning incense and dismissed me from the altar. The congregation laughed, I grinned sheepishly and took an imaginary bow. Thus vanished any possibility that the Fathers might earmark me as a future candidate for priesthood. I had launched my career as an entertainer.

COMING OF AGE

"It's time we found you a summer job," said my mother, pointing to the classified ads in the *Evening Mail*. "Here's one that says they need waiters, waitresses, cooks, housekeeping staff, shop assistants and other staff at Red Island. You should apply."

I was in my second-last year of secondary school at Oatlands College. Though a middling student with unexceptional grades in history, algebra, trigonometry, Latin, French and chemistry, I had never been asked by my parents to take any tutoring or summer refresher courses. Hence my mother's desire to get me out of the house and keep me busy in other ways.

I looked at the Red Island ad. "But you have to be 18, Mammy." I was four months shy of my 17th birthday.

"You're tall," she said. "You'll pass for 18."

My mother, bless her, was stage-managing my life again. She had done it six years earlier when she told Mr. Mackey, the man who owned the newsagent's shop on Kilmacud Road, that I should be given a paper route because I was a 10-year-old with the maturity of a 12-year-old. She did it again when I was 13, first getting me a summer job washing dishes by hand at the Salthill Hotel in Monkstown, and then – when I quit that job after one unhappy day trying to keep up with the endless flow of dirty plates and cutlery – getting me a job as a caddy at Elm Park Golf Club. The following year, when I was 14, she got me the job as church organist in Mount Merrion. I should have made her my agent for life.

I got the Red Island job, thanks to my mother's help with the application form, and the coaching she gave me for the interview. "Make sure to smile," she said. "And take off your cap." I would spend the summer working as a lounge waiter at this holiday camp in Skerries, a small seaside town in North County Dublin, about a two-hour bus ride from our home in Mount Merrion.

Red Island was an all-inclusive resort – a kind of Club Med for the working class – modelled after the popular Butlins Holiday Camps in England. The guests came for a week or two of dining, dancing, miniature golf, talent shows, fancy-dress balls and sunbathing on the rocky beach nearby. They never left the site. Red Island provided them with all their meals and entertainment. Whatever attractions the rest of Skerries had to offer were never seen by the Red Island guests.

"You'll write every week, won't you?" said my mother as I boarded the bus for Skerries. It was to be my first time living away from home. The childhood summers of socializing with my pals, bowling my hoop around the neighbourhood and playing pickup soccer on the street were now behind me. I felt as if I was moving to another country, where the only communication with friends and family would be by mail.

My job entailed greeting the guests when they arrived by tour bus on a Saturday afternoon, carrying their bags to the rooms, serving them drinks and waving them goodbye when they left on the bus the following Saturday morning. The wages were low – £2.50 a week, paid to us in cash – but the tips tripled that amount. The shifting arrangement seemed most peculiar to me. It called for us to work for 24 hours straight with a six-hour break for sleep, and then to be off for 24 hours when we could enjoy all the amenities of the camp. My workday began at noon, when I restocked the bar with bottles and kegs from the warehouse. The shift continued through the afternoon and evening, when I served drinks in the bar, sun lounge and dining room, and ended at midnight, when I took my last order. I then slept for six hours in the stone Martello tower on the property that was used for staff accommodation. I was up again at 6:00 a.m. to spend the morning in the bar clearing out the empties from the night before.

Red Island was the kind of place to which my mother would never have sent me if she had known how red-blooded young men and women carry on when they work and live together. Or perhaps she *did* know and thought the experience would be good for me. It was indeed an eye-opening experience for a 16-year-old. Older male colleagues – who could not have been much more than 19 – told me where you could go in Skerries to buy condoms under the counter. Contraceptives were illegal in Holy Catholic Ireland then. They also told me which of the female staff members were amenable to seduction.

This was all a bit shocking to me, but I did take a tentative step in the direction of young adulthood by forming an innocent romantic attachment with the pretty 17-year-old who worked in the camp's souvenir shop. She too must have lied about her age when she applied for the Red Island job. We sat on the beach under the stars chatting and necking, hesitantly and awkwardly, on the nights when I was not serving drinks. Her convent-sheltered upbringing and my own upbringing of limited social contact with girls had us relating to one another as if we were appearing in a musical comedy by Rodgers and Hammerstein. The Catholic education system in Ireland had been designed, with the approval of parents, to keep the sexes apart until the end of high school. After that we could interact socially but were expected to suppress our sexual urges until marriage.

My romance with Miss Souvenir Shop ended when I left Red Island. After that I moved to Cork to rejoin my parents and siblings. The reunion with my father in Cork was marred when a pickpocket stole my wallet from my back pocket while I was standing on the Dublin railway platform waiting to board. To the thief's undoubted delight, I had squeezed all the cash I saved from Red Island into my wallet (I was too young to have a bank account). My father was not happy to learn he would now have to cover my bus fares, coffee breaks and other incidental day-to-day expenses during my last year in secondary school.

I had mixed feelings about moving to Cork. Though I had few close friends in Dublin, there was one in particular – John MacManus – whom I regretted leaving behind.

He had been a part of my life since I was nine years old. We met at Oatlands when we were both in the fourth grade, walked to school together every day and competed with one another for top place in every class. John was good at math and I was good at English. It seemed to have been in the cards from early on that he would eventually become a scientist and I a writer.

I have no recollection now of what John and I talked about during those long walks up and down Trees Road, back and forth to Oatlands. Girls? Soccer? The Top 20 hits on Radio Luxembourg? If I were a novelist, I could recall the conversations in detail. But I cannot remember what books we might have discussed, nor any movies we might have seen together. I do know, however, we shared a mutual hatred of Gaelic football, the national sport played at Oatlands as at most institutions run by the black-soutaned Christian Brothers. And I do know that John could pick a potential pop hit before anyone else in the school. He would have made a fortune in radio programming. I remember once, in the early 1960s, when John picked up a broom in his kitchen, strummed it like a guitar and sang an off-key version of "Love Me Do" that sounded just awful. He then tried to convince me that the group responsible for this dreadful song would some day become the hottest pop act in the world. I didn't believe him.

After I had been in Cork for a few months, John wrote and asked if I had acquired a Cork accent. "The voice that reads your letters to me will always echo with the sounds of Dublin." By that time, he and I were already going our separate ways, but we would always maintain a connection. Today, John is contentedly retired in Ottawa, pursuing an interest in photography that also happens to be a late-blooming interest of mine.

I spent a celibate (as well as money-challenged) year in Cork, without any regular social contact with young women because I was busy with my studies. I graduated from secondary school in the summer of 1961, and that – according to Catholic Irish convention – would normally have been my cue to start looking for a girlfriend. But I was posted to Claremorris, County Mayo, after being hired as a railway ticket clerk by Córas Iompair Éireann, the national bus and rail company. Claremorris did not seem like the kind of place where a young man from the big city could expect to meet the woman of his dreams. The last train from anywhere arrived at two o'clock in the afternoon. "A graveyard with lights" is how I characterized the town in a homesick letter to my mother. I lived in a rented room above a clothing shop that turned into an illegal pub after hours. My evenings were spent sitting in the kitchen, drinking bottles of Guinness with my fellow boarders. Also enjoying the conviviality were single male members of the local constabulary, who allowed the landlady to serve booze all night as long as she didn't charge *them* for the drinks.

The Claremorris job, mercifully, lasted only a month. After that, I returned to Dublin to take a clerical job with Aer Lingus, the national airline. I rented a one-room furnished flat in Harcourt Street, a 15-minute walk from the Aer Lingus office, and relished the fact that it was my first bachelor pad. No longer living at home with my parents, or sharing a bedroom with some other lonely guy in a soulless boarding house, I now had a place to which I could bring a young woman for tea and conversation. It had a single bed, one chair, a hot plate, a shilling gas meter for the heat and a bathroom down the hall. What more could a young man ask for?

The Aer Lingus job lasted until November 1961 when my placement number came up and I received the call from the Irish civil service to come and work as an executive officer. To earn that job I had written a national entrance examination, at which I did quite well despite the fact that the only subjects for which I had any real facility were Irish – which I had learned through immersion starting at age ten – and English, which was always my favourite subject in school. In secondary school I had prepared for math and history exams by spending five to six hours nightly cramming information into a highly resistant brain. By dint of hard slogging, I set academic standards that my poor siblings were expected to match in the years following. I'm sure they must have resented me greatly for this. I wish I could have told them that the work I put in as a plodding student ultimately brought me nothing more than a civil service job that I eventually grew to hate.

University was not an option for me after high school, because my father simply didn't have the money to pay for my tuition or support me through four more years of schooling. I did win a small scholarship to University College Cork, but Dad discouraged me from going because it would only have covered the fees for my first year. So I sat in my bedroom, night after night, memorizing the dates of the battles in the Wars of the Roses in preparation for the national exams. Career success in Ireland depended on doing well in the exams, and the jewel in the crown – according to my parents, at least – was the civil service job. This was the Brennan family business, after all, and they were very pleased when I joined the firm.

Being back in Dublin meant that I could now, for the first time in my life, start attending the dances sponsored by university student groups and rugby clubs, where I could meet young women, and hopefully invite them back to my bachelor pad. The accepted mating ritual was for the man to pick out a woman from the group standing at the back of the hall, invite her onto the dance floor and, if she was agreeable, dance with her several times over the course of the evening. If she was not agreeable, he would try the same routine with another prospect. If a young woman signalled her interest by inviting him to dance with her during the "ladies' choice," that would be his cue to ask for her telephone number. The next step after that was for them to go out on a date, usually to the movies. That much I knew from comparing notes with my male friends. What I didn't know was what happened next. Life in Ireland never seemed to unfold the way it did in the romantic comedies of Rock Hudson and Doris Day. Some of my more worldly friends bragged about "getting tail," but that was not where I wanted to go. I wanted to know how you got from the movie house to the place where love and marriage resulted, not to the place where bedroom gymnastics resulted. I was still sufficiently influenced by my parents and priests to believe that sex, however it worked, was something you saved until after your wedding day.

The problem for me was that I had never been given any information on how to form a mature loving relationship with a woman, much less how to make a woman happy in the bedroom. I received no sex education in school and no information from my parents about sex or about courtship and marriage. My friends weren't much help either. One claimed with a straight face that he could maintain a five-hour erection when sleeping with his landlady, and for a while I almost believed him. Where was *Sex and the City* when we needed it? I guess my parents thought I would figure it out for myself in the fullness of time. Once, when I was about 15, I asked my mother about "the facts of life." I didn't even know what the phrase meant; a friend had suggested I ask her. My mother said she would tell me everything on the night before my wedding. That was our first and last conversation on the subject. I had to make my discoveries on my own. I dated a few of the young women I met at the dances, but wedding bells never rang for us. I was always sensitive about the size of my acne-scarred nose – a paternal family inheritance I could well have done without – and I felt sure the nose had to be the reason some women found me unappealing.

The university dances, sponsored by students from the engineering and agricultural faculties, seemed at first glance to be the best places to meet members of the opposite sex. They were held in downtown ballrooms that could accommodate many hundreds of dancers. This seemed like the answer to my prayers until I discovered that most of the women who attended had no interest in dancing with me. In fact, they seemed to have no interest in dancing with *any* of the men who attended. If they danced at all, it was with the women who accompanied them to the dance. I watched this seemingly misandristic behaviour every week for a couple of years until I finally realized what was going on. *They were not there for the men; they were there for the music!* The featured musical groups, known as showbands, were a particularly Irish kind of entertainment phenomenon: nine-piece combinations of horns, guitars, keyboards, drums and vocals, much like the disco-funk outfits that became popular in North America during the 1970s. They always featured charismatic lead singers who could impersonate Elvis and Cliff Richard, and the female fans adored them. These showband singers were as well known throughout the country as any politician or sports hero. The most popular included Brendan Bowyer of the Royal Showband, Dickie Rock of the Miami Showband, and Brendan O'Brien of the Dixies Showband. They toured extensively, playing in rural community halls as well as appearing regularly at the big ballrooms in Dublin, Cork and Galway. Though they came from the urban working class, their constituency was universal.

I did not find the woman of my dreams at the big ballroom dances. Nor did I find her at the rugby-club dances. These were smaller affairs, usually held on Saturday and Sunday nights, catering to what I thought were my kind of people – i.e., from a college-educated, middle-class background – and featuring a five-piece band in which everybody sang and most doubled on other instruments. Like the showbands, these groups covered the pop hits of the day and had a strong show element in their performances. A plus for me was that the women who went to these dances seemed to have more interest in men than many of the women who followed the showbands. But I, for whatever reason, just didn't fit in with this rugby-club crowd. Perhaps it was because I didn't actually play rugby. If I had been a star fullback for Old Belvedere, I might have had better luck.

As it turned out, it was not the dances but my piano-playing in the pubs that eventually brought me the female companionship I sought. If a group of young women was out on the town and one had a talent for singing, another would come over to the piano and ask if I could accompany her friend singing "Down by the Sally Gardens" or "She Moved through the Fair." I would strike up a conversation with them during my next break, and that would sometimes lead to dating. However, because I always ended up telling the young women that it was my dream to travel and live abroad, I never struck any of them as being a good prospect. Only one ever accepted my proposal of marriage – a young woman who sang with me one summer during a seaside vacation at the Towers Hotel in Glenbeigh, County Kerry – and, while she would have been willing to accompany me to Canada, she could not go against the wishes of her mother, who wanted her to stay in Ireland.

If going to Canada was just a pipe dream before my engagement to Miss Towers Hotel, it became an imperative after the engagement was broken off. Now I had another reason – besides my tedious job in the civil service and a general desire to explore – to add to my list. In Canada, I told myself, I would find a new woman to love as well as job satisfaction, excitement and adventure. A change of scene would bring me everything I couldn't get in Ireland. I had a friend, Michael Murphy, who felt similarly restless and wanted to share the adventure.

Murph and I talked for a few years about it. We had a little routine that we did. The dialogue usually went something like this:

"Let's go to South Africa, Brennan."

"Nah, it's got apartheid there."

"How about the States, then?"

"Nah, I don't think so either. They send you to Vietnam."

"How about Australia?"

"Nah, it's too far away. Besides, I hear they don't have a lot of women down there."

"How about Canada?"

"That might be a possibility. We should look into it."

We did, in fact, look into Australia first. We talked to the embassy people in Dublin and discovered it would cost us 10 pounds apiece to fly to the Australian destination of our choice. "Let's see if we can get a better deal at the Canadian embassy," said Murph. There, we discovered we could fly for free, as long as we paid back the cost of our airfares within three years. *Such a deal!* Canada was eager to attract newcomers, especially educated, white, British subjects like Murph and me. The interest-free assisted-passage loan was an incentive I could not pass up. Neither could Murph. He had already left the civil service job his father had encouraged him to take after secondary school, and he'd gone to work for Jacob's Biscuits as a work-study officer. But he wasn't any happier there than he had been in the service.

Murph and I were bosom buddies. We first met when we were both 18, at a civil service Christmas dance in Dublin where we both had our eyes on the same girl. Murph, ever the dashing Corkman, stole her attention with his captivating line of blarney. We became firm friends shortly afterwards. We were part of a group that included Murph's older brother, Mahon, and a trainee accountant named Niall Deasy, who had lived in the same neighbourhood as the Murphy family in Cork. I qualified for membership on the strengths of having spent my last year of high school in Cork and being able to sing all the verses and choruses of such popular Cork anthems as "The Holy Ground" ("Fine girl, you are"), "The Boul' Thady Quill," and the ever-popular "Banks of My Own Lovely Lee."

As a group, we did everything together. On summer weekends, we pitched our tent in the sand dunes at Brittas Bay, slept on inflatable mattresses, went to the toilet in the tall grass, bathed in the sea and cruised the beach for girls. My Corkonian comrades had been friends since schooldays, so I felt privileged to be admitted to their ranks. I had lost touch with John MacManus and my other Dublin school pals after moving to Cork, and I felt the need to belong to a group. These gregarious Corkmen were my salvation. We learned the songs of The Beatles and The Clancy Brothers, taught ourselves how to play guitar, sang in pubs, discussed the novels of Saul Bellow and Albert Camus, attended premieres of plays by Samuel Beckett and Harold Pinter, read *The Economist* and *New Statesman*, vacationed in a cabin cruiser on the River Shannon and climbed the Sugar Loaf Mountain.

Girls entered our lives from time to time. But girls had to understand that friendship with one of our group meant friendship with all of us, i.e., membership in our circle. Our commitment to one another was such that no girl was ever likely to do what Yoko Ono later did to The Beatles. But that's not to say we avoided serious relationships for the sake of the group. When Miss Right came along, the group just got larger. One of our members, Denis O'Leary, acknowledged this as the accepted convention when he became the first in the group to marry. Denis was a Mayo native who became an honorary Corkonian like myself when he worked with Michael Murphy in the Department of Lands. He fell for the daughter of a Swedish doctor when posted temporarily to Stockholm as a junior diplomat. Denis's wife, Susanne, said later that when he brought her over to Ireland for the first time, he warned her that the other five members of our group would be at the airport to "check her out." I can well believe it. Under the circumstances, it's a wonder she didn't get on the next plane back to Stockholm.

When Murph and I embarked for Canada, we did what no girl had ever succeeded in doing. We broke up this group of male buddies, this circle of Corkonian comradeship, for once and for all. That was not our intention, of course. We just wanted to set out on an adventure across the sea. Instead of backpacking around Europe as some of our friends were doing, we would wander around Canada for a couple of years. But when we dined for the last time at the Lamb Doyle's restaurant in the Dublin Mountains, and then sang choruses of "Whispering Hope" around the piano for Murph's mother, we surely sensed that things would never be the same again. Never again would we spend our Sunday afternoons at the Murphy home playing chess, trying to crack the *Observer* crossword puzzle, learning the words of the new Bob Dylan song or applauding Mahon's clumsy efforts to master the Pete Seeger style of frailing banjo. Never again would we talk about buying a stone cottage as a summer retreat in the Wicklow hills. Never again would we gate-crash girls' parties with impunity, defending our actions on grounds that men with guitars should never be turned away. Never again would we return to the state of innocence we shared as single Irish men in our early 20s. For innocent we truly were, unwise in the ways of the world, possessed of a naive faith in our abilities to succeed at whatever we turned our hands to. We had been protected from the harsh realities of life by caring, supportive parents who sacrificed much to keep us in school and give us hot dinners and good clothes and who allowed us as much time as we needed before giving us wings to fly. So even if we believed we could make it on our own – and some of us had actually taken a step in this direction by moving into apartments where we paid our own utility bills – we were still essentially unprepared to deal with the kinds of economic and other problems our parents had faced during the 1930s and 1940s.

Did we appreciate what our parents did for us? I don't think I did. I wasted away my time in the civil service drinking pints of Guinness at Murt Leonard's pub every weekday from noon to three o'clock, and playing snooker in the back room with my pal and fellow executive officer Tom Duffy. No wonder the principal officer had us transferred from Division Four to Division Three, with "considerably less dutiable headings from the Brussels Tariff than those administered by one executive officer in Div. 4." The principal must have had tongue poked firmly in cheek when he wrote that letter of reference for me:

Mr. Brian Brennan has worked satisfactorily under my supervision for several years in the administration of Customs duties. He is capable, industrious and imaginative and the use of initiative is habitual with him. He is a man of high integrity and invariably courteous, considerate and co-operative.

(D. DUNNE)

(PRINCIPAL OFFICER)

And what did I do when the service gave me time off with pay to complete a degree in public administration at University College Dublin? I spent my time hanging out with the fine arts crowd, writing satire and playing piano in pub cabarets. My father had worked overtime for 20 years to give his children a good education and a good start in life. I took that gift and squandered it. Then I ran away to Canada.

Of course, I could always have done something else, something that would not have involved leaving Ireland. I could, for example, have taken advantages of the service's university education subsidies and earned a degree in drama or English literature. But Canada had an enticing aura of mystery and opportunity about it. I romanticized it as an exotic destination, thousands of miles away from people who knew me, where I could reinvent myself as, well, I didn't yet know.

Finding the

Right Chords

in Canada

COMING TO CANADA

We arrived in Canada on an Aer Lingus flight from Shannon. My travelling companion and fellow immigrant was Michael Murphy, who had been a friend for five years. We were both 23, dressed in our Sunday best and looking very respectable. We had gone for haircuts and shaved off our beards because my uncle in Boston told me no American employer would look at us twice if we had long hair and beards. We travelled light. We each checked one medium-sized suitcase, and I brought my guitar as a carry-on. The cardboard guitar case was too flimsy to risk putting it in with the checked luggage, so I asked the woman at the check-in counter if I could take it with me on the plane. I had never been on a plane before so I thought it would be just like taking the guitar aboard a train. She told me there would probably be an empty seat at the back of the plane where I could stash the instrument during the flight. Jet planes didn't have overhead bins in 1966.

We landed in Montreal first, with plans to make a side trip to Boston before carrying on to Vancouver, our final destination. We went through customs and immigration, had our passports stamped and answered a few questions.

"Anything to declare?" asked the officer.

"Not really," I said, mystified by the question.

"Any liquor or cigarettes?"

"Oh, just a couple of packs of Players and a bottle of Irish Mist for my uncle in Boston."

"Irish Mist? For your uncle? You're giving him *perfume*?" said the officer.

"Oh, no," I said, blushing. "It's not perfume or anything like that, it's a liqueur."

"What are you going to do with this?" asked the officer, pointing to my guitar case.

"I'm going to play it," I said. "That's my guitar."

"You're not going to sell it?"

"Oh, no, nothing like that."

"Welcome to Canada, sir. Make us better."

That's all it took. The officer shook hands with us. We were now officially recognized as landed immigrants. No lengthy wait before being admitted, no big interrogation, no third degree. Just a simple handshake, and welcome to Canada. Easy as that. *"Make us better"*? How were we going to do that? We didn't know, of course. But we still had plenty of time to figure that out.

Murph and I didn't really view ourselves as immigrants. Though we had applied for landed immigrant status at the Canadian embassy in Dublin, and received an interest-free assisted-passage loan from the Canadian government to cover our airfare, we saw ourselves more as travellers and temporary visitors than as immigrants. Our intention was to fulfil our commitment to stay in Canada for at least two years and then move on to our next adventure. We might even return to Ireland, though I had no particular desire to do that. I had left behind an undemanding job as a civil servant, and I wanted to try something else. So I was in Canada as a happy wanderer, *a gypsy rover*.

We ordered our first Canadian drinks – a sweet martini for me and a pineapple juice for teetotaller Murph – at the Queen Elizabeth Hotel. The waiter demanded to see ID.

"What's ID?"

"I need proof that you're over 21."

"I'm 23. We're both 23."

"I still need proof. That's the law."

"Would our passports be acceptable?"

"I don't know. I'll have to ask the bartender."

The bartender accepted our passports as proof, and we raised our glasses in a toast to Canada.

We spent the next few days in Boston with my uncle, who got a kick out of the Irish Mist story. We then resumed our journey to Vancouver, landing there on Remembrance Day – November 11, 1966. Such a date you never forget. We collected our landed immigrant documents – two little pieces of yellow paper that the officer pinned to our passports in a manner much like a mother attaching a name tag to a child's lapel – and asked the officer where we could find cheap lodgings for the night. He said there were several inexpensive hotels along Hastings Street. We opted for a six-dollar hotel with a well-scrubbed lobby, where men in shabby clothes sat in armchairs and smoked cigarettes. I think it was probably a single men's hostel.

In 2011 I ask myself the question Why did we come to Canada? In 1966 I had a ready answer, bit of a pat one, really: Because I saw the future and didn't like it. Because I worked for the civil service in Dublin and hated every boring minute of it. Because I shared an office with a man in his 60s whose job it was to sign the letters I was responsible for drafting. If the best I could aspire to after 40 years in a job was a move across the room to sign letters drafted by some 20ish junior executive officer, then it seemed to me I should be doing something else with my life.

I still believe this was a valid rationale for leaving, although it wasn't my only reason. If pressed, in 1966, I might have advanced other, more high-minded reasons for leaving Ireland: state censorship, hidebound provincialism, a repressive Church culture that saw sex rather than money as the currency of sin, treatment of women as second-class citizens, too many shops selling souvenir leprechauns made of bog oak. Okay, that last one might have been a bit of a stretch. Escape from the civil service was undoubtedly my most compelling reason. The civil service was stultifying. The psychological choke was more than I could bear. I left because I felt there had to be *something better someplace else*. There were some interesting opportunities in the Parliamentary Secretariat and the diplomatic corps, but those jobs were only available if you could first suffer through years of mindless paper shuffling in one of the less exciting branches of the civil service. I couldn't do that. No sooner had I landed in the Office of the Revenue Commissioners, Customs and Excise Division, Dublin Castle, than I wanted out.

If I had been older and wiser, I might have realized – as the novelist Flann O'Brien and the playwright Hugh Leonard did – that in this slough of sloth I had the perfect pad for launching a career as a writer. But at age 23 I just wanted to get away from a job defined by tea breaks, *Irish Times* crossword puzzles and earnest debates about the ambiguities of the Irish customs regulations: Should beach balls be classified as toys or sporting goods? Should linoleum be classified as a floor covering or a petroleum by-product? My job was to make rulings on such weighty matters, seek affirmation from my principal officer, have my clerical assistant fill in the blanks in the appropriate form letters and then submit those letters to my higher executive officer – the man in his 60s – for signature. The whole enterprise was labour-intensive to the point of wastefulness. But then, this was the Irish civil service. All the clichés were true.

Murph and I chose Vancouver partly because it was the farthest distance from Dublin we could go on our subsidized Aer Lingus flight, and partly because we expected the weather to be much the same as in Dublin. It wasn't. Vancouver was wetter. Between mid-November and Christmas it rained for 40 days and 40 nights. *If we had wanted weather like this, we could have stayed at home.* But the rain was little more than a minor inconvenience for a couple of gabardine-clad travellers from a country where the difference between winter and summer was that the rain felt warmer in summer. "With the changes in weather here, you never know what clothes to pawn," my father used to say. We had plenty to discover and plenty to enjoy.

We arrived in the middle of Grey Cup week. The Ottawa Rough Riders were playing the Saskatchewan Roughriders. I had never heard these names before. Nor had I heard that Vancouver's mayor was popularly known as "Tom Terrific," or that the federal Opposition leader was known as "Dief the Chief." So much to learn. Bars in hotels were not pubs; they were "beer parlours" or "beverage rooms." They had separate entrances for "men only" and "ladies and escorts." The women got to drink in a room with soft seats and rug on the floor, while the men had to be content with something resembling a construction site, with sawdust floors and no seating. No wonder there was no limit to the number of "escorts" a "lady" could bring with her.

We soon learned that Vancouver was the centre of the Canadian universe. Forget Toronto and Montreal; they were somewhere way over there on the far side of the Rocky Mountains and didn't figure in the thinking of Vancouverites. A Toronto guest on Jack Webster's CKNW Radio open-line program tried to make the point that Vancouver was "nothing more than Winnipeg with mountains." A columnist for the *Province*, Eric Nicol, responded in the next day's paper. "British Columbia," he wrote, "is a large body of land entirely surrounded by envy."

I had enough money to live on for about a month, no job and no immediate prospects. But I was not worried. The man at the Canadian embassy in Dublin had assured me I would have no difficulty finding work in Canada. He had an ulterior motive, of course. He knew the Lester Pearson government was actively encouraging immigration because it believed that immigrants of a certain kind – young, well educated, employable and fluent in English or French – would contribute to the national objectives of maintaining a high rate of population and economic growth. All Murph and I had to do was show the man our college diplomas and we were eligible for assisted passage.

Would our fathers have done the same thing? If they had been working in well-paid jobs, would they have left Ireland just because they were bored and restless? Would they have gone gallivanting off to another country just for the sake of seeing what things were like on the other side? Likely not. The words "job satisfaction" did not exist in that generation's vocabulary. The children of the First World War era were grateful to have jobs during the Depression, and if the jobs brought them cradle-to-grave security, so much the better. Security meant they could plan for the future: plan to get married, raise families and buy houses, furniture and cars. But none of this entered my thinking when I decided to quit my job and leave home. Mine had been a comfortable, urban, middle-class childhood, with trips to the movies every rainy Saturday afternoon and a bag of greasy french fries awaiting me at Stillorgan Fish & Chips whenever I had an extra sixpence to spend. I had never been through a Depression; I had never known deprivation or want. The concept of cradle-to-grave security meant nothing to me. I just wanted to escape.

Though my background as an Irish civil servant qualified me for nothing advertised on the bulletin boards at the Canada Employment office, I felt confident there was a job waiting for me somewhere. In fact, I was so convinced of my ability to succeed that I walked into the office of CKNW – the top-rated AM station in Greater Vancouver – and asked to be a news announcer. Such hubris. It never occurred to me that my lack of radio experience, not to mention my Dublin accent, might be an impediment. My accent was no different from that of Dublin-born Dave Abbott, and he was one of the featured talk-show hosts at CKNW. The personnel man at CKNW, to his credit, didn't laugh me out of his office. He politely listened to my request and promised he would get back to me in a few days. Needless to say, he never did. Irish and Scottish accents, I subsequently discovered, were fine for talk-show hosts but not for news announcers, who were expected to sound like Lorne Greene.

Within a few weeks, though, I did have a job. I applied to various finance companies and banks where the managers were eager to interview me but never actually offered me anything. I'm sure they only wanted to hear me talk about Ireland, because they all seemed to have family connections with what they called the "old country." Then I walked into the office of Ross & Kerr Customs Brokers on Pender Street. It was lunchtime. Mr. Kerr interviewed me as he munched on his apple and bologna sandwich. He said he had a job for me as brokerage clerk if I was interested. It didn't sound very exciting. In fact, it sounded just as dreary as the civil service job I had just left behind in Ireland. But it would pay for my living expenses in Vancouver until something better came along. I took the job and remained there for the next seven months. It entailed doing the paperwork for imported goods consigned to bonded warehouse, and using an electric calculator to figure out the customs duty payable when the goods were released from warehouse. I enjoyed the company of my colleagues, but the work was boringly repetitive.

Murph too landed a job – as a work-study specialist for a company manufacturing steam pressure gauges for ships' boilers. He got the job after we were invited to sing some Irish songs at a Grey Cup party where one of the guests was the company president. The president took a liking to Murph and offered him the job.

At this point, Murph and I were staying with the McCarron family in New Westminster. They were generous Catholics who took us in after learning we had recently arrived from Ireland. A colleague at Dublin Castle had given me the name of an Irish-born nun, Sister Josephine, living in a New Westminster convent. As soon as I contacted her, she put the wheels in motion to find accommodation for us. The McCarrons already had three grown children of their own, all still living at home. But still they found room to accommodate two more. Murph and I stayed in their attic bedroom for a month or so until we had saved enough money to rent a walk-up apartment in Kitsilano, closer to where we worked. We liked living in New Westminster with the McCarrons but found the commute, to and from Vancouver by bus, somewhat tedious.

My father must have found it strange that I wanted to live in a place halfway across the world, working in a dead-end office job clearly inferior to the secure, pensionable, civil service job I had left behind. From his point of view, Ireland had everything that Canada could offer and more. Why would I want to live in Canada? What would possess me to abandon a career with great promotion prospects for some misguided adventure in a land across the sea? Had I taken leave of my senses?

We had never talked about this before I left Ireland. My father must surely have been disappointed. I had entered the civil service at a level that was not possible for him because he lacked the education—he dropped out of secondary school at 16 to write the exam for a clerical officer's job in the Revenue Commissioners—and I threw it all away after less than five years.

Years later, I asked my father if he had any concerns at the time about me going to Canada. "Not really," he said. "You were a smart boy, and smart boys always do well." But I could sense he felt I had made the wrong decision. "You could have been a principal officer if you had stayed," he said. "You could have been earning £30,000 a year by now."

My dad was partly right. Indeed, I could have done as well financially, if not better, by staying in the Irish civil service than by moving to an equivalent job somewhere else. But that wasn't the point. I didn't leave Ireland to do the same kind of job someplace else. It was an opportunity to see if life had more to offer than what I had experienced of it thus far. If Canada had turned out to be wrong for me, I likely would have tried another country, England or New Zealand perhaps. I never would have returned to the musty halls of the Irish civil service.

Murph felt differently. He never saw going to Canada as making a permanent commitment to expatriation. He always intended to return home when his Canadian sojourn was over. In fact, he did eventually return to Ireland after making an eight-year detour to Africa as a volunteer with CUSO. However, he soon discovered that the Dublin he left in 1966 was not the same city he returned to a decade later. Life had moved on and old friends were moving in new social circles. Murph eventually came back to Canada and settled in Saskatoon, where he remains to this day, happily retired.

I never gave any serious consideration to going back, except during a brief period after my mother's death in 1977, when I was motivated more by homesickness than by right-mindedness. When I visited with former colleagues in Dublin in 1975, nine years after leaving for Canada, I feigned interest when they told me about their regular trips to Brussels to work on tariff reduction programs linked to Ireland's entry into the Common Market. I smiled and nodded and told them I wished he had stayed around long enough to start collecting the frequent-flyer points. But I was lying. I wouldn't have swapped positions with them for all the tea in Liptons. *Níl dada dá aiféala orm* (I have no regrets about it), as they say in Ireland. Canada, by then, had given me the opportunity to do many of the things I had always wanted to do in Ireland, including making my living as an entertainer.

JOURNEY INTO
SHOW BUSINESS

When Shay Duffin died in Los Angeles in April 2010, of complications following heart surgery, I uttered a silent prayer for this talented and ambitious performer who had made it possible for me to realize a long-cherished dream. I had the desire and Duffin had the drive. He also had the contacts. His Vancouver agent, Ben Kopelow, gave us our stage name, Dublin Rogues, and got us the gigs. Kopelow dressed us up in green corduroy pants, white sweaters and tweed caps, and had us performing at every corporate banquet job that called for an Irish tenor to hit the high notes of "Danny Boy" and "Macushla." Duffin was the Irish tenor. He didn't always hit the high notes but the crowds loved him anyway. I played piano and accordion. I also sang bass harmony and strummed a little on acoustic guitar.

We were a cabaret duo, with a focus on Irish ballads, comedy patter and musical parodies. The Irish Rovers, also bringing a taste of Celtic music to Canada in the 1960s, had a similar focus – folksinging and comedy – but they were more deeply ensconced in the folkie tradition, playing banjo, harmonica, accordion and tin whistle, while we played piano and did percussion on the spoons. Originally from County Antrim, the Rovers started out as a foursome in Calgary – brothers Will and George Millar and their cousin Joe Millar, along with a burly baritone named Jimmy Ferguson. Will Millar paved the way for the others by landing one gig as a Saturday morning children's entertainer on CFAC television and a second gig singing nightly at Phil's Pancake House. When the others arrived in Calgary, Will featured 'them as guests on his television show and had them singing with him nightly at Phil's. He also featured them at a Calgary coffeehouse called The Depression, a booze-free folk club later best known for having given Joni Mitchell her start in music.

Pancake restaurants were popular entertainment venues in those days. In Vancouver, Duffin played Sunday brunches at an eatery on Kingsway called Little Black Sambo's Pancake House. At least, that's what the place was called when I first arrived in Vancouver in November 1966. A sign on the outside of the restaurant depicted a caricature of a curly-haired black child. When the BC Association for the Advancement of Coloured People complained, the owner removed the offending sign and changed the name to the less offensive Sambo's Family Restaurant.

The customers at Sambo's didn't have much interest in Irish folk music. Although Duffin was getting some airplay on Vancouver radio stations with a self-produced recording of an old IRA marching song called "Off to Dublin in the Green," he discovered that the Sambo's customers preferred listening to popular vocal selections from the musicals *The Fantasticks* and *The Sound of Music*. He sang "Try to Remember" and "Climb Ev'ry Mountain." His pianist played "A Walk in the Black Forest" and "Lara's Theme" from *Dr. Zhivago*. The customers applauded and the restaurant management was happy.

Duffin was keen to work full time in show business. A 36-year-old upholsterer from Dublin who claimed to have once installed leather padding on a toilet seat in Princess Margaret's Kensington Palace apartment – you could never tell if Duffin, an inveterate teller of tall tales, was making these things up – he did bit parts in movies and television shows shot in Vancouver, sold boxes of his 45-rpm singles on consignment at The Bay, and did his Irish tenor routine at golf club dinners and trade fairs.

We met one Sunday at Sambo's, where I went to hear him sing. I introduced myself and Duffin invited me to play a couple of tunes on the piano. A couple of days later, he phoned to say that his regular accompanist was no longer available and wondered if I would be interested. I jumped at the chance. The Sambo's job paid us $15 each every Sunday. Our other casual musical engagements brought us between $10 and $20 apiece. Hardly enough to live on, but enough to keep me in cigarettes and the occasional glass of Johnnie Walker Red Label.

Before meeting Duffin, I had done a little performing around Vancouver with Murph, singing Irish ballads at private house functions put on by fellow members of Vancouver's Irish Sporting & Social Club. But we never advanced beyond the party setting because we didn't know how to break into the commercial scene. In Dublin, it had been simply a matter of commandeering the piano in a singing pub, taking requests in return for free drinks and earning a few pounds if the proprietor happened to like our act. In Vancouver, there were no singing pubs, and – as I discovered after meeting Duffin – you needed to have an agent if you wanted to work in hotels or restaurants. Duffin had the Sambo's job because of Kopelow. His other gigs were also booked through Kopelow's agency.

I continued to perform with Murph at private parties after meeting Duffin, but that was now mainly for fun. With Duffin I was able to turn a hobby into a moonlighting occupation. I joined the musicians' union, went into partnership with Duffin and started earning money as a performer.

The chance to quit our day jobs came in June 1967. A Vancouver impresario named Fran Dowie heard Duffin and me performing at Sambo's and booked us for a two-month summer gig at the Palace Grand Theatre in Dawson City. Duffin was to be the emcee, telling jokes and doing some solo singing on stage. I would be in the pit, playing piano accompaniment as musical director. A second piano would be pushed out on stage when we did our 10-minute Dublin Rogues routine. By this time, Duffin and I had released our first album of Irish ballads, *Off to Dublin in the Green*, on the RCA Camden label.

Dawson City, located two thousand miles north of Vancouver and 70 years behind the rest of the world, looked for all the world like the set of a Klondike Gold Rush movie. We arrived there after a one-hour flight from Whitehorse aboard a 16-passenger Beechcraft that gave me new insight into the meaning of the word turbulence. The plane tossed around in the clouds like a dinghy on the high seas. Not normally a nervous flier, I came close to losing my lunch on that trip. The pilot took two passes around the Dawson airfield to ensure there were no moose or other wildlife on the dirt runway, and when we stepped off the plane we moved back in time. Dressed up in 1890s fashion, volunteers from the Klondike Visitors Association were at the airport to welcome us.

My armchair-travelling father loved the descriptions of Dawson I gave in my letters home that summer. With its wooden sidewalks and streets paved with mud after every rainfall, the town struck my father as being the kind of wild and woolly place where gunslingers would be exchanging fire at high noon. The members of the Klondike Visitors Association had done an admirable job of making the town an echo of the past. Not only did they have the Vancouver entertainers performing in the nightly Gaslight Follies revue at the Palace Grand Theatre but they also pressed us into service as interpretative guides during the day. Magician Anthony Taylor played the role of a riverboat gambler, performing the three-card trick for tourists visiting the permanently docked SS *Keno* sternwheeler. Actor Wally McSween recited the poetry of Robert Service on the porch of the hillside cabin where Service had lived for a couple of years before the First World War. I sat surrounded by imitation ingots in the gold room of the Bank of Commerce where Service had worked as a teller. My job there was to explain to visitors how to pan for gold and tell them about the history of the region. My teaching guide was a well-thumbed copy of Pierre Berton's book *Klondike*, loaned to me by the local pharmacist.

There were 11 of us in the Gaslight Follies show, including four young women who danced the can-can, an English-born singer named Gillian Campbell who played the role of Klondike Kate, a drag artist named Garfield White who played an opera singer called Madame Olga Petrovitch and an old, rubber-faced vaudeville entertainer named Frank (Pop) Dowie who also happened to be the father of impresario Fran Dowie. Pop was billed in the program as the creator and director of the show. But the actual creative genius was Fran Dowie, who spent just two days cobbling together a disparate collection of variety acts into a cohesive stage presentation. He arrived from Whitehorse after a four-hour drive in a rental car, strode into the bar where the cast members had gathered for an evening of socializing and asked, "Why are we not rehearsing, ladies and gentlemen?" My recollection of his sudden appearance may be faulty, but I would swear now that Dowie was wearing a black top hat and cloak, and that he twirled the ends of his moustache like the villain in a silent movie. It's the kind of image that tends to lodge in your memory after you have spent a summer dressing up nightly in period costume, recreating a style of stage entertainment popular around the turn of the 20th century.

Two more images from that summer of 1967 linger in the memory. One shows a bag of lead shot sitting on the smashed keys of my stage piano. The bag, used as a counterweight to fly props and sets on and off the stage, broke free of its moorings one night and came crashing down on the piano just before the curtain was to rise on the Dublin Rogues segment of the Gaslight Follies program. Normally, I would have been sitting at the piano waiting for the curtain, but on this particular night I had left the stage momentarily to fetch my cap. Stage manager John Howe almost had a heart attack when he heard the crash. So did actor Wally McSween, who talked about the incident for years afterwards. I carried on with the show as if nothing had happened. I was able to get the instrument to work even with four important keys out of commission.

The other image from that summer that is clear to me now shows me and two friends standing atop a hillside overlooking Dawson, spontaneously singing a chorus of "O Canada." On a Sunday afternoon when the three of us – a Montrealer, a Newfoundlander and I – walked to the top of Midnight Dome to take in the view. Beyond the town, this place carved out of moose pasture and Indian fish camp, we could see the creeks of gold and the scars of old dredger and placer mining operations. Beyond that, we could see the forested green of the Ogilvie Mountains, the slate-coloured lakes, the unspoiled valleys, and we sensed the emptiness of the great North. Not only was it Dominion Day in Canada, it was also Canada's hundredth birthday. The world had come to Expo 67 in Montreal to toast us. Singing "O Canada" seemed like the right thing to do.

After just eight months away from Dublin I felt eager to embrace what I already knew would be my home away from homeland. I felt temperamentally suited to the gentle pace of life in this young country. After singing the national anthem, the three of us on Midnight Dome sang a new song, Bobby Gimby's "Ca-na-da," written for the centennial. The words were hokey – *four little, five little, six little provinces* – but we sang them anyhow. *Merrily we roll along, together all the way.* With the three of us joined together in song, it seemed inconceivable to me then that Quebec separatism could ever threaten Canadian unity. If Canada were ever in danger of breaking up, I believed, the problem would be resolved in civilized fashion with a group of politicians sitting around a table trying to find middle ground. Or maybe they would be singing along to the chorus of "Ca-na-da." That was the time-honoured Canadian way, as I saw it. We didn't shout, we didn't confront and we didn't reach for our guns whenever we wanted to fix things.

The Dawson gig gave Duffin and me a great opportunity to expand our musical repertoire and create a tight show. Every night after the Gaslight Follies performance we went over to the Westminster Hotel to play music in the bar until closing time. We tried out new parodies we had written – including one about Lyndon Johnson and one about the Queen's visit to Expo 67 – worked up arrangements of Irish songs we had not performed before and added to our program a local audience favourite that we would never sing anywhere else: "Squaws along the Yukon." It told the tale of a "salmon-coloured girl" who "rubs noses" with gold miners and American airmen. Nobody in Dawson seemed concerned that the song, as well as being sexist, reinforced a racial stereotype. Certainly, we heard no complaints from members of the Dawson Indian Band who came to the bar nightly and sang along to the chorus in their native Han language. Like the original version of Jerome Kern's "Ol' Man River," which referred to "niggers" working on the Mississippi, "Squaws along the Yukon" was a period piece written to entertain, not offend. However, Duffin and I did drop the song from our repertoire after we left Dawson. In Dawson, we could treat the song like an anthem. In Vancouver, we would have been viewed as a couple of Irish bigots who glorified racism.

By the time we left Dawson we had developed enough Irish material to fill four one-hour sets without repeating ourselves. We quietly retired "Try to Remember" and the hits of *The Sound of Music* from our program, and in their place offered renditions of "The Garden Where the Praties Grow," "Johnnie, I Hardly Knew Ye" and "The Boston Burglar." We drew simultaneously from the repertoires of the great Irish tenor John McCormack and the popular Irish folk group The Clancy Brothers and Tommy Makem. That made it difficult for the music industry to pigeon-hole us. We moved between the genteel Victorian draw-ing-room style of musical performance later depicted in the John Huston movie *The Dead* and the raucous style of pub singing that one associates with the rhythm of clinking bottles and tapping feet. How do you categorize a hybrid like that? One minute we were all decanted port and pianos draped in brocade. The next we were doing percussion with spoons ("stolen only from the finest restaurants," quipped Duffin) and encouraging the crowd to shout out the words "Fine girl, you are!" The record company and the radio stations called us a folk act. But we viewed ourselves as supper-club entertainment, as a Vegas-type act that should be featured on *The Ed Sullivan Show*.

We dispensed with the stage-Irish tweed caps and green corduroy pants after we returned to Vancouver. We replaced them with tuxedos for a while but later opted for more casual dress: green blazers, grey pants and white turtleneck shirts. The Dawson experience had left us hungry for more full-time work in the music business, so in October 1967 we quit our day jobs for the second time. I had been welcomed back by Ross & Kerr for what I suspected would be the last time, because I clearly had no long-term commitment to the brokerage.

"Why don't we see if we can make it in Toronto?" asked Duffin. Why not indeed? He had a wife and four children. I was single. I had a lot less to risk.

Initially, we stayed at the rundown Ford Hotel in Toronto. When Duffin's cash reserves were depleted, we moved to the even cheaper YMCA, where Duffin dined daily on a diet of chocolate bars and Coca Cola. I could afford a better class of meal because I still had most of my savings from Dawson City. Duffin was almost broke because his money had gone toward paying for his family's accommodation and living expenses in Vancouver. Then came what we hoped would be our big break. The Moxie Whitney talent agency booked us as the opening act for the touring Abbey Tavern Singers, an Irish edition of the New Christy Minstrels who had scored a hit in Ireland with their recording of "Off to Dublin in the Green." The Singers became well known on this side of the Atlantic after they were featured performing the song in a Carling's Black Label lager commercial, and they capitalized on that exposure by doing a concert tour of Canada. We had recorded the same song as the title track of our album but were told we should drop it from our program for this tour.

Getting the tour was a coup for us. The Singers were such big news in Canada that when their spoons player arrived in Toronto without his instruments, the story made the front page of the *Telegram*. The hapless percussionist tried out every spoon in the kitchens of the Royal York Hotel, but none of them would do, he said. Didn't have the right weight or tonal quality. The tour had to be delayed for two days while he waited for a replacement pair to come from some cutlery establishment in Dublin. Press photographers were on hand at the airport when the precious cargo landed. "The spoons have arrived," said the front-page headline in the *Telegram*.

Duffin and I played just two concerts with the Singers before being booted off the tour. We should have known better. We were doing parody versions of the maudlin Irish songs the Singers were trying to sing straight. The audience would laugh loudly at our politically incorrect reworking of "Galway Bay" – *"she had me driven crazy with her naggin' and she had a mouth as big as Galway Bay"* – and then start giggling again when the Singers tried to sing the straight version later in the show. The Singers complained to the tour manager, and we were dispatched back to Toronto, chastened but unrepentant.

We met up with the Irish Rovers while waiting for our next break. They were playing a gig at Theatre in the Dell, a popular Toronto nightspot. The crowd was small – no more than a dozen people, if that. "Did ye all come in the same Volkswagen?" quipped Will Millar, the leprechaunish leader of the four-man group. I looked at Duffin and said, "We'll have to remember that line."

The Rovers had enjoyed some success in California, playing for twenty-two successive weeks at the Purple Onion in San Francisco, and were now trying to recreate that success in Toronto. But it was a tough slog for them. Discouraged, button accordionist Joe Millar soon left the group and returned to his old day job, working in the shipping and receiving department at Eaton's. According to local legend, Timothy Eaton had once pledged there would always be work in his stores for fellow immigrants from Northern Ireland.

The Rovers hired a replacement accordionist – All-Ireland Champion Wilcil McDowell. They released a single recording of "The Unicorn," a novelty song by *Playboy* magazine cartoonist Shel Silverstein that Will Millar had sung for the kids at Phil's Pancake House in Calgary. The Rovers' recording of the song, with country singer Glen Campbell playing anonymously on lead guitar, sold enough copies to secure their future as recording artists and television performers. Cousin Joe turned up the radio in the Eaton's warehouse whenever "The Unicorn" came on the air. "That's me and the lads doing the singing there," he told his colleagues, beaming broadly. "Then why aren't you still playing with them?" they asked. Why not, indeed? The story goes that Joe then phoned Will and inquired about returning to the group. "Sorry, Joe," said Will, "but we've already got Wilcil." They did not, however, have a bass player. Joe went home to learn electric bass. Two months later, he was back in the band.

"The Unicorn" opened the door for the Rovers to tour the world, appear on American television shows hosted by the Smothers Brothers and Merv Griffin, and eventually get their own weekly variety show on CBC television. Duffin and I, meanwhile, hit the Canadian nightclub circuit, playing one- and two-week gigs across Ontario and Nova Scotia. The work was steady, the compensation was good – $300 each per week, plus meals, travel and accommodation – and the audiences were receptive. But after five months of playing clubs in such places as Sudbury, Ottawa, Renfrew, Sault Ste. Marie, Halifax and Antigonish, Duffin and I were impatient to start performing on a bigger stage. We wanted to do big concerts and network television shows. Heck, we wanted to be on *Ed Sullivan*. Only problem was, we didn't have a hit single like "The Unicorn" to get us there. "Off to Dublin in the Green" would always be associated with the Abbey Tavern Singers, not the Dublin Rogues.

We did get some airplay with a satirical song, "Pierre, the Kissing PM," which we recorded at a radio station, CKCY, in Sault Ste. Marie, Ontario. The newspapers were filled with stories about the "charismatic" bachelor prime minister who wore a red rose in his lapel and kissed every young woman who approached him in public. We also sold enough copies of the *Off to Dublin in the Green* album to warrant doing a second album for RCA. But none of this brought us any closer to our dream of playing on the big stage. Or if it did, it wasn't happening quickly enough for me.

I remember hearing a story once that the original leader of the Kingston Trio, banjo player Dave Guard, quit the group after four years because he was tired of singing their hit song, "Tom Dooley." I eventually came to feel that way about "Off to Dublin in the Green." When I first sang it in the pubs of Ireland, I felt a strong sense of nationalistic pride because it told the story of a "merry ploughboy" who left the farm to join the Irish Republican Army and fight for his country's freedom. After being educated by anti-English Christian Brothers, I had become – like most of my schoolmates – a closet republican. At the time, I truly believed I was blessed to be living in this free, independent sovereign state made possible because the heroes of the past – the freedom fighters of the IRA – had made the supreme sacrifice for us. Like Jesus these freedom fighters were. Or so the Brothers told us. They laid down their lives so that future generations of Irish boys and girls could live in freedom and peace, without the "yoke of British imperialism" fastened around their necks. These were not the reprehensible IRA terrorists of the late 1960s who bombed pubs and killed unsuspecting civilians. These were the original soldiers of destiny, the followers of Michael Collins and Richard Mulcahy, who participated in the struggle for independence from Britain in 1916–21. I would never have joined them myself, because I am fundamentally a coward. But I loved their passion and their bravery, and I loved the songs that celebrated their struggle. "Off to Dublin in the Green" was one of those songs.

However, when I sang "Off to Dublin in the Green," night after night, week after week, month after month in the lounges of Nova Scotia and Ontario, the lyrics began to lose all emotional appeal for me. I had told this story too many times. There were nights when I felt like following the lead of crooner Rudy Vallee when he played Vancouver's Cave Supper Club in 1966. After 30 years of singing "Life Is Just a Bowl of Cherries," Vallee decided he didn't want to do the song any more. In fact, he didn't want to do *any* song any more. Instead, he wanted to do a comedy routine with a ventriloquist's dummy. The audience did not welcome this development, and neither did the manager of the Cave. He sent Vallee packing after one night.

Duffin and I would have been fired too if we had dropped "Off to Dublin in the Green," or even "The Wild Rover," from our repertoire. So we were stuck performing the same material night after night unto perpetuity.

On the one hand, I suppose I should have counted myself lucky to be working steadily in the music business, earning good money and not having to worry about paying utility bills, buying groceries or covering the costs of owning a car. Other musicians considered themselves fortunate to get occasional weekend work while they struggled to keep body and soul together. I lived comfortably and kept my expenses to a minimum because I carried my house on my back. My worldly goods consisted of a guitar and two suitcases filled with clothes and books. I had money in the bank, no house or vehicle to maintain, and contracts to keep me busy for three months at a time. But I simply took all this for granted. I was impatient to move up to the next level because this musical career was only taking me around in circles, from one club gig to the next. I had always wanted to be in show business, but not *this* kind of show business. The occasional variety concerts did little to appease me, though they did provide an opportunity to rub shoulders with such top Canadian performers of the period as Tommy Hunter and John Allan Cameron. At one charity show in Halifax I found myself standing in the wings next to a young blonde woman who was about to go on. "What do you do?" I asked. "I'm a singer," she replied. I told her that I sang, too: "I'm Brian Brennan from the

Dublin Rogues." She shook my hand and said, "I'm Anne Murray." Two years later Anne's recording of "Snowbird" became the first disc by a female Canadian artist to exceed a million sales in the United States.

Although I still loved to be on stage, after nine months of steady travelling I grew to hate the nomadic aspect of the music business, especially after meeting Zelda. We met when Duffin and I were playing a gig at the Black Knight Lounge in Halifax. Zelda came with two of her female roommates. All three were single and in their early 20s. Duffin made a beeline for their table during our first break. I did the rounds of the bar, visited with other people I knew and didn't join them until 1:00 a.m. after our final set. "I've been trying to get over here all night," I said. Zelda laughed at my audacity. But she and her friends invited us back for coffee at their apartment, and Zelda later agreed to go out with me. A few months later I met her parents. They lived a small farm on Prince Edward Island, a couple of kilometres from Green Gables, the historic home that author Lucy Maud Montgomery used as a setting for her celebrated novel *Anne of Green Gables*. Zelda's parents, Angus and Melina Pineau, were devout Catholics who said the rosary every night and received Holy Communion every Sunday. I must have seemed very exotic to them. They lived in an Acadian community of farmers and fishermen, where music was played only in kitchens and at church. *What in God's name is our daughter doing with this weird guy from Ireland who wears a goatee and plays music for a living?*

But I was Catholic too, so I guess I can't have seemed all bad to them.

Our courtship was mainly by mail and long-distance telephone. While Zelda worked at an insurance office in Halifax, I continued travelling but liked it less and less. The feelings of rootlessness and loneliness I had at this time caused me to drink more Scotch than was good for me – before, during and after every performance. Another six months of this nomadic existence and I would have become an alcoholic. I wanted to get off the road, make a home with Zelda and do something else with my life. The music and the travelling had been fun for a while, but I finally realized I was too much of a homebody to spend the rest of my life as a wandering minstrel. Even playing on the big stage, I realized, would still have meant living out of a suitcase.

Duffin and I discussed the possibility of putting together a theatrical show based on the life of the booze-loving Irish playwright Brendan Behan, with Duffin impersonating Behan and me providing onstage accordion accompaniment. But that would have taken goodness-knows how long to research and write, with no guarantee of getting any workshop money or production commitments when the show was ready for staging. It seemed too much of a gamble to me. I opted out of the project before it began. Duffin, to his credit, took the idea and ran with it. He developed the concept as a one-man show and later performed it to critical and audience acclaim throughout Canada and the United States. "Mr. Duffin, if not Behan, has given us a memorable evening," said *The New York Times* after he played the Astor Place Theater in 1981.

In early 1968, I told Duffin I wanted to quit the Dublin Rogues after we had discharged our existing contract obligations, a couple of months hence. He was not happy to hear this. Neither was RCA, which had just paid for the costs of recording our second album. My departure meant the planned cover photo would have to be scrapped and the album released as a recording by "Shay Duffin and the Dublin Rogues." I had no proprietary claim on the Dublin Rogues name, so it didn't bother me to leave it behind. The call from Ed Sullivan had never come, so the name had no currency beyond the cocktail lounges of Ontario and the Maritimes. What had been a duo would now be promoted as a solo act, with me listed in the liner notes as a supporting musician. I didn't mind the demotion. I wouldn't be around to promote the album when it came out. I had done my musical thing – at least for the time being – and was moving on. Within a few months Duffin would be performing with two other players as Shay Duffin and the Dublin Rogues, and I would be on my way to a new life in Vancouver with Zelda. I chose Vancouver, with Zelda's agreement, because it had been a good place for me to begin life as a new Canadian in 1966. I felt it would also be a good place to start anew.

JOURNEY INTO JOURNALISM

When I first started working as a newspaper reporter, the only tools I carried were a ballpoint pen and a spiral-bound notebook. Occasionally, I brought along a portable cassette recorder, but mostly I relied on the old police interrogation trick of asking questions first and documenting the responses later, jotting down the answers while they were still fresh in my memory.

Life was simpler then. I didn't have to deal with the technology – smart phones, laptops, text messages – that now make it possible for people to communicate instantaneously. I didn't have to do what many reporters do today: write stories for the print edition of a newspaper while simultaneously providing content for the paper's website.

Meeting the 24/7 deadline requirements of today's Internet-wired newspapers would have been a struggle for me. Print journalists now have to be as quick, efficient and light on their feet as their colleagues in the electronic media. They have to deliver the news within minutes of it happening. Sometimes they even have to deliver it *while* it is happening. They ad lib it to the cameras before they have a chance to script it, and live-blog it on the web while it still has the immediacy of a chat-line conversation. They have no time for second thoughts or second drafts. I could not do journalism that way. I am so obsessed with choosing the right words and putting them in the right order that it takes me 20 minutes to compose a four-sentence e-mail.

Seeking the right words and trying to put them in the right order became my career focus after I quit the music business and went into journalism. You didn't need special qualifications to get a newspaper reporting job in Canada in the 1960s. The basic prerequisites were a high-school education, some fundamental writing skills, a sense of curiosity and a love of storytelling. I landed my first job in the business because a trusting soul named Gary White took a chance on me. He was the editor of the weekly *Interior News* in Smithers. His only reporter had just quit. I was a 25-year-old first-semester dropout from the journalism program at Vancouver City College. I had left the program early because my savings ran out.

Gary must have been desperate. There was nothing in my resume to suggest I might be a worthy replacement for the reporter who had left. I had no experience, no references and a mere two months of journalistic training. And I'm sure Gary would never have hired me if he had known about my sloppy first attempt to land a reporting job in Canada. I had written a letter to the television columnist at the *Vancouver Sun* asking if one of the paper's editors might be interested in hiring me. I said I had a plausible manner, some literary ability and a burning desire to write news stories. *In your dreams, Brennan.* The columnist wrote back saying my "idiosyncratic" spelling of his last name, MacGillivray, left me with a major credibility gap. Bad move on my part. I had just broken the first law of journalism: I had gotten the name wrong.

The *Sun* would not have hired me anyway, even if I had spelled MacGillivray's name correctly. It was a big-city paper staffed with Fleet Street veterans and such Canadian luminaries as Allan Fotheringham, Paul St. Pierre, Barry Broadfoot and Christopher Dafoe. The *Sun* wanted reporters who had paid their dues with the best of them, not J-school dropouts with stars in their eyes. I needed to lower my sights.

I took greater care with the application I sent to Gary White. I made sure every word was spelled correctly and enclosed some clippings of feature stories and theatre reviews I had written for the student newspaper at Vancouver City College. Gary read the application and hired me over the telephone. Just like that. "When can you get here?" he said. "Probably in a couple of days," I said, giving the thumbs-up sign to Zelda. In Canada, everything was possible. This was a place where dreams came true.

That night, Zelda and I sat at the table in our Kitsilano bed-sitter and celebrated my good fortune with a bottle of Mateus Rosé. Zelda had encouraged me to go into journalism because she felt there was literary merit in the letters I had sent her from the road while touring Ontario singing Irish ballads. *Literary merit?* What did I know? Of course I wanted to believe her. You want to believe *everything* told to you by the woman you love. Zelda had identified what seemed like the logical next step for me to take on my journey through life. Journalism would give me another way to express myself. The urge to write had always been there, starting in childhood when I made up stories for my brother Michael at bedtime. It had also been there when I tried to be a cartoonist, crudely imitating the funnies that appeared in the popular *Beano* and *Dandy* children's comics. Performing as a pianist and singer had been the first professional manifestation of my need to express myself. Journalism would be the next.

Occasionally, as a teenager, I had fantasized about becoming a reporter, a professional teller of stories. But my parents wanted me to become a civil servant, and I dared not disappoint them. Now, after the phone call from Gary White, I was poised to do what I never had a chance to do in Ireland. When I wrote to my parents to tell them I had landed a job as a newspaper reporter, my father wrote back to say he was glad to hear I finally had employment again after being out of the workforce for more than a year. I couldn't convince him that, in Canada, playing music for a living was actually a real job.

Zelda and I pored over the British Columbia road map, worked out the mileage and calculated that we should be able get from Vancouver to Prince George – eight hours of travelling at 60 miles an hour – on the first day. Four hours of driving the following day would take us to Smithers. We didn't take into account the fact, nor did we know, that once we turned north after Hope – an hour and a half's drive out of Vancouver – we would be motoring through ice and snow for the rest of the journey. Our vehicle was a 10-year-old Austin Cambridge. Great little car for rainy

Vancouver. Not so great for the frozen roads of the Cariboo country in November. Zelda was five months pregnant; should we have been worried? We didn't even think about that. What babes in arms we were.

Predictably, we broke down. The hood flipped up as we drove through the Fraser Canyon, and then the engine quit. "Do you have snow chains?" asked the kindly passing motorist who drove us into Lytton to find a tow truck. "What are snow chains?" I said. "You'll need them if you don't have studded tires," said our Good Samaritan. I had never heard of studded tires either. How would I? We didn't have such things in Ireland.

We spent the night at a motel in Quesnel. The check-in lady gently corrected me when I pronounced it "Kweznell." She said the "s" was actually silent. A man in the bar told us we would never make it to Smithers without a spare can of gasoline in the trunk. "They only have gas stations every two hundred miles up there," he said ominously. "Many of them don't even open in the winter." This was the kind of news we did not need to hear. "I think we should go back to Vancouver," said Zelda.

We continued our journey toward Smithers the next day after finding room amidst the pots, pans and suitcases in our already overstuffed vehicle for our newly acquired snow chains and can of gasoline. The hood flipped up and the engine stalled again just before we reached Prince George. The catch on the hood was supposedly fixed in Lytton. I phoned Gary at the *Interior News*. "We're on our way but we've been delayed," I said. He could barely conceal his impatience. "I need you to be here, like, yesterday," he said. "I've been without a reporter for two weeks now."

We spent the next night at a motel in Burns Lake. We tuned in the Smithers radio station, CFBV, and heard Tammy Wynette, that wonderful country singer with the teardrop in her voice. She was singing "Stand by Your Man." Best country song ever written. Wynette had the perfect voice for it. She began the song on the A below middle C – I know this because I have played the song for singers with voices much better than mine – and then soared through an octave and a half as the tune built to a final, triumphant C sharp that made your skin tighten and the hairs rise up on the back of your neck. As we left the Burns Lake motel the next morning, the CFBV announcer was saying, "It's nine o'clock, and the first batch of hot bread is just coming out of the ovens at Overwaitea." Zelda suggested we stop at a coffee shop and order some toast and jam.

The car made it from Burns Lake to Smithers without further incident. It had become clear to us by then, however, that this fragile English sedan, this delicate saloon, would have to be traded in soon for a sturdier North American coupe. A Ford Fairlane, perhaps, or maybe a Chevy Impala. *Oh, we'll never get to heaven in an Austin car. 'Cos an Austin car won't go that far.*

Arriving in the Bulkley Valley was like reaching the Promised Land. Snow-capped Hudson Bay Mountain stood watch over the neatly laid-out town, which looked like an Alpine village I had coloured on a paint-by-numbers canvas as a child. I ran out of white paint before I could finish the canvas. I had used far too many coats on every snow-covered roof. The cars on Smithers's Main Street sported bumper stickers urging people to contribute to a community fund for a heated swimming pool. Tammy Wynette was on the radio again, singing her other big hit of 1968, "D-I-V-O-R-C-E." A battered sign in the window of an autobody repair shop said "Slow down and live – in Smithers." This, I thought, was going to be a good place to begin a career in journalism.

I knew nothing about the *Interior News* before arriving in Smithers. We didn't have Google then. Gary White told me that an adventurer named Joe Coyle – best known as the inventor of the cardboard egg carton – had founded the paper during the first years of the 20th century. The proprietor in 1968 was Bill Yorke-Hardy, a retired prospector who had staked a significant molybdenum deposit on Hudson Bay Mountain. He came into the newspaper office once a week to drop off a story about local prospecting activities written in technical language only a geologist could love. "Bill's story always runs without editing," warned Gary. "Say no more."

Gary hadn't told me this before I left Vancouver, but it turned out I would be more than just a reporter at the *Interior News*. Beyond covering the news, I would be collecting sports results, writing the occasional editorial commentary and taking photographs. In other words, I would be a one-man newsroom operation. No wonder Gary had sounded impatient when I phoned him from Prince George. "No problem, Gary, I'm here to learn. Just show me how to work the f-stops on that Nikon and I'll be taking good pictures before you know it."

Gary was a roly-poly guy of 28, with a big toothy smile and an infectious giggle. His staffers included the two women in the front office who handled subscriptions and classified ads, the ad salesman who spent most of his day away from the office doing the rounds of the merchants, and the two brothers in the print shop who knew *everything* about sports. After introducing me to them all, Gary said, "Let's play." That's how he did newspapering. For him, it was about having fun. I liked his attitude.

Gary held my hand for the first couple of weeks. He accompanied me to the town council and chamber of commerce meetings, introduced me to the people I would be quoting in the paper and told me what stories I should write. I needed this guidance because I didn't know anything about the issues important to the people of Smithers.

Those issues, I soon learned, were mainly those of the local business community: snowmobile dealers who wanted zoning bylaw changes to expand their operations, or hotel owners who sought council permission to put live entertainment into their taverns. You didn't read much in the *Interior News* about the problems of the Natives or the goals of the anti-pollution activists. You knew that these people existed because you met them in the drugstore or the coffee shop, but the paper never acknowledged them as significant community groups. The Natives only made the news when the paper did a feature story about the pole-carving artisans at nearby New Hazelton; never when they complained about the lack of affordable housing in town. The anti-pollution types were dismissed by the paper as a bunch of greenie nutbars who impeded commercial progress. The most prominent of these environmentalists, a professional guitar player named Joe L'Orsa, would later have a public wilderness cabin named after him to recognize his contribution to ecological awareness. But in 1968, L'Orsa's publicly expressed concerns about emissions into the Bulkley River from a proposed pulp mill at nearby Houston were shouted down by chamber of commerce members who claimed that the treated effluent would be safer to drink than tap water. One of the chamber types even drank a glass of the effluent as a publicity stunt to assure local residents that fish and people would not be at risk. He could have saved himself the bother. The American owners of the forest products company soon ran into financial difficulties, and the proposed pulp mill was stillborn.

Zelda and I lived for a week at the Sandman Inn before we found a furnished apartment to rent. It was located above the post office on Main Street, and the daily life of the town streamed below our window like sockeye salmon migrating up the Moricetown Canyon to spawn. Within a few weeks we were able to recognize almost everyone who walked by.

"Oh, look, there's the drugstore guy, Jimmy You-know-who. Moving a little slowly this morning, isn't he? I guess he did a little too much dancing at the Hilltop Hotel last night."

"And look, there's old Doctor Moneybags. Shouldn't he be retired by now? He's got to be older than any of his patients."

"And there's that big guy with the buckskin jacket again, lumbering down the street like a prowling grizzly bear. Do you really think he killed someone with his bare hands and then beat the murder rap? Gary swears by the story, but I haven't been able to find anything in the files about it."

This was a new experience for me. I had always lived in cities where I moved in limited circles. The only people I knew were those I had met either through school or work. Here, I knew everybody and everybody knew me. That left me with mixed feelings. On the one hand, I was grateful to be welcomed into this close-knit forestry and mining community where every family had access to a snowmobile and a hunting rifle. But in the process I had to surrender some of the privacy I had cherished while living in bigger places. I preferred the sense of being relatively anonymous. I didn't like everybody in town knowing what I was doing or where I was going.

Our second home in Smithers – the one to which we brought Nicole shortly after her birth – was a rented one-bedroom fourplex across the road from the high school where we could see the community leaders of tomorrow practising their smoking skills during recess. The apartment was barely big enough to accommodate a single person, much less a family of three. When we put Nicole's crib next to our bed, there was no room in the bedroom for any other furniture. We got in and out of bed by crawling over the foot. Zelda actually liked this intimacy because she could reach across and touch Nicole whenever she cried in the night. The small living room doubled as our dining room and kitchen. It was a tight squeeze but we managed.

Nicole's arrival, after a difficult Caesarean delivery, put us in seventh heaven. "A bouncing, healthy, arms-and-legs-thrashing little bundle of French and Irish stock," I wrote in Zelda's diary while she was in recovery at the Bulkley Valley District Hospital. "The happiest thing ever to come into our lives." We brought our beloved baby home, and we all fell asleep nightly to the easy-listening sounds of James Last's *Classics Up To Date* album. The record player shut off automatically when the needle reached the end of the last track: the adagio from Bruch's G Minor Violin Concerto. What amazing technology, I thought.

We moved out of the tiny fourplex a few months after Nicole was born. An enterprising realtor named Ted Bishop found us a fully furnished, two-storey, three-bedroom house on a gravel street a couple of blocks from the newspaper office, selling for the bargain-basement price of seven thousand dollars.

We soon learned why the selling price was so low. The house had a few problems. The roof needed to be reshingled, the water didn't drain properly from the bathroom sink, the upstairs toilet needed to be replaced and the crawl space under the main floor needed to be insulated. The problems made it difficult for us to secure a mortgage. The Central Mortgage & Housing man insisted on holding back some of the money until we had the problems fixed. But even with a second loan from the bank to cover the repairs, it still was a great buy. We loved our big backyard with its unobstructed view of *our* mountain, Hudson Bay.

I quit smoking when we moved into the house. Zelda encouraged – nay, ordered – me to do so. Nicole had been into the hospital twice with bronchial pneumonia, and Zelda thought it would be best for the baby's breathing if I gave up my beloved smokes. We didn't know about the dangers of second-hand smoke then. It just seemed logical that if cigarettes could cause me to hack and splutter every morning, any fumes I exhaled inside our home – especially during those long cold periods when the windows and doors were sealed tight – would aggravate Nicole's bronchial condition.

Craven "A" was my brand of choice. In Dublin, I had been a Peter Stuyvesant man. I used to smoke Gitanes and Gauloises when I was going through my European intellectual phase but eventually gave them up because I found them hard on the throat. So I switched to Pall Malls, and then to filter-tipped Peter Stuyvesants, which I bought at a little tobacconist's shop on the Lower Rathmines Road that sold illegally imported smokes under the counter. I liked these American cigarettes mainly because of the packaging. When my father reached for a Players Navy Cut, he had to use both hands. He used his right hand to flip up the cardboard lid and his left to pull out the cigarette. I could achieve the same result with just one hand, shaking the cigarette out of the pack with my left while nonchalantly flicking the Zippo lighter with my right. Very cool! Very Steve McQueen!

My father smoked cigarettes until he was 45 and then switched to plastic-tipped cigarillos. His doctor had found a growth in his throat and warned Dad he would be dead of cancer within 12 months if he didn't give up the cigarettes. I don't know why Dad thought the cigarillos would be any safer. He still inhaled, which meant he never lost his smoker's cough. But the switch to cigarillos did spare his hats from further damage. They were riddled with the burn holes Dad caused when he smoked in the cinema with his hat in his lap and was distracted by the action on screen. The cinema management permitted cigarette smoking but would not hear of patrons smoking cigars or cigarillos, so my father's hats were spared.

I was never tempted to switch to cigarillos. That would have meant exchanging one habit for another, and I felt no need for a substitute. I quit the Craven "A"s without saying anything to colleagues or friends. If I was to fail, I only wanted Zelda to know about it. Not for me the public confessions of the 12-step recovery programs or the tabloid TV talk shows. In Ireland, we used to joke about the difference between being a drunk and an alcoholic: when you were a drunk, you didn't have to attend all those show-and-tell meetings. I quietly quit smoking for one hour at a time, one cigarette at a time, and told myself I had the freedom to relapse at any time.

Although I was kicking a nine-year habit of 30 cigarettes a day, the withdrawal felt more psychological than physical. Smoking was what I had done to create a persona, not feed an addiction. It was like combing my hair straight back or wearing a cravat. As a teenager, I had taken up smoking to be sociable. My rite of passage occurred when someone stole my bicycle from outside Mount Merrion Church and I reported the theft at the local police station. The desk sergeant offered me a cigarette "to calm your nerves." I was 14. The following day, I bought my first packet of unfiltered Woodbines. "Coffin nails," we used to call them, though we never actually believed they could kill us. We were immortal then. We liked the Woodbines because we could buy them singly or in packs of five and they were cheap.

Giving up smoking meant reimagining the latest character I had chosen to play in the drama of my life. As a club musician, I had performed with an ashtray sitting atop the piano like Liberace's candelabra. As a reporter, my routine was to light up before typing the first sentence. Now I had to envisage myself as a writer without that familiar grey plume encircling my head. I stayed off the cigarettes first for a day, then for a week, then for a month. After that, Zelda went through the house and threw out all the cigarettes and matches she could find. I have not smoked since. Good riddance to bad rubbish.

It is now 2011, and I wince as I reread some of the first articles I produced for the *Interior News*. I am grateful that newspapers in 1968 had no way of archiving their stories in electronic databases; that my early scribblings did not become fodder for a blog about bad journalism in Canada. Newspapers then were never bastions of literary excellence. Most of the writing was leaden and cliché-ridden, produced by hacks who learned their techniques by imitating the wooden prose styles of other hacks. But in 1968 they did have a tried-and-true formula for delivering the news in a readable manner. Taken from the creativity-stifling *Canadian Press Stylebook*, it was a formula that, I confess now, I knew nothing about. Nor did I know anything about the technique of conducting interviews: always ask open-ended questions. I guess they must have taught the interviewing and story-structuring skills the day after I left Vancouver City College. Or maybe I was just sleeping in class.

I didn't know, for example, that according to *Canadian Press* the important stuff was supposed to appear at the top of every news story – patterned according to the so-called "inverted pyramid" structure of news writing – and that every story had to answer the "five Ws" (who? what? when? where? why?) before being considered complete. I wrote my pieces like shaggy-dog stories, backing into them when I should have been getting to the point, and trailing off when even I could see they had reached the point of terminal inconsequentiality. Typical of these was a story I wrote about a rancher whose favourite riding horse had been shot to death by an unknown assailant. After several paragraphs of introductory pablum about how much he loved his horse, I eventually got around to mentioning that the horse had been killed, and then went on for several more paragraphs about how upset he was. Boring!

I did know how to touch type, however. That was a skill my mother had taught me when I was 14. She had learned touch typing at business school before entering the civil service as a clerical officer. How did she know I would ever get to use it? "Why do you want me to learn this, Mammy?" The only people in Ireland who touch typed were secretaries, clerks and desk sergeants at police stations. Even journalists didn't touch type. They punched out their stories on manual typewriters using the old two-fingered, hunt-and-peck method. Administrators like my father didn't type at all. He – like all of his executive colleagues – did his paperwork in longhand. He was proud of his copperplate penmanship. I don't know if he ever took lessons in calligraphy, but Dad had the skill of a master engraver and could produce beautiful handwritten documents. The civil service, with its inkwells, fountain pens and stacks of foolscap paper, was the perfect place for his scripting talents. It seemed to have been my destiny from childhood to become a longhand writer of memos, as well. Why then did my mother want me to practise touch typing on the old black Underwood she used when typing out my father's monthly newsletter for the Association of Officers of Taxes? She must have thought that if I ever became the editor of a civil service newsletter, touch typing would be a useful skill to have.

If Gary White had been an experienced newsman, he would have seen how bad my news writing was, pulled me aside and offered me some coaching. But Gary was a former ad salesman who had never worked as a reporter. For him the newspaper functioned primarily as a vehicle for selling ads, not as a medium for crusading journalism or compelling news writing. His idea of a great front-page story was a puff piece about the opening of a new car dealership. My lack of news-writing ability – if he ever noticed it – was of no concern to him. He was just pleased that I was "feeding the goat" for him, generating enough copy to fill the 16-page newspaper and keep the advertisers happy. That was the key to success in small-town newspapering. It had nothing to do with great journalism or writing, and everything to do with giving the local businessmen what they wanted.

I didn't mind writing these advertorials. They gave me an opportunity to practise a new craft. The fact that they were little more than columns of promotional bumf was of no matter to me. They made me think and organize and choose my words carefully, and as long as I left out the adjectives I could convince myself they were respectable pieces of writing. They gave me the right to call myself a working newsman. With this job, I was getting paid to express myself in print, and that was a far better place to be than in the Irish civil service or even on the road playing music. When I sat down at my metal desk, loosened my tie, did the imaginary washing of the hands (a nervous tic that always seemed to bring forth the right words) and started to type, I imagined myself to be following in the footsteps of Ernest Hemingway and Pierre Berton.

In Vancouver, Zelda had supported me with the income from her insurance clerk's job while I went to school. In Smithers, I became the breadwinner while Zelda stayed home to care for Nicole. But truth be told, although I sometimes felt I wrote acceptable copy, I was still going to school. My instructors were the reporters who worked up the road at the daily *Prince George Citizen*. Every day, I combed through the *Citizen's* city pages, studied how the reporters wrote stories about court cases, labour disputes and regional district meetings, and tried to catch the rhythm of their styles. I needed to learn because I was parading my deficiencies weekly in the *Interior News*.

One week, I felt rather proud of myself because I had just published my first hockey story. I went to the rink and described the game action as if I were writing about a hurling match in Tipperary. The boys in the back shop quickly brought me down to Earth. "You don't say the referee *threw* in the puck, Brennan," said Laurie Moore, the linotype operator. "The correct expression is *dropped* the puck. Even the Queen knows that." Her Majesty, it transpired, had visited Canada in 1964 to mark the commemoration of the first Confederation meetings in Charlottetown, and as part of her royal duties "dropped the puck" at a hockey game in Quebec City. So much for bringing an Irish sensibility to the coverage of things Canadian.

It was at this point that I realized that if I was going to become a good reporter and eventually work for a paper larger than the *Interior News*, I would have to learn the language of sports, commerce and local politics, as well as the essentials of news writing technique and story structure. I already knew about such Canadiana as toques and block heaters and separate schools and weather offices, but clearly that was not enough. I was lucky to be learning my craft at a newspaper so small that I could make my mistakes in public without too many people noticing. My only small consolation about the botched hockey story was the discovery years later that Pierre Trudeau knew as little about hockey as I did. The story goes that the prime minister once placed a call to an aide who said he could only talk for a few moments because he was preoccupied watching the hockey playoffs. Trudeau hesitated for a moment and then said, "Oh, I see. What inning are they in?"

Aside from not knowing anything about hockey, I also knew nothing about the laws of libel and defamation. I guess I missed those classes at Vancouver City College, as well. This got me into trouble on two occasions. In the first instance, I wrote an editorial accusing the Smithers chamber of commerce president of "being imbued with a sense of his own self-importance" because he reportedly used scare tactics to warn storeowners they could be prosecuted under an obscure municipal bylaw covering opening and closing hours. He threatened to sue me for libel. I'm grateful he didn't because I probably would have lost.

I should have learned a lesson from that episode, but I didn't. A few weeks later, I wrote a graphic account of a hockey game in which one player sucker-punched another. The lawyer for the alleged attacker sent me a letter saying I had defamed his client. I wrote back saying I simply reported on what I witnessed. "I was there; I know what I saw." The case went no further than that. Count me lucky.

Count me lucky, too, for keeping my job at the *News* after I dodged the libel bullet that second time. Gary wanted me fired. The paper could ill afford a lawsuit and I was becoming a potentially expensive liability. He changed his mind, however, when he talked it over with Keith Marshall, the paper's darkroom technician. Gary and Keith were about to buy the paper from the retiring Bill Yorke-Hardy, and they had already lost one key employee, ad salesman George Bramsleven, who left to sell cars for a living. Losing its only reporter would have put the paper in an even more precarious state, said Keith. So instead of firing me they offered me a small raise, from $400 to $450 a month, and told me to stay out of trouble.

Learning from the *Prince George Citizen* undoubtedly helped me improve my performance as a news writer. But it also gave me some bad habits. Hackneyed phrases began to pepper my copy. The *Citizen* had taught me that such clichés, the lingua franca of the news business, were acceptable. Rain invariably "failed to dampen spirits." Victorious softball players "came through with flying colours." Heavy snowfalls brought several inches of "the white stuff." "Raging" fires "swept through" abandoned buildings. Skydiving competitors were "cool, calm and collected." Terminal patients died "after a long battle with cancer."

This was prosaic writing of a kind that makes me shudder now, but I don't think it upset Gary White. Certainly, it didn't bother the readers of the *Interior News*. They bought the paper because they wanted to read about themselves, see pictures of their kids receiving prizes for winning essay contests and find out what was happening at town council without having to sit through the boring meetings. They expected the newspaper to cover all the local news and sports important to them. They didn't care about the elegance of the sentences as long the paper included as many names as possible in every story. The best-read section of the paper, compiled from phone calls to the front office, was the social-notes column, which told about the comings and goings of local residents, the visits from out-of-town relatives, the 50th wedding anniversary celebrations, the growing of big vegetables and the trips to the hospital for hip surgeries.

If I had brought with me the kind of jaded cynicism you find nowadays in big-city newsrooms, where reporters have seen and heard it all, I would not have lasted five minutes in Smithers. I would have quickly drowned in a sea of apathy, bored with the banality of life in a tiny town where the most serious crime prosecuted by the RCMP in 1969 was a count of simple possession levelled against three brainless marijuana smokers who took delivery at the post office of a small parcel of cannabis mailed to them by a friend in Kelowna. As it turned out, I worked at the *Interior News* for close to two years, mainly because it gave me a chance to develop my writing skills. After that, it was on to our next adventure, accompanied by our most precious souvenir of the town: dear beloved Nicole.

We sold our house to a buyer from Prince George who came to Smithers to work both as a funeral director and driving instructor. This seemed like an odd combination of jobs, but Smithers attracted people like that. Our buyer didn't trust banks. He saw our advertisement in the *Interior News* – we had made a point of mentioning the flowering rose bushes and ripening raspberries in our back garden – and drove over to pay us the full amount in cash: $14,000. Zelda and I looked at one another in amazement. "Twice as much as we paid for this house, can you believe it?" We had never seen so much money before. We did what they always do in the movies. We sat on the bed surrounded by piles of 10- and 20-dollar bills, and tossed handfuls into the air like autumn leaves. "Wheeeeee!"

By the time we left Smithers in the summer of 1970, I had mastered the house style of the *Prince George Citizen* so well that I had no difficulty fitting in when I went to work there as a reporter in 1972. But first I had something else to do. I had never worked in broadcasting and I wanted to give that a try. The owner of the Smithers radio station, Ron East, was opening a new station in Prince George and he had a job for me there.

NIGHTS ON AIR

It was a cold March 1971 evening in Prince George, with snow flurries flying and a wind-chill temperature of 14°F. I was doing my regular nightly news shift at CJCI Radio, pulling stories off the wire and preparing them for broadcast. A state of emergency had been declared in Quebec after a blizzard raged through the province. Dave Barrett, the headline-grabbing leader of British Columbia's New Democratic Party, had been expelled from the Legislature for a week because he refused to comply with the committee chairman's ruling that he take his seat during a budget debate. Then the bulletin alarm bell sounded on the Broadcast News wire machine. The news gave me a shiver of excitement. Canada's 51-year-old prime minister, Pierre Elliott Trudeau, had secretly married 22-year-old Margaret Sinclair, the daughter of a former federal fisheries minister.

I ripped the Trudeau story from the wire machine, sprinted into the news studio, asked the deejay to interrupt the regular Thursday-night broadcast of the *Back to the Bible* religious program and read out the short announcement. "Good evening, this is a news bulletin from CJCI Radio. Prime Minister Trudeau was married in North Vancouver tonight. More details coming up on the news at 10 o'clock."

My phone was ringing off the hook when I got back to the newsroom. I had committed a no-no it seems. The first five callers were *outraged* that had I cut into *Back to the Bible*, the popular evangelical program directed by former

Alberta premier Ernest Manning. These listeners didn't want to hear anything about Trudeau. They wanted to hear Manning preach. But the sixth caller was different. He was in a jubilant mood. "I'm ready to celebrate," he said. "Did you say Trudeau was *murdered* tonight?"

Blame it on my Dublin accent. I wasn't really looking to become a news announcer when I applied for the job at CJCI. I just wanted to be a news writer, putting together stories for others to read on the air. But while that was the practice at Radio Éireann, Ireland's national broadcaster, it was not the way things worked in commercial radio in Canada. The person who wrote the stories also read them on air. Once I learned this, I asked if I could write advertising copy for the deejays who voiced the commercials. The news director, John Ashbridge, suggested, however, that first I tape a sample newscast so he could hear how I sounded on air. I recorded the audition tape, mailed it off to Ashbridge and he promptly hired me as a newsman. "We can give you some tips for smoothing out the accent," he said. In Vancouver, where the sonorous voices of the on-air announcers sounded like they were modulated at the Lorne Greene School of Broadcasting, my accent would have been a liability. In Prince George, it was a badge of distinction.

I was one of four newsmen Ashbridge hired before CJCI went on the air in August 1970, though I wasn't actually there for the station opening. Zelda and I had taken the proceeds from the sale of our house in Smithers and spent the money on a trip to Ireland to introduce Nicole to my family. So I started at the station when we returned in September, and things were already up and running. Did we regret having spent the money on a vacation when we might have done the sensible thing and used it to buy another house? Not at all. We were still young. Another house could come later. We were quite content to return to apartment living for a while.

CJCI's four-man newsroom operation made for an unusually large setup compared to that of other regional stations, where two-man newsrooms were the norm. The CJCI station manager, Ron East, wanted his newsroom to have a big-city feel to it, and that's why he hired Ashbridge to run it. We were all in our early to mid-20s. Regional radio, then as now, was a young person's business.

Ashbridge was an experienced and accomplished newsman. Though only 23, he had actually worked in broadcasting for 10 years. He had started doing evening and weekend shifts at a Victoria radio station while still going to junior high school, and became a general announcer with Vancouver's CJOR at age 17. A year later, he moved to New Westminster's top-rated CKNW, where his boss and mentor was Warren Barker, one of the pioneers of commercial news broadcasting in British Columbia. When Ashbridge moved north to Prince George in 1970, lured by the prospect of establishing the first radio news network in the BC interior, he brought with him the values he inherited from Barker.

The competing station in town, CKPG, had a lazy approach to the news. The announcers assembled their newscasts from the hourly summaries issued by the Broadcast News agency, ripped the prepackaged copy from the wire machine and read the stories without editing or adding local context. At CJCI, this "rip and read" practice was strictly forbidden. To ensure our newscasts would sound fresh and different, Ashbridge insisted that every piece of wire copy be rewritten before being read on-air. The only exceptions to this rule were the breaking-news bulletins like the one announcing Trudeau's marriage. With a newscast at the top of every hour and headlines every half-hour, each of our news stories had to go through a total of three rewrites before being discarded. After three airings the stories were not considered news anymore.

I read my first newscast on a Tuesday night in mid-September 1970. Early on Wednesday morning, to be precise. Ashbridge put me on the air at midnight so I could make my mistakes when only a few people were listening. I got through the news part of the broadcast without too many stumbles – though my reading did sound stilted and monotonic. A United Auto Workers strike against General Motors had put 240,000 workers on the picket lines in Canada and the United States. Canada's federal and provincial leaders were commencing the fifth in a series of ongoing talks aimed at patriating the constitution. Search efforts were being stepped up for four young boys in a canoe who had gone missing off the coast of Vancouver Island.

Then came the sports, starting with the baseball results. In the National League, New York had defeated "Mtl" by a score of nine-to-five. I stopped dead when I hit the abbreviated word "Mtl" in the Broadcast News wire copy. *Oh God, what does this mean?* I paused for what seemed like an eternity. "It's MONTREAL," the deejay in the control room finally yelled out. Thanks a lot, Broadcast News! I struggled through the rest of the sports scores, gasped out the temperatures from around the province and staggered back to the newsroom, mortified and ready to start looking for another line of work.

The next day, Ashbridge was all smiles and sympathy. "It will get better," he assured me. "Just one thing to remember for the moment. You don't say '*far*-ty *far*-est fires' are burning out of control in northern BC. You say '*four*-ty *four*-est fires' are out of control. Get it?"

After those soothing words of advice, I made a conscious effort to change my vowel pronunciations to sound more like a Canuck on the air. I felt I had succeeded when I went back to Ireland on a holiday the following summer and a cab driver said I was the only "American" he'd ever met who could correctly pronounce the title of an Irish-language drama playing at the Abbey Theatre.

Reading the news was one of my daily duties at CJCI. Reporting from city hall was another. Ashbridge told me I should go to council's committee-of-the-whole meeting at 9:00 a.m., take plenty of notes and be ready to file my first report, live over the telephone, at 10:00 a.m. "But the meeting won't be over yet," I protested. "That's how we stay ahead of 'PG," explained Ashbridge. "They won't file until after the meeting. We file *during* the meeting. That way, we have the jump on them all morning." He added that if I planned to record any interviews with aldermen or city administration members, he would show me how to dismantle the receiver of the city hall pay telephone so I could wire it directly into my tape recorder. This man was a veritable gold mine of big-city broadcasting tricks!

Stealing listeners and advertising revenue away from CKPG was the primary goal of CJCI when it started broadcasting in August 1970. It wasn't an easy task. 'PG was a well-established radio and television operation backed by the financial might of Vancouver's CHQM Radio. Its only handicap, from the point of view of some Prince George listeners, was its affiliate relationship with the CBC, which required CKPG to regularly broadcast what a *Prince George Citizen* writer described as "such long-winded horrors as *Cross Country Checkup*." These same public affairs shows were carried simultaneously on a local CBC repeater station, CBU. That meant it was all talk all the time on the Prince George airwaves during certain hours of the day until CJCI arrived on the scene. CJCI station manager East hoped to woo the disaffected listeners by programming blocks of country and western, light rock or easy listening music when the other two stations were airing *Cross Country Checkup, Assignment* and *As it Happens*. He confidently told the *Citizen* there was plenty of local advertising money available to sustain two commercial stations in Prince George. But in reality, he was worried about CJCI's survival chances. A local beer baron, Ben Ginter, had tried and failed earlier in the year to cut into the *Citizen*'s advertising revenue budget with a short-lived newspaper called *North Star*. CJCI, in the weeks before going on-air, was faced with the tough task of trying to sell advertising contracts for a new station that promised something different but had yet to deliver on that promise.

CJCI launched a pre-emptive strike against CKPG by hiring away the station's popular morning announcer, Don Prentice, a chain-smoking comedian whose appeal was linked to his fondness for Raquel Welch jokes and laugh tracks. ("What do you get when you cross Raquel Welch with Santa? A big thank you from Santa!" Ha-ha-ha-ha-ha.) Prentice brought several of his listeners with him, and that helped draw a few advertisers into the CJCI fold. Then CJCI did something inane. It hired a big-voiced Vancouver announcer to do a series of promotional spots, all ending with the vaguely threatening tag line, "We're not the *only* radio station in town – but we're working on it." CKPG complained to the CRTC, Canada's broadcast regulator. The CRTC responded promptly and the offending spots were soon pulled off the air.

After surviving that early confrontation with the CRTC, CJCI remained on the air for 33 years. At the end of that time, in August 2003, the station moved from 620 on the AM dial to 97 on the FM band, changed its name to "The

Wolf," and switched its music format from middle-of-the-road to "modern country and the best southern rock." The call letters CJCI disappeared into the annals of broadcast history. CKPG Radio also changed its format and its name in 2003, to a news–talk station called "The Drive." I felt a tinge of sadness when I discovered this while surfing the net recently. It was as if a part of my life had been erased.

I worked full time at CJCI for 18 months. The biggest story I covered during that period involved an angry hockey fan who forced CKPG's television station off the air at gunpoint because it wasn't showing the NHL game in which his son was playing. Normally, because of the competitive nature of the media business, we would never have mentioned the name of CKPG in our newscasts. If we had to make any reference to it, we would have called it "a local radio and TV station." But this was different. The listeners would have considered us unnecessarily petty if we had run a story about this incident without naming the station in question. They probably thought we were petty anyhow for routinely referring to CKPG – the only other station in town – as "a" local station. CKPG was "a" local station and the *Citizen*, the only daily in town, was "a" local newspaper. We seemed to believe that if we never publicly named them, these competing media would somehow cease to exist.

The irate hockey fan in question was Roy Spencer, the 50-year-old father of Brian (Spinner) Spencer, a 21-year-old left-winger with the Toronto Maple Leafs. When called up from the minors in December 1970 to play in his first NHL game, Brian phoned his father in Fort St. James. He said his father should be sure to watch the Saturday game on CBC's *Hockey Night in Canada* because Brian was going to be interviewed on the air at intermission. CKPG, however, was not carrying the Toronto–Chicago game that night. Like other British Columbia stations, it was telecasting the game between the Vancouver Canucks and the California Golden Seals.

Roy Spencer phoned CKPG to demand that it drop the West Coast game and show the game in which his son was playing. When an employee said the station had no control over network programming, Spencer grabbed a loaded pistol, a bottle of whisky and a couple of loaded rifles, got into his truck and drove the 150 kilometres to Prince George. He confronted the station's news anchor, Tom Haertel, in the CKPG parking lot. He ordered him to turn around, stuck the pistol in his back, cocked the hammer and said, "There is going to be a revolution all over the country because of the CBC." Earlier that day, Spencer had installed a new antenna on the roof of his house so he could get a clearer picture of his son on the black and white TV.

The gunman told Haertel he wanted the station off the air. "If I can't watch my son playing hockey tonight, nobody gets to watch hockey tonight." He ordered Haertel and three of his colleagues to line up against the newsroom wall. "I don't want to kill anybody," he said, waving the pistol. "I've killed before. I killed many times in the commandos. Turn the TV off."

The station went off the air at 7:40 p.m. The radio dee-jay saw what was happening in the TV newsroom, locked himself into the control room, kept the music playing and phoned the RCMP. Several officers arrived in three patrol cruisers and were waiting for Spencer when he left by the front door. The station employees hastily exited by the back door.

One of the officers, Corporal Roger Post, ordered Spencer to drop the gun. Spencer responded by open-ing fire, hitting Post's holster with one bullet and hitting Constable Dave Pidruchny in the foot with another. Post and Constable Steve Lozinski returned fire, hitting Spencer in the chest with three bullets. He was dead on arrival at hospital.

The station went back on the air at 7:54 p.m., just 14 min-utes after being shut down. I would have sworn it was much longer than that. A blank screen on the television makes time stand still. Haertel headed straight for the bar at the Inn of the North, ordered a Scotch and announced he was taking the rest of the night off. "The barrel on that gun looked like a cannon, like it was 50 feet around," he said when I caught up with him after my evening news shift. The CJCI studios were in the ninth-floor penthouse suite of the Inn of the North – "at the top of the town," as the station promos described it – and the lounge downstairs was a favourite haunt of local radio and television staffers. Haertel gave me a full account of what happened, and the story led every newscast the next day.

An amusing sequel to this story occurred a week later. Two RCMP officers were listening to CKPG as they drove around Prince George in their patrol car. The music stopped and the station fell silent. "Here we go again," said one officer. After radioing for backup, they arrived at the station with guns drawn. They checked the control room and found it empty. "Where is the deejay? Has he been kidnapped?" It turned out he had decided in the middle of his shift that he didn't want to work at CKPG anymore. Too dangerous, he thought. He put a Christmas LP on the turntable, inserted the needle into the first groove, left by the back door, got into his car and started driving toward Vancouver. His car skidded off the icy highway near Quesnel. That's where the police eventually found him, stuck in the ditch.

Not so amusing is the story of what eventually happened to Spinner Spencer. He left hockey after nine years in the NHL, moved to Florida and struggled with drug addiction. He lived in a trailer park with a prostitute who later accused him of murdering one of her clients. He was acquitted after a 1987 trial in which a guilty verdict would have sent him to the electric chair. Three months after the acquittal, he was shot dead by a mugger who refused to believe he had no money. Spencer was 39.

I didn't follow Spencer's NHL career moves after the Prince George incident, mainly because I only pay attention to hockey during Stanley Cup playoffs. But when I heard about the murder charge against him and his subsequent brutal death, I was haunted by the thought of what had happened to his father and how that must have affected the young hockey star. Just prior to the Prince George shooting, Spinner had two reasons to celebrate. His wife had given birth to their first child, a daughter, and he had joined the elite club of hockey players who get to demonstrate their talents in the NHL. The night after the shooting, Spinner opted to play in Buffalo in a game against the newly franchised Sabres rather than fly home to be with his wife and new baby. "My father wanted me to be a hockey player more than he wanted anything in the world," he said. "I think he would want me to play, and that's what I'm going to do." And play he did, with reckless fury and abandon, during a time in NHL history when some players became stars more because of their ability to fight than because of their ability to score points. Spinner played violently, lived violently and eventually died violently – just like his tormented father.

I switched from full-time to part-time work at CJCI in early 1972 because I wanted to take one more shot at quenching my still-burning thirst to play piano for a living. Old habits die hard. Being on the road with Duffin had opened my eyes to the downside of being a working musician, but it hadn't quite cured me of the obsession.

GIVE MY REGARDS TO
OLD PRINCE GEORGE

It was a Wednesday night at Teddy's Pizza Parlour in Prince George. I had moved from full-time to part-time on-air work at CJCI, and was back to playing piano as my main paying gig. The CJCI sales manager, Doug Johnston, had asked me to become his resident musician after he bought a majority share in Teddy's, and I jumped at the chance to give the music biz one more shot. Much better than being on the road, I thought. I put together a brand new repertoire for the entertainment of the Teddy's regulars – "Bye, Bye, Miss American Pie," "Help Me Make It Through the Night," "Sunday Morning Coming Down" – and packaged myself as a pop-country singer, without a single Irish ballad in my program. I learned the new material by taping the songs at the radio station and having Zelda transcribe the lyrics.

Why no more Irish ballads? Mainly because I didn't think there would be much of a market for that music in Prince George. This was a country-and-western town, and I wanted to fit in.

My father was disappointed to hear I was "unemployed" again. "I'm sure I can still get them to open up a spot for you in the civil service," he wrote. "It disturbs me to know that you haven't been able to find steady work since you went to Canada." I tried to assure him that everything was fine, that I wasn't going on the dole, but I don't think he believed me. If a job had no pension plan, it was not a real job as far as Dad was concerned. My mother, on the other hand, seemed to be okay with my latest career move. Nicole was in daycare and Zelda had returned to work as an insurance clerk, so my mother didn't see any cause for concern.

I didn't recognize the man sitting alone in the shadows at the back of the restaurant. He called me over during my break and held out his hand.

"Hi, I'm Tony Skae. I'm the editor of the *Citizen*."

"Hello Mr. Skae. I'm pleased to meet you."

"'Tony,' please. You play a mean piano there, Brian."

He knew me from my city hall reporting on the radio. I was still doing that while working as a pianist at Teddy's. Somehow, I felt that this musical gig – while enjoyable to a fault – might not last forever because of the ups and downs of the restaurant business. So I was still keeping my hand in as a broadcaster.

"We're looking for a reporter at the *Citizen*. Would you be interested? I saw your piece in *Content* magazine and liked your writing."

Content was a monthly publication for journalists distributed across Canada. My whimsical piece about Prince George's "press club" had appeared in the magazine. In the absence of an official club, a couple of Prince George reporters designated part of the sprawling Inn of the North tavern as our city's unofficial club. I wrote about aldermen announcing their re-election plans in the tavern, labour leaders unveiling strike plans there and dope dealers selling bags of pot without getting caught. At the end of the piece, I described myself as a freelance journalist on the lookout for full-time work. I didn't tell my Teddy's boss, Doug, that I was spreading my wings again. He had been so pleased to have me entertaining his customers that I wanted to delay my departure announcement until I had someplace else to go.

"Greg McIntyre tells me you used to work at the *Interior News*. That's the kind of experience we like to have at the *Citizen*."

Greg was a *Lethbridge Herald* reporter, formerly with the *Citizen*, who had become a good friend when we covered Prince George city hall together. He had encouraged me to return to newspapering, but at that point I was still enjoying broadcasting and not ready yet for a move back into print.

"I'm very flattered by your offer, Tony. Let me talk it over with my wife, and I'll get in touch with you tomorrow."

Skae's job offer came at just the right time for me. After six months of six-nights-a-week performing at Teddy's I had finally worked the music bug out of my system and was ready to try something else. I had sent broadcast clips of my newscasts to radio stations in Victoria and Vancouver, but the responses were discouraging. My Dublin accent, though somewhat neutralized after 18 months of on-air work in Prince George, was still obvious to the news directors who listened to the audition tapes. Thus evaporated my chances of ever getting a job in big-city broadcasting.

I hadn't considered applying for another newspaper job after leaving Smithers. It never struck me that less than two years of experience at a community weekly would be enough to make the editor of a daily paper want to hire me. Yet, here I was now with a job offer from the *Prince George Citizen*, the paper that had taught me what little I knew about the essentials of news writing. I gladly accepted the offer and began a career in daily newspapers that kept me stimulated and engaged for the next 27 years. My father was greatly relieved when I wrote to him and said there would be no more bopping around from one type of work to the next. At age 28, I was finally settling into a career that came with health benefits, unemployment insurance and a company pension plan.

There were six reporters at the *Citizen*, each with a different beat. I was assigned to cover city hall because I already knew the territory from my CJCI work. In the absence of an arts critic, I also assumed responsibility for reviewing theatre productions and pop music concerts. These brought me many free tickets and a few angry letters to the editor. The letters were the price I had to pay for my free tickets. I didn't mind. I had my opinion and the readers were entitled to theirs.

I enjoyed covering city hall for the paper. It gave me an opportunity to add context and depth to stories that necessarily had to be truncated when I wrote them for radio. But after a few months back at the typewriter I started to realize that what I liked best about being a newspaper writer was the storytelling process. As much as I enjoyed covering some of the issues debated by council, these were merely grist for the storytelling mill. I was an entertainer at heart, and this was just another type of public performance.

The same held true for the reviews. They gave me an opportunity to have some fun, albeit often at the expense of those I was writing about. But while I may have skewered some of the individuals I reviewed – and I seem to recall upsetting more than a few readers with my dismissive critique of a New Seekers ("I'd Like To Teach the World To Sing") concert – it was never out of a sense of malice that I wrote these pieces. I was a little bit like the New York theatre critic who dropped in to Sardi's restaurant one night, eager to show his review of a Broadway opening to the actors before it appeared in the newspaper the next day. The review was negative, and the actors showed their displeasure by pelting the hapless critic with dinner buns. "But didn't you like the writing?" he wailed as he hightailed it out of the restaurant.

Reviewing gave me an opportunity to stay in touch with the performing business, from which I knew – as the kid who always had stars in his eyes – I would never want to entirely divorce myself. Interviewing visiting performers was another way for me to stay in touch. One of my favourite subjects was an 89-year-old Hollywood bit player named Burt Mustin, who had started acting professionally at age 67 and described himself as "the best 'they went that-a-way' actor in Hollywood." Another was an Edmonton pianist and TV talk-show host named Tommy Banks, who later became a Canadian senator. I also enjoyed talking to Jay Silverheels, the Aboriginal actor who played Tonto in the long-running American television series *The Lone Ranger*.

Silverheels told me – and I've no reason to doubt him – that he was the originator of the well-travelled story about the Lone Ranger and Tonto being surrounded by thousands of warring Mohawks. The "masked rider of the Plains" turns to his "faithful companion" and asks, "How do we get out of this mess, Tonto?" The usually taciturn Native replies, "What you mean *we*, white man?" Silverheels said he came up with this line during an off-camera banter session on the set, when he and co-star Clayton Moore were kibitzing between scenes. "A member of the crew must have been eavesdropping because, a few weeks later, I was surprised to hear someone using the line in a joke."

The offbeat stories from city hall were as much a source of fun for me as the reviews and the interviews with visiting entertainers. Typical of these was a story I wrote about a complaint to city council alleging that hundreds of young swimmers were committing the perfect crime daily by answering nature's call in the municipal pool instead of using the public toilets. It was more than just a *piddling* matter, I wrote. One of the aldermen had vowed to *flush* the problem into the open. I had an arrangement with the *Vancouver Province* at the time to rerun any of my stories from the *Citizen* that the editor considered well written. This one, to my delight, made the *Province*'s front page. When I left the *Citizen* a couple of years later, one of my colleagues – a thoughtful and sophisticated prose stylist named Bill Graham – inscribed these words on the pewter mug traditionally given to reporters when they move on: "Like the perfect crime that you exposed, your words spread far, touched many." I was moved by that little accolade.

Before leaving the *Citizen* in April 1974 I spent three months in Ottawa as an intern with Southam News. This was the news agency for the Southam newspapers, which included the *Citizen* and such papers as the *Province*, *Calgary Herald*, *Ottawa Citizen* and *Montreal Gazette*. The purpose of the internship was twofold: to give young reporters from the papers an opportunity to write about federal politics, and to let the Southam people identify those writers with the potential to become top correspondents in the future. As well as covering Ottawa, Southam News also covered international affairs from bureaus in London, Paris, Washington and elsewhere, so it was a good gig for anyone who wanted to move from the local stage to the national and international stages.

I knew after watching a few sessions of Question Period in the House of Commons that I would never want to cover Parliament the way it was being covered by most members of the Parliamentary Press Gallery. The reporters were much too earnest for my liking, embalming the bafflegab of politicians as if it were something to be taken seriously by the readers and listeners. While I enjoyed some of the political theatre enacted daily in the Commons, I preferred to be in a real theatre where the actors were more accomplished and the lines less predictable. So, just as I had done in Prince George, I looked for the offbeat stories with which I could amuse myself.

Among these was a piece I wrote about the installation of a new concert organ in the National Arts Centre. After playing a few bars of "Panis Angelicus" on the big instrument, I wrote what purported to be an open letter to syndicated political columnist Charles Lynch. He was the star of the Southam News Ottawa bureau in those days, a serious journalist who wrote in a disarmingly folksy style and boasted of "slipping the reader mickeys of information along with the entertainment." A man after my own heart, in other words. He played the harmonica in his spare time. In my piece about the National Arts Centre organ, I said that the feeling of power I got from playing this massive three-manual instrument transcended anything Lynch could possibly get from a two-octave mouth organ that he carried around in his back pocket. One of the other correspondents in the Southam Ottawa bureau dismissed my piece as "esoteric." But the roars of laughter I heard from Lynch's office as he read the piece told me I was on the right track. All the papers in the Southam chain printed the piece in their next-day editions.

One of the more serious pieces I wrote during my three months in Ottawa was a takeout on the Canada Council, then in its 16th year of fostering the growth of arts and culture in this country. It ran to a total of more than three thousand words. When I look at it now, I note that many of the arguments employed then by the council's critics to discredit the organization are still being used by its critics today. "I don't want to see my taxpayer's dollars being wasted in support of weirdo artists and out-of-work poets," went a typical argument. "The money should be spent on important things like pensions and health care."

The loudest complaints were usually voiced when the council put money into what the critics regarded as frivolous projects: piano smashing or playing the fool. When an American artist named Ralph Ortiz received Canada Council money to chop up a piano with an axe, and a jester named Joachim Foikis received funding to spend a year acting as Vancouver's town fool, the opposition politicians and the newspaper critics were furious. Yet none saw fit to acknowledge that while Ortiz received just $284 for his piano-smashing routine, the Vancouver art gallery where he staged his so-called "act of destructivism" received four hundred times that amount in annual funding. Nor did anyone point out that Foikis's one-time grant of $3,500 was a mere pittance compared to the money the Manitoba Theatre Centre was giving to star actor Len Cariou for a single three-week appearance in Winnipeg. The council's associate director, Tim Porteous, explained it this way to me:

> You have to support a limited amount of experimental work in the hope that out of it will come something of lasting quality. It's something similar to a person managing an investment portfolio. He puts

most of the money into blue-chip stocks, and a limited
amount into penny mining stocks that may or may
not yield a fortune. We put the vast majority of the
funds into established, recognized areas, and occa-
sionally dabble in the penny stocks.

More specifically, said Porteous, the council spent most of its $45-million annual budget supporting such mainstream arts organizations as the Montreal Symphony and the National Ballet, while spending just a few thousand on the offbeat and the experimental.

How many of these experimental artists eventually produced something of lasting quality? I think it's probably fair to say that those with genuine artistic talent and enduring audience appeal did go on to make significant contributions. In 1996 Ralph Ortiz was still being commissioned by such galleries as the Whitney Museum of American Art in New York to re-enact his piano-smashing routines of the 1960s. And while Joachim Foikis disappeared from public view after hanging up his jester's costume and belled cap in 1969, he was fondly remembered at the time of his death in 2007 as someone who shook his rattle in the face of authority and drew attention to what many saw as the hypocrisies and high-spending habits of Vancouver City Council.

After writing the Canada Council piece in December 1973, I started to envisage the kind of home I wanted to build for myself in journalism. But I wasn't going to be able to build it in Prince George, where the arts and entertainment scene was confined to local amateur theatricals and the occasional concert by visiting professionals. I would have to move to a larger city, and I assumed that city would be Vancouver. But when I applied for a job at the *Province*, to which I was already contributing regularly as Prince George correspondent, I was told that under the paper's contract with the Newspaper Guild all new editorial hires had to serve a three-month probationary period before being considered for full-time employment. This seemed like too much of a gamble to me. If I had been single, I might have taken the chance. But I was not about to quit my full-time job at the *Citizen*, uproot Zelda and five-year-old Nicole, and pay the expenses of moving to Vancouver without some guarantee that my job at the *Province* would last more than three months.

Then came a job offer from Calgary. It came out of the blue, just like *Citizen* editor Tony Skae's offer had in 1972. It came courtesy of my good friend Greg McIntyre, who had become a reporter at the *Calgary Herald* after working for a couple of years at the *Lethbridge Herald*. "If you were ever thinking of moving to Calgary, now's the time," said Greg. "They've just lost some senior reporters here and they're scrambling to find new people."

I wasn't thinking of moving to Calgary. Zelda and Nicole and I had spent a week there one summer visiting with Greg and his wife Val and family, and nothing about the place particularly appealed to me. It seemed hot and dusty and dry, and somewhat characterless. But the Vancouver door had banged shut, and I wanted to get out of Prince

George. Though seven times larger than 4,000-person Smithers, and a very good place for young reporters to polish their skills, Prince George was still too much the small town for me – the eternal big-city boy.

For some, such as *Citizen* editor Skae and the paper's talented photographer, Dave Milne, Prince George was a final destination. They liked the gentle pace, the uncrowded ski hills and the absence of rush-hour traffic. For me, it was little more than a way station. I missed the big-city bustle, the bookstores, the Italian restaurants. City living was in my genes. As a child I had been lulled to sleep by the sound of traffic outside my bedroom window. "Why don't I get Peter Matthews to give you a call," said Greg. Matthews was the *Herald*'s city editor. He was looking to fill four senior reporter positions following a move by the incumbents to jobs in Vancouver and Toronto.

Matthews hired me over the phone, just like Gary White of the *Interior News* had done six years earlier. I seemed to be living a charmed life when it came to job offers from Canadian newspapers. Matthews told me that the *Herald* would pay me the top-of-the-grid salary for a senior reporter – about $1,200 a month, as I recall – and cover my moving expenses from Prince George to Calgary. And the job would be permanent. There was no union in the *Herald* newsroom to keep new hires on tenterhooks for three months before granting them full-time status. "But I need you to send me a backdated application in writing before I can put you on the payroll," said Matthews. "We're not supposed to poach employees from other Southam papers."

"Let's go there for a year," I said to Zelda. I still had my heart set on moving to Vancouver. After a year in Calgary I would be ready to move on. The *Herald* reporters who moved to Vancouver seemed to have found a way to get around the union restrictions on new hires. I figured I might be able to do the same.

We arrived in Calgary on April 15, 1974. The snow was still on the ground in Prince George, but the McIntyres had put away the boots and parkas and were already enjoying backyard barbecues. Spring had seemingly arrived. But in Calgary you never stow away the snow shovels until the beginning of May at least. On April 28, a snowstorm dumped 45 centimetres on the city, disrupted power and phone service, rendered highways impassable and closed Calgary International Airport.

We lived in the McIntyres' basement for about a week until we found a duplex to rent in the same community, Huntington Hills. It was then the most northerly suburb in Calgary, a newly built neighbourhood on the edge of the bald prairie, with some depressing aspects. The landscaped median strips were dotted with spindly poplar trees recently planted by the city, which would not attain maturity for another 20 years. But it had lots of couples with young children, and Nicole quickly made many friends. It was a safe neighbourhood for children. When Nicole was in kindergarten, she could walk to school with one of her classmates, and we never had to worry about them being accosted.

While our initial plan was to make Calgary just a temporary stop on our way to Vancouver, we soon started thinking of setting down roots. We were coming to see Calgary as a city where the future promised nothing but brightness.

Harmony and

Discord at the

Calgary Herald

REMEMBER ME TO
HERALD SQUARE

We went to the 1974 Mother's Day brunch, Zelda, Nicole and I, at the penthouse restaurant of the 12-storey Sheraton Summit Hotel, then one of the landmark buildings in downtown Calgary. The featured entertainment was by a tuxedoed jazz singer whose name I've long forgotten. Between songs he said, "Please put your hands together, ladies and gentlemen, and welcome one of our special guests today, the distinguished columnist for the *Calgary Herald*: MR. JOHNNY HOPKINS!"

Distinguished columnist? Hopkins was one of my colleagues. I wanted to tell the people sitting at the next table that I worked for the *Calgary Herald* too. For a few moments I felt as if I had just come to work for a newspaper as important as *The New York Times*.

Johnny Hopkins was typical of *Herald* scribes in those days – a widely read metro columnist who had never been to university or to journalism school but knew how to listen and to write. His subject was people. If Johnny had an opinion on an issue, you never read about it in the *Herald*. But you would read about the first person to climb the inside steps to the top of the Calgary Tower, or about the last elevator operator left working downtown. Or you might read about Hopkins himself. One column was about his trip to hospital for abdominal surgery. ("Hey, that's me you're cutting.") He wrote it as part of his ongoing "attempt to brighten up this corner of the page."

Hopkins had his own office at the *Herald*, one he shared with a fellow columnist named Ken Liddell. An office, shared or otherwise, was a status symbol at the paper. Every senior newsroom manager, every editorial writer, every columnist had one. The rest of us were corralled in the so-called "open-concept" newsroom – which meant that the place looked for all the world like an office surplus showroom, with desks pushed too close together and piles of yellowing newspaper clippings stacked up on the floor like stooks in a wheat field. Toronto journalist Ian Brown, who writes columns for *The Globe and Mail*, has wryly characterized such a setting as a "congenial place to write – as abattoirs go."

The building manager regularly complained that the newsroom was a fire hazard, but nobody paid him any heed. Reporters kept tear sheets close to their desks because they thought they might have to refer to them some day for a story they were researching. Even though they usually couldn't remember what actual stories were stuck at the bottom of the piles, the reporters would never have considered throwing them out. Heck, there might have been something important down there. Nor would they ever *dream* of asking a newsroom librarian to help them with their research. They firmly believed that if an assignment editor were to ask them to do a story on, say, water fluoridation plebiscites or heroin use in prisons, they would simply gaze at the pile of papers gathered around their desks and the needed reference material would magically ascend from the bottom of the stack like the queen of hearts arising from a conjurer's deck of cards.

I began my *Herald* career as a reporter on the police beat, the traditional proving ground for new editorial employees. My byline said I was a "*Herald* staff writer," and that simple designation spoke volumes. At the *Citizen* I had been a "staff reporter," signifying that my job was simply to report the news for publication, no creative writing expected. The editors in Prince George cared nothing about literary style; they expected the stories to be written clearly and concisely, in plain, understandable language, with all the most important points covered in the first four paragraphs. At the *Herald*, things were different. Newsroom job applicants had to pass a word comprehension and writing test before being hired. "Remember that *pulchritude* means *beauty*!" a newsroom wag, Bob Blakey, would yell in a loud stage whisper to an applicant waiting nervously to write the test for Merv Anderson, the assistant news editor who did the hiring.

Anderson was one of the few *Herald* editors with a college education. Most were like Bill Gold, the paper's 38-year-old, self-educated editor-in-chief, who used to boast that he was "surely the last editor of a major paper in Canada to own no certificates of school completion beyond grade eight." Gold compensated for his lack of formal education by bringing uncommon intelligence, curiosity and keen powers of observation to his work as a newspaperman. He was living proof that the road to journalistic excellence did not have to be paved with sheepskin. By dint of reading widely and thinking deeply, Gold carried the torch for truth, integrity, humanism and all the other qualities that epitomized the best in Canadian journalism.

In a newsroom where many of the senior managers were amiable and incompetent drunks, Gold stood apart from the pack and led by example. He wrote with grace, insight and passion, and encouraged other *Herald* writers to do the same. He urged us to use all the stylistic techniques at our disposal to produce our best prose and to "go long" on stories where in-depth treatment seemed warranted. There was plenty of room to accommodate these longer stories, because on any given day the volume of ads left us with plenty of white space to fill. My way of feeding this insatiable goat was to step away occasionally from my day-to-day coverage of major crimes to write a lengthy news backgrounder about the increasing incidence of alcohol-induced rapes and murders in the city, or to put together a major feature about the heroin trade on downtown Calgary streets.

Years later, a new generation of *Herald* managers would dismissively accuse me and my contemporaries of alienating advertisers by purveying so-called "advocacy journalism" – raising public awareness and promoting the need for social change. However, we believed we were on the side of the angels because our first mentor had been a respected editor who flatly refused to sacrifice journalism at the altar of advertising revenues. Gold had taught us to play a serious and important role – a public- interest role that today has no place in a business driven more by private profit than by public debate – acting as the conscience as well as the eyes and ears of our city.

As well as writing about the rapes, murders and drug dealings, I also moonlighted during my first year as an occasional pop concert reviewer and book reviewer for the *Herald's* entertainment editor, Jamie Portman. He rewarded me for my efforts in 1975 by offering me a full-time job in the entertainment section when he left the department to become national arts correspondent for Southam News. My friends in the newsroom were surprised when I transferred to what they disparagingly called "the pansy patch." But I had no desire to write about the "oil patch" – the main industry in town – and I certainly didn't want to write about politics. My brief internship as parliamentary correspondent with Southam News in Ottawa in 1973 had convinced me that Canadian politics was too bewildering for words.

Portman had been an eclectic arts writer at the *Herald*, covering theatre, classical music, opera, ballet, movies and books. The other writers in the department cherry-picked from this smorgasbord of cultural beats before I arrived, so I was left to find my own niche. I chose writing about nightclub entertainment. Given my background as a club performer, it was a good fit for me. Portman's successor as entertainment editor, Al Rach, ran the stories with my photo-byline up top, which meant I was now, like Johnny

Hopkins, a "distinguished columnist." Hopkins obviously had some concerns about this, because shortly after I started writing the *Nightscene* column he invited me to lunch to talk about it.

Hopkins was worried that I might be moving in on his territory. One of his regular beats was the Calgary hospitality industry. In the elliptical "three-dot journalism" style popularized by *San Francisco Chronicle* columnist Herb Caen, Hopkins introduced his readers to the new chef at the Guv'nors Grill or the new maître d' at the Sheraton Summit, with their names highlighted in boldface type. He worried that my column might be possible competition for him, but I quickly assured him it was not. I said I was interested only in the entertainment presented at these venues; the staffing changes were his bailiwick. Having thus explained my position, I continued writing about the visiting country rockers and bump-and-boogie bands for the next couple of years.

I also wrote about some bigger-name entertainers who invariably agreed to sit down with me between sets and talk about their careers. Fats Domino was an exception. He seemed to mistake me for a fan, or perhaps a visiting plainclothes officer, because he signed a photograph to me – "Good luck to Mr. Brennan" – and then refused to answer any questions. Others were more forthcoming. Kenny Rogers, whose fortunes had taken a dive after he left the First Edition and went solo in 1976, treated me to an impromptu green-room performance, a cappella, of a pop–country song he predicted would restart his then-stalled recording career. He obviously knew what he was talking about. "Lucille" reached number one on the pop charts in 12 countries, sold more than five million copies and put Rogers on the road to becoming a much bigger star than he was when he hosted the Canadian TV variety show *Rollin' on the River*.

A couple of older entertainers, comedy pianist Victor Borge, then 66, and fan dancer Sally Rand, then 71, told me, when I asked the question between sets, that they would never give up performing. "Retire from what?" asked Borge, obviously insulted by the question. "Retire from life? Performing *is* my life. Age is emphasized too much. Some people are old when they're 22. Others are still young when they're 80. It all has to do with the spirit. I feel stronger now than I did 20 years ago." I was 31 when I asked Borge the question. I am older now than he was then. With the passing years, I have learned not to ask the retirement question.

In the case of Sally Rand, I thought the question, though rude, was legitimate. She was almost as old as my grand-mother, and she was still taking her clothes off in public. "Why are you still doing this?" I asked. "If I were to give it up, what would I retire to?" she replied impatiently. "Sitting on a patio doing needlepoint? Yecch!" I described her striptease performance as graceful, tasteful and elegant, and said that the body stocking she wore – made of a gauze material called *mousseline de soie* (I got this information from her press kit) – created the kind of illusion that you see in motion pictures where reality is softened by diffusion filters. She was obviously upset by this comparison, because she phoned me the day after the column appeared. "I was not wearing a body stocking," she insisted. "I was nude!" So there.

I had a lot of fun with the *Nightscene* column. So did entertainment editor Rach, who tried to match every column with a witty headline. One of his best topped a column I wrote about a group billed as The Platters, who offered a mediocre impersonation of the famed black vocal group that had exploded onto the pop scene during the mid-1950s with such monster hits as "Only You," "The Great Pretender" and "Twilight Time." When I checked with the Buck Ram organization in Las Vegas, which held the rights to the name, I discovered that this Vancouver-based group playing in Calgary had no permission to call themselves The Platters. The only officially sanctioned Platters group at that time was playing a gig in London, England. Rach wrote the only headline that seemed to apply under the circumstances: "Oh, yes, they're the Great Pretenders." We never heard back from the imitators.

It may have been the non-threatening atmosphere of the Calgary clubs that encouraged candour, or perhaps because they thought they were playing in some hick town where they wouldn't have to worry about the tabloids distorting their stories, but I found that many visiting entertainers dropped their guard and revealed little-known details about their lives and careers when they sat down with me and chatted between sets. Crooner Al Martino, for example, told me he became a social pariah in Hollywood when the producers of the movie *The Godfather* signed him to play the singer Johnny Fontane – a character based on Frank Sinatra – because the director, Francis Ford Coppola, had wanted Sinatra protégé Vic Damone to get the part. "I think a lot of the anger was due to the fact that I was a newcomer to the motion picture industry, and the movie people don't like outsiders invading their domain," said Martino.

Chuck Berry told me that all of his songs were autobiographical and that he had no interest in following current trends by sweetening his tunes with pop-disco orchestrations. "There are no violins in my music," he said. "No sir-ree, and you can put the emphasis under the 'ree.'" Tammy Wynette said that her songs too were autobiographical. Then married for just two months to Nashville real-estate executive Michael Tomlin, Wynette admitted between shows at the Ranchman's Steakhouse that the marriage, her fourth, was already on the rocks. "It's very hard to travel and life a normal life," she said. Her trademark songs of heartbreak and despair – "Stand By Your Man," "D-I-V-O-R-C-E," "Another Lonely Song," "It's All Over," "I Don't Want To Play House," "Your Good Girl's Gonna Go Bad" – revealed the story of her troubled private life. "Every line is true," she said wistfully.

Chubby Checker, meanwhile, used his Calgary appearance to publicly denounce the fans for not sticking with him through a succession of increasingly silly dance records after he had made "The Twist" one of the biggest pop hits of the 1960s, prompting millions of youngsters to dance as if towelling their backs dry after a shower. Checker was clearly upset that the disco generation of the 1970s had no appreciation for what he had given the world: "Hank Ballard wrote the song ("The Twist") but Chubby made it a dance. Einstein made only one great discovery in his life, too." And so it went.

I wrote *Nightscene* until editor Rach asked me to become the *Herald*'s full-time theatre writer. I was already covering some theatre in addition to my duties as columnist, so I welcomed the opportunity to make theatre my specialty.

I wasn't the fastest writer at the *Herald*, so I was greatly relieved when Rach said he didn't expect me to churn out a quick theatre review while the final applause was still ringing in my ears. I could spend all night on the review if necessary because the *Herald* was then an afternoon paper, which meant it wasn't put to bed until sometime after 10:00 a.m. The morning *Albertan* worked to a much tighter deadline, covering opening nights the same way it covered school board meetings and hockey games: always making sure that a review of some kind, however groan-inducing, was in the paper the following day.

I took time with my reviews and soon began to fancy myself a worthy successor to George Bernard Shaw with my dazzling displays of verbal brilliance. I now realize that it was hardly ethical for me to have launched a career in theatre criticism based on getting show-off prose and undergraduate humour into the newspaper: "There's less to *See How They Run* than meets the eye . . . The audience should cry 'fowl' and *The Birds* should spread their tiny wings and fly away." But at the time it seemed to me that the spirit of irreverence that prevailed in the *Herald* sports pages and in some of the editorial opinion columns should also be a defining characteristic of the arts and entertainment pages.

What were my qualifications as a theatre critic? In the beginning, they were much the same as the non-existent credentials I brought to the job of journalism when I first started writing for the *Interior News* in 1968. I could claim a little more expertise than the average theatrical neophyte because I had acted in a few semi-professional stage productions in Dublin and done a few theatre reviews for the *Prince George Citizen* when I wasn't busy covering city council meetings. I had also seen a fair amount of professional theatre in Dublin. During the early 1960s I attended the first Irish performances of plays by Pinter, Beckett and Tennessee Williams, including one memorable night in the Pike Theatre when the Dublin morality squad shut down *The Rose Tattoo* on grounds that the play was "indecent and profane." The theatre ran afoul of the Catholic Irish police because the director committed the unpardonable sin of allowing the young actress playing Rosa to appear on stage in her underwear. But still I have to admit that my superficial type of theatre criticism could have been produced by almost anyone who had read a few scripts and attended a few shows. It consisted mainly of allowing the waves of a performance to wash over me and then analyzing the markings in the sand. In any other specialty branch of journalism, if I had tried to pass myself off as competent with a similar lack of qualifications, I would have been denounced as a fraud. But at the *Herald*, I got away with it.

My situation was fairly common in Canadian daily newspapers at that time. If I had applied for a job in the sports department, I would have been expected to know something more about curling than the fact that the national championship was called the Brier. If I had applied for a position as a business writer, I would have been expected to know how to make sense of a simplified prospectus. Yet anyone with a smattering of knowledge about acting and production values could become a theatre reviewer. "Do you think you would recognize it if Willie Shakespeare were writing in Calgary today?" my *Herald* colleague Don Truckey provocatively asked after I had been reviewing for a few years. Perhaps not, but then neither would those who had been entrusted with the artistic leadership of the major professional theatres in town.

The Canadian actor Barry Morse, who became well known across North America during the five years (1963–67) he played the dogged police detective Philip Gerard in the American television series *The Fugitive*, had an amusing routine he liked to use to demonstrate the philistinism of Canadian newspaper theatre critics. Whenever he encountered one who had given him a negative review, Morse would challenge the critic to answer three questions: "What was Molière's real name?" (Jean-Baptiste Poquelin) "Who was Joseph Jefferson?" (A Philadelphia-born actor-comedian [1829–1905] who became one of the most popular 19th-century personalities of the American stage.) "What was *Caste* and why was it important?" (A play by the Anglo-Irish dramatist Thomas William Robertson [1829-71], one of the earliest attempts to put contemporary "cup-and-saucer" realism on the English stage.) He told me that if the hapless critic failed to answer his questions, Morse would dismiss him from the room with the following rant:

> *Your bottomless ignorance has reinforced my opinion that the majority of theatre critics in this country are refugees from writing about dogs' funerals. How can you presume to pass judgment on my work when you don't even know the ABC of theatre? What would your newspaper have to say to someone who wanted to be a sportswriter if he had never heard of Gordie Howe? Or to a business writer who didn't know anything about preferred shares? Yet you presume to write about theatre as somebody who is supposed to be informed. Get out of here!*

There was a good reason for this philistinism. The people who ran the newspapers knew little about the theatre, and they didn't really care how well it was covered. They were happy to pay us to write about arts and entertainment, but they never took us seriously as journalists. They tolerated our contributions to the papers only because someone told them they should. This would start to change during the 1980s, when newspapers began to develop higher standards for all aspects of their journalistic coverage, and the newspaper bosses began to see that the arts were vital to an integral part of Canadian life. But in the mid-1970s the standard for arts coverage at most Canadian newspapers was no higher than it had been in the 1950s, when it was not unusual for police reporters who had never seen a play to be pressed into service as critics. Theatre coverage in those days was what Toronto cultural commentator Robert Fulford has called a "suburb of journalism," and it hadn't moved any closer to the city centre of political, business and crime reporting by the mid-1970s. But the suburb was a great neighbourhood for people like me who didn't want to spend our working lives turning the press statements of politicians and police officers into news stories. We got to put on our opera cloaks every night and bask in the glow of the footlights. It was also great for Zelda, who accompanied me to most of the productions for adults, and for Nicole, who received an education in family-oriented theatre that made her the envy of all her friends.

Lack of knowledge was a failing I felt I had to remedy once I decided to make theatre reviewing my calling. If I had needed some justification for my ignorance, I might have taken consolation from George Bernard Shaw, who once wrote there was no way of becoming a theatre critic except by accident. "And when the accident happens, it happens to a journalist . . . someone who can write and who knows the ways of newspapers." But I didn't want to settle for the role of accidental critic, wearing my ignorance on my sleeve and using it as a pretext for identification with the "average theatregoer." I wanted to know more than the average theatregoer and, if possible, more than the average theatre practitioner. I bought an external reader's library card from the University of Calgary, borrowed books about acting, directing and set designing, and began to study the essays of Shaw, Dryden, Matthew Arnold, Kenneth Tynan, Lionel Trilling and Northrop Frye.

My studies helped make me a more informed critic, but they didn't help me in all aspects of my job as a reviewer. Nobody had ever written a primer on how to write reviews on deadline for a daily newspaper. That was something I had to learn on the job. Every review had to combine journalism with criticism. I had to tell the reader what the play was about and then say what I thought of the script and the production. Finding the right balance between chronicling and critical analysis was something I struggled with in the early years.

New Canadian plays were a particular challenge for me. If a play was already in print, I could borrow the script from the university library and bone up before attending the performance. But if the script was unpublished, I had to try and digest it in one sitting while simultaneously taking note of the acting, directing and other production values. Not an easy task, as I discovered. If I focused too much on the felicities of the language or the inventive plot twists, I missed a lot of what the actors were doing with the material. Conversely, if I concentrated on the acting and directing, I missed much of what the playwright had written down for the actors to perform.

Professional theatre in Calgary was still in its childhood then. The oldest and largest of the three main theatres, Theatre Calgary, had been operating for only seven years in 1975, and its artistic director, New York–trained Harold G. Baldridge, had been with the theatre for just three years. Alberta Theatre Projects (ATP), founded by actor-director Douglas Riske, his playwright wife Paddy Campbell and manager Lucille Wagner had been operating for only three years, with a focus on new Canadian plays. The third company, Lunchbox Theatre, was a brand new addition to the Calgary scene, founded by the husband-and-wife team of director Bartley Bard and actress Margaret Bard to provide noon-hour entertainment for brown-bagging patrons. Some other professional theatres, such as the university-based Image Theatre Company and a group called Alternative Theatre Company, attempted to gain a foothold in the city during the same period. However, the audience for theatre in Calgary was small, and funding from private and government sources was in short supply, so these new companies quickly folded.

Whenever I liked a show, which happened often in the case of Lunchbox Theatre during its first three seasons, I trumpeted my enthusiasm in the paper and encouraged readers to attend. Whenever I didn't like a show, usually because Theatre Calgary or ATP had failed to deliver the "excitement" their artistic directors had promised when announcing their seasons, I became a tough and often unyielding reviewer. I might have adopted a more sympathetic approach had I been there to witness and chronicle Calgary theatre's transition from amateur to professional in the late 1960s and been aware of its growing pains. But I was a relative newcomer in town and not about to make allowances for the difficulties involved in producing what I viewed as bad work. I was a journalist, not an apologist. My duty was to the readers who relied on the paper for independent coverage. This was supposed to be professional theatre, after all. I was being paid by the *Herald* to offer an opinion on whether or not a show was worth the ticket price. I was not being paid to be Caspar Milquetoast. To waffle would have been to deceive. Or so I felt at the time.

I suspect now I may have drawn blood with my early negative reviews, squelching promising talents while trying to impress readers with my wit, intelligence and the fruits of my reading list that week. Because negative criticism often has a direct and immediate effect on a theatrical production, I fear some actors, directors and playwrights may have been wounded by these hard-hitting critiques. Yet when I mentioned this to the playwright and librettist John Murrell a few years ago, his response was characteristically generous. "Perhaps we weren't very good," he said. "Remember, we were learning our craft too."

Murrell, now one of the distinguished senior members of Canada's playwriting fraternity, with works translated into many languages and produced around the world, is an example of someone who suffered at my hands during the early years of my career as a *Herald* reviewer. He had two plays premiered at ATP in 1976–77 when he was playwright-in-residence at the theatre. I panned them both. I described *A Great Noise, A Great Light* – about a group of vagrants reacting to the religious and political propaganda preached by Social Credit premier William Aberhart during the Depression – as a talky play that "makes a lot of statements but doesn't really say anything." Murrell's second play, *Waiting for the Parade*, offered a series of interlinked vignettes about life on the home front for five women in Calgary during the Second World War. I described it as a "photo album of staged nostalgia . . . as unstructured as a raw egg spilled on the kitchen floor." I was not alone in this opinion. The *Albertan* reviewer, Scott Beaven, said much the same about *Parade*. And when the play later moved on to Toronto's Tarragon Theatre, the *Toronto Star* critic, Art Cuthbert, described it as "annoyingly domestic and vague."

If Murrell had allowed himself to be shattered by the negative reviews of *Parade*, chances are he would have quit the theatre – he was 32 when the play was produced at ATP – and taken up another line of work. But Canadian theatre, unlike its embattled New York counterpart, was not made or broken by critics. The theatre critic of *The New York Times*, no matter who holds the job, is always known as the "Butcher of Broadway." Murrell was hurt but he didn't let the negative reviews slow him down. After revising the *Parade* script, he had it remounted and toured across Canada by the National Arts Centre. I described the NAC version as "more edifying, more amusing and more fully realized" than the version I had seen in 1977, but the reality is that it may have just been a better production than the Calgary original. It was also filmed for television, produced in New York and London, and won the Chalmers Award for best Canadian play of 1979.

So, did I get it wrong when I gave a negative review to *Parade* in 1977? Only to the extent that I failed to consider the possibility that the play might be improved with rewriting, more imaginative direction and a stronger cast. I wrote in 1977 that the play was basically a work-in-progress, and I still believe this was true. The constraints of a pre-sold season and an inflexible opening night had put *Parade* in the position of being presented before it was ready.

As for *A Great Noise, A Great Light*, it was never staged again. Murrell seems to have acknowledged that the characters could never amount to anything more than faceless mouthpieces for the different sides in the Social Credit debates of the 1930s, because he put the script back in his drawer and turned his mind to other playwriting endeavours. These included *Memoir*, a bittersweet play about the life and art of Sarah Bernhardt that would eventually be translated into 15 languages and performed in 30 countries. When the play toured Ireland and England, the role of Bernhardt was played by the distinguished Irish actress Siobhan McKenna. This play struck a particular chord with me when I saw a revival in 1981 – the year I turned 38 – because it got me thinking about mortality, self-preservation and the unreliability of memory. Would I, like Bernhardt, start losing it as I got older? A friend of mine, the playwright Sandra Dempsey, told me jokingly that when I reached that point my writing would simply turn into experimental poetry!

Sharon Pollock was another playwright of the time whose works were later produced internationally. Predictably, I panned her plays when I first saw them in Calgary and Edmonton. For example, I found 1979's *The Komagata Maru Incident*, about the 1914 confrontation between Canadian immigration authorities and a boatload of Punjabi Sikhs stranded in Vancouver's Burrard Inlet, to be a "didactic history lesson, filled with righteous attitudinizing and laced with propaganda." *Mail versus Female*, presented at Lunchbox in 1979, was a "confused mess," combining a comedy sketch about the 1935 On-to-Ottawa Trek by disgruntled relief-camp residents with an unrelated sketch about Prime Minister Trudeau and the Canadian postal authorities. "Pollock obviously doesn't like the federal government (any government) too much but never actually gets around to telling us why," I wrote. I also disliked her 1980 prison-hostage drama, *One Tiger to a Hill* ("a propaganda piece masquerading as a realistic drama"), because, much like *The Komagata Maru Incident*, it invited only one kind of knee-jerk response, and I didn't happen to go along with Pollock's anarchic line in political ideology. I didn't have much good to say either about ATP's 1980 premiere production of *Generations*, adapted from a Pollock radio play about a young Alberta farmer justifying his reasons for staying on the farm as his father and grandfather did before him. I had some problems with the script of *Generations* ("too much self-righteous sermonizing") but my main difficulty was with the ATP set, which reduced the sweeping landscape of the Prairies to "Munchkin Land proportions."

Then, in 1980, came *Blood Relations*, Pollock's mystery drama about the Lizzie Borden axe murders, and finally I had reason to celebrate. After attending the premiere production of the play at Edmonton's Theatre 3, I declared that the playwright "for a change, has given us a play about real people instead of bombarding us with propaganda in her efforts to dramatize a pet theme." The first four Pollock plays, to my mind, had amounted to little more than polemics, ideological exhortations, expressions of moral judgments. *Blood Relations*, by contrast, was a play laced with ambiguity that prompted us to make up our own minds. "Did Lizzie, or didn't she?" Pollock provided the clues and we got to supply the answer.

If Murrell and Pollock were upset by my first-night reviews of their early work, they certainly didn't hold grudges. Both became regular lunch companions of mine during the rest of my stint as *Herald* theatre critic, with the unspoken understanding that this growing friendship of ours would not compromise my independence as a critic. I had a similarly friendly relationship with others in the theatre community. We would meet over lunch or drinks and often agree to disagree, but never to the point where we stopped communicating. Then in 1992, four years after I left the drama beat, Pollock paid me a terrific compliment. She invited me to play the pianist/narrator in a production of *Billy Bishop Goes to War* that she was directing at Calgary's Garry Theatre. "I always knew you were a great piano player, but I had to wait until you got off the theatre beat before I could use you," she said. That production, dramatizing the achievements of Canada's top fighter pilot in the First World War, brought me a taste of my own medicine when my successor as *Herald* theatre critic, Martin Morrow, reviewed my performance: "His singing voice, while pleasantly lilting, proves too slight to hold up his side of the vocals." Ouch!

My negative reviews usually brought a few letters to the editor from patrons who disagreed with me. They brought me some additional notoriety in May 1983 when I was barred from Stage West, a professional dinner theatre that had been operating in Calgary for about two years. Stage West's programming formula was to pick a comedy that had been a hit in New York or London and turn it into a starring vehicle for a television actor such as Don Adams (*Get Smart*) or Gary Burghoff (*M*A*S*H*). After I had given negative reviews to half a dozen Stage West productions, the owner of the theatre, Howard Pechet, sought a meeting with *Herald* publisher Pat O'Callaghan aimed at having me taken off the beat. "He doesn't like dinner the-atre and we don't like him," said Pechet to O'Callaghan's secretary. "You don't send someone who hates Italian food to review an Italian restaurant. You shouldn't send some-one who dislikes dinner theatre to review our theatre."

O'Callaghan refused to meet with or even talk to Pechet. "Tell him I don't get into pissing matches with skunks," he said to his secretary when Pechet demanded a reason. Pechet retaliated by first refusing to let me have compli-mentary review tickets and then having me ejected from the theatre when I bought my own. The story of my ban-ishment ran in newspapers across Canada and also in *Variety*, the show-business trade weekly. The *Herald* car-ried letters from readers cheering the Stage West move. "It's time someone ended Brian Brennan's ego trip. I'm sick of Brennan's snobbish flatulence."

To get around the ban, I considered shaving off my beard, putting on a wig, and going to the theatre in drag. The *Herald*'s fashion writer, Bernice Huxtable, even managed to find a dress large enough to accommodate my 6-foot-4-inch frame. O'Callaghan, however, would not hear of such a scheme. "We either go through the front door or not at all," he said. "We are the *Herald*, not a bunch of undercover agents."

For O'Callaghan, the Stage West ban was not a hill to die on. He had more important things to worry about than the *Herald* being denied entrance to a profit-orient-ed, commercial dinner theatre that served over-the-top productions and nondescript food. A crusading journalist who compensated for Alberta's lack of significant representation in Parliament by making the *Herald* the voice of Alberta, O'Callaghan only took up the cudgels on behalf of a free press when the public's right to know was seriously threatened. If Stage West had been something more than a marginal player in the local theatre scene, O'Callaghan would have assigned another critic to review its shows.

I was just as happy to strike Stage West off my list of things to do. It offered the kind of mundane entertainment that works better on television. I had run out of words trying to describe the same formulaic experience ("yet another tired small-cast comedy," "yet another superannuated Hollywood actor") repeated over and over again. I did, however, continue to write news items about Stage West from time to time – without any residual rancour on my part. As long as Pechet was competing with the city's other theatres for the production rights to West End and Broadway hits, he was a legitimate news subject for my theatre column.

The theatre column, which I filled with news and commentary, was an extension of my work as a critic. In it, I was able to do extended interviews with theatre people who were still active in the business, as well as some who had moved on to other things. One such graduate of the theatre scene was retired English barrister John Mortimer, best known as the creator of the televised *Rumpole of the Bailey* stories, who had once described himself – accurately – as "the best playwright ever to represent a murderer at the Old Bailey." When I met him in Calgary in 1985, he was doing a regular column for the *Sunday Times*, interviewing such well-known and diverse personalities as Mick Jagger, Graham Greene and the Archbishop of Canterbury. My interview with Mortimer, in the lobby of the Westin Hotel, was supposed to last only 20 minutes, but it went on for considerably longer than that after I asked my first question:

"If John Mortimer the award-winning journalist were sent to interview John Mortimer the playwright and novelist, what kinds of questions would he ask?"

"Mr. Brennan, I think we should go and have lunch," Mortimer replied. "Do you like to drink wine?"

Of course I liked to drink wine. When we had ordered our meals – oysters Rockefeller for him and beef on a bun for me – he gave me his answer: "I would ask me if I believed in God, because that's what I ask all my people." Why? "Because they don't expect to be asked the question. And I think it's quite a good test of somebody's character, to ask them whether they believe in God, because it brings them up against some sort of basic reality."

When I asked him how Mick Jagger responded to the question, Mortimer just laughed. "Mr. Jagger said, 'What a question to throw at me in the middle of the World Cup!'" But did he answer? "In fact, he did," said Mortimer. "Mr. Jagger said he supposed he'd have a bit of Christian, a bit of Muslim, a bit of Buddhism in him. But not just *one* religion."

I already knew the answer when I asked Mortimer my opening question. He was on record as being the self-styled "captain of the unbelievers." But I was surprised when he told me he had tremendous respect for religion and for religious people. "In some ways, I do feel very Christian. There's something to be said for Christian ideals and tradition. The only thing I can't get on with is actually believing in God. Because of my legal training, I suppose, I need more proof." Mortimer sipped from his glass of Beaujolais and laughed as he contemplated the idea of cross-examining Jesus Christ about his religious beliefs. "But I do have a great feeling that religion is important to people, and often I wish I could join in. I go to church on Christmas Eve in the village near where I live, and I feel very moved. One of the contradictions in my character, I suppose, is that I would hate England without churches. I would loathe living in a country that didn't have village chapels and cathedrals."

Mortimer gave me a valuable journalistic tip that day. In future interviews, I would make a point of asking people about their spiritual beliefs, especially when I felt the answer might reveal something hitherto undiscovered about the individual. When Ralph Klein, then mayor of Calgary, told me during a magazine interview in 1988 that he left the worries of city hall behind and sought inner peace, not by praying or going to church, but by fly-fishing on the Bow River, I felt I had discovered a side of the man that had not previously been revealed in the many newspaper articles written about him. Klein didn't take his spiritual cues from the words of Scripture; he looked into the glacier-fed waters of the Bow and found the answers there.

Many of the interviews were great fun for me. I often felt like a talk-show host who had landed Robin Williams as the featured guest. The actor Richard Harris, for example, gave me a wonderfully amusing account of what it was like to give up drinking after years of bar-hopping with the likes of Peter O'Toole, Richard Burton and Dylan Thomas. "It's especially difficult for me when I go back to Ireland," said Harris, in Calgary starring in a 1985 touring production of *Camelot*. "Going back to Ireland and not having a drink is like going to church and not saying a prayer."

I also enjoyed chatting with the famously reclusive humourist Tom Lehrer. He had been widely (and erroneously) quoted as saying that political satire became redundant when Henry Kissinger was awarded the Nobel Peace Prize in 1973. However, when he came to Calgary in 1980 to oversee the first production of *Tomfoolery*, a theatre revue based on his songs from the 1950s and 1960s, Lehrer gave me his real reason for dropping out. The liberal consensus was divided, he said. "In the 50s, we had a common enemy. We agreed Adlai Stevenson was good, Eisenhower was foolish and Joseph McCarthy was evil. Then the liberals got in and you couldn't really joke about those people anymore." For political satire to work, Lehrer said, an audience had to agree with the sentiments expressed by the satirist. "It's hard to write a funny song with a lot of 'howevers' in it."

As well as doing the interviews, the critiques and the theatre column, I also covered the theatre scene by writing season-end and year-end retrospectives to put the theatre seasons in perspective for the readers and myself. An Edmonton academic, Diane Bessai, has accused me of being sometimes revisionist ("in an unacknowledged and irritating flip-flop of his original opinion") in these look-back summaries, but I prefer to think of them as sober second thoughts. The next-day reviews had been composed and written in relative haste, and my verdicts – as I looked back at them – were not always clear. As I once explained in a *Herald* column, the reviews were written under deadline pressure, with emphasis on promptness and clarity. This induced a disciplining of the mind and a concentration on what I viewed as essentials. For the sake of dispatch, the mind grasped for easy solutions, looking for sermons in stones and ultimate truths where often there were none. Complex ideas lost layers of meaning. Scholarly musings about literary craft were often sacrificed to simplicity.

I believed that while the articulation of an immediate response in a next-day review could be exhilarating and carry its own kind of special authenticity, there was also a danger of misrepresentation through oversimplification. The reviews appeared in black and white (literally and metaphorically), which could sometimes result in unfair treatment of a work presented in several shades of grey. Hence, in my view, the need for the season-end second looks. The season-enders provided me with an opportunity to clarify and expand on my original assessments and resolve the apparent contradictions that Bessai attributes to my struggle to decide whether I was Brennan the journalist or Brennan the critic. The retrospectives also contributed to the historical record. As time went on, they served as a useful reference guide whenever I wanted to compare, say, the Harold Baldridge era at Theatre Calgary to the era of Rick McNair, his successor as artistic director.

To round out my duties as *Herald* theatre critic, I reviewed movies showing in Calgary that had begun life as stage plays. I also did some outrageous things. In 1981 I conducted a poll of Calgary theatregoers, inviting readers to nominate their favourite plays, best leading actors, supporting actors and so on. For reasons that escape me now, I also asked the readers to nominate the *worst* plays, actors and directors. I even offered a list of suggestions for them to draw from. Mercifully, I came to my senses before proceeding any further with this exercise in cruelty. I never publicized the results. I kept hidden the depressing fact that most of the respondents thought the staging of Canadian plays was, as one reader put it, "an exercise in misguided patriotism." The artistic directors at our largest theatres – Theatre Calgary's Rick McNair and ATP's Doug Riske – were dedicated to showcasing the best in Canadian drama. I realized I would be hurting them unnecessarily if I were to publicize the negative comments of a few jaundiced theatregoers who only saw merit in English and American plays. The Canadian theatre had given us John Murrell's *Memoir* and

Sharon Pollock's *Blood Relations*. Those were just two of the reasons why we should celebrate not disparage local theatre.

I was the *Herald*'s theatre critic for 13 years (1975–88). During that time I came to appreciate that occasional refresher courses in practical theatre were a useful way for me to stay sharp as a critic. I gained some valuable knowledge during the summer of 1981 when I was selected to be a visiting critic/fellow at the Eugene O'Neill Theater Center in Waterford, Connecticut. I worked as script adviser on *Johnny Bull*, an autobiographical play by New York's Kathleen Betsko Yale about a pregnant Cockney woman who accompanies her American serviceman husband to his home in Pennsylvania with the expectation that life will be like what she'd seen in a Doris Day movie. I also left the aisle seat occasionally to participate in Calgary theatrical projects. I attended workshops, play readings and rehearsals to keep in touch with the mechanics of script development, direction and performance, and I used these experiences to deepen my understanding of the production process. In all of these instances I was pleased to discover that a critic could sometimes cross that invisible boundary between artist and audience and make a different kind of contribution to the art form he loves and serves.

The *Herald* theatre critic's job was a dream posting in many respects. I never had any difficulty convincing a succession of managing editors to spend money on sending me to Broadway or the West End to write about shows that Calgary artistic directors were long-listing for future seasons. These trips were a wonderful way of recharging the creative batteries and keeping me motivated whenever I felt jaded by the Calgary theatre scene. The trips also provided a great opportunity for Zelda and Nicole to see some of the best that New York and London had to offer. After Zelda went back to university in 1981 to earn her education degree, she and Nicole were able to accompany me on my summer trips, and we would spend several happy months afterwards reminding ourselves of how hilarious Kevin Kline was in the Broadway production of *The Pirates of Penzance* or how realistic the actors were in the London production of *Cats*.

If I didn't have the occasional opportunity to soothe my soul with some of the best theatre in the English-speaking world, I'm sure I would have quit my gig as *Herald* theatre critic a few years after starting it. Theatre criticism can burn you out quickly if you allow bad productions to get to you. George Bernard Shaw spent barely three years as drama critic for the *Saturday Review* before deciding he could write better plays than the ones he was seeing on the London stage.

Kenneth Tynan wrote some brilliant criticism for the *Observer* before crossing the footlights to become Laurence Olivier's literary manager at the National Theatre. Criticism, Tynan quickly realized, was viewed as an unsavoury occupation by those who worked in the theatre, as third-rate thinking by those who worked in academe, as third-rate literature by those who wrote novels, and as esoteric nonsense by those who ran newspapers. The theatre he wanted to influence never really trusted him, and the newspaper editors whose support and encouragement he needed made him so paranoid and uncertain of his talent that he couldn't put pen to paper without a glass of white wine next to his typewriter and a cigarette burning in the ashtray. So he went to work for Olivier only to discover that the famous actor had created the literary manager's job "just to get you off the damn *Observer*."

I didn't see an opportunity for myself either as a playwright or as a literary manager. I would have made a terrible playwright, because I had been a journalist for so long (20 years) that it would have been virtually impossible for me to reinvent myself as a theatre artist. But I did know that a change of assignment was essential for me after I had been spoiled by all the great performances at the Calgary Olympic Arts Festival in 1988. I had witnessed the best and worst the Calgary theatre scene had to offer between 1975 and 1988, and I had nothing more to say on the subject.

Shortly before I left the theatre beat I was surprised to see a letter to the editor from Sharon Pollock, whose play *Walsh* had been produced at Theatre Calgary as an Olympics presentation. The play, set in a North-West Territories police fort in the wake of Custer's Last Stand, dealt with the dilemma of a buckskin-jacketed Mountie ordered by his Ottawa superiors to dispatch the fleeing Sitting Bull and his Sioux warriors back to the United States. I wrote in my review that the police officer's quandary, involving a conflict between conscience and duty, was "sketchily defined and too neatly resolved." I expected Pollock to admonish me with one of her characteristically blunt put-downs. Instead, to my surprise, she wrote that my review simply made the same points about the script and the production that she had seen in reviews elsewhere. (I hadn't seen these other reviews.) "Brennan must call a production as he sees it based on his experience and expertise, which is considerable," wrote Pollock. "I respect Brennan as a critic and journalist even when I disagree with him and am the butt of his critical wit and occasional venom." Pollock concluded with a call for me to carry on reviewing: "May he continue to serve the theatre and the public without pandering to any one theatre or individual, and thus enhance the *Herald*'s entertainment section, one of the best in the country." I silently thanked her for that vote of confidence, but I had already made up my mind to move on.

I had another reason for wanting a change of scene. The landscape of arts and entertainment coverage had changed at the *Calgary Herald*, as it had at other regional newspapers across the country. While the level of expertise and authority had risen among those of us writing about the arts, the space available for serious arts journalism in many Southam newspapers – arts journalism that discussed ideas and issues as well as covering the opening nights – had shrunk considerably since I started writing about theatre in 1975. The papers only had room for first-night reviews of theatre productions (not of dance, opera or classical music), coverage of pop culture and showbiz gossip. Jamie Portman, the former *Herald* entertainment editor who had paved the way for me to become a full-time arts journalist at the *Herald*, was now a national arts correspondent in name only. His Southam News bosses had told him, after conducting a poll of entertainment editors across the Southam chain, that they would prefer to have him doing interviews with Hollywood starlets than being an advocate for the arts in Canada. In 1988 I was told, by a penny-pinching *Herald* assistant managing editor, that if I wanted to continue being an arts critic and analyst with a company-subsidized travel budget, I should seriously consider applying for a job at *The Globe and Mail* or *The New York Times*. I could see where things were going and opted instead for a new challenge. It was time to redefine my role as a writer. I moved into general feature writing, first with the *Herald's Sunday* magazine, until it folded in 1991, and then with the paper's Lifestyles section.

The *Sunday* magazine position was a gift, the best job at the *Herald* for someone who wanted to try doing the kind of long-form writing that Christina McCall and Peter Gzowski had done with great success at *Maclean's* and *Saturday Night* magazines. I didn't presume to be in the same league as these nationally known Canadian writers, but I did learn a lot from them, studying their articles to see what worked and what didn't and then applying some of their techniques to my own work as a magazine writer. Among my favourite projects was a behind-the-scenes story I wrote about the filming of a $50-million samurai movie, *Heaven and Earth*, and an operating-room story I wrote about open-heart surgery that won me the national Hollobon Award for "excellence in medical reporting." These were great stories to do, because I didn't have to meet a daily or even a weekly deadline. I could take up to a month if necessary, to work on an article and make it as definitive as possible. So I was very disappointed in 1991 when *Herald* publisher Kevin Peterson announced he was shutting down the magazine for economic reasons. I was still able to write features for the paper, but the thrill of being able to stretch out on a story was gone. At that point in my journalistic career, I seemed destined to be remembered as the Salman Rushdie of the Calgary theatre scene: the guy who incurred the wrath of Stage West and spent a dozen years trying to keep the plays of Neil Simon off the local stage.

Then, in September 1992, a notice appeared on the newsroom bulletin board saying that the *Herald* was planning to follow the lead of the *Daily Telegraph* in London and appoint a writer to produce a regular feature obituary column that would be "anecdotal, sharp, witty and wise."

The features editor, Reg Vickers, thought I was crazy when I said I was leaving the department to write about dead people. "Why would you want to do that?" he asked. "That's a job for kids and old hacks who are just spooling out their lines. You're a talented writer, Brennan. You're doing some great work for this section. Why would you want to give that up?"

"I appreciate the compliment, Reg, but it's time for me to move on," I said. "I like the feature writing but I really want to try something different."

Vickers's reaction was predictable. Obituary writing at most North American newspapers was viewed as a thankless chore, a boot-camp assignment given to untried juniors or jaded seniors with an attitude problem. "Duffy," says the city editor to a struggling reporter in Ben Hecht's *The Front Page*, "if you don't smarten up, I'll send you to obituaries." Every obituary followed the same tired formula: the opening paragraph cited one of the deceased's most notable achievements; the next couple of paragraphs quoted the platitudes from friends and family saying what a wonderful person the deceased was; and the rest recorded the bare facts of the individual's life, with a strong focus on achievement. If there was a human being in the midst of all this, he or she was usually lost in a pool of solemn prose about oil wells drilled or companies founded.

I wanted to do it differently. I didn't see obituary writing as punishment; I saw it as opportunity. What I envisaged was still uncharted newspaper territory. Nobody had ever done the kind of obituary writing I had in mind. That meant I had the chance, rare in daily newspapering, to *invent* the column and put my own stamp on it. The great Alberta social historian Grant MacEwan had written books about the homesteading "sodbusters" who came to Alberta to till virgin land and "ride five hundred miles in any direction without opening a gate." In the process, they helped build a province. I would become a journalistic "sodbuster" and perhaps help build something, as well.

THE *TRIBUTE* COLUMN

In my introductory *Tribute* column for the *Calgary Herald*, October 13, 1992, I told the readers that this new obituary feature – due to appear in the paper five times weekly – would commemorate the lives of "ordinary" individuals who had "made a difference." They had not made the headlines, nor did they have a public stage on which to score popularity points with a mass audience. They had just quietly gotten on with the business of living and making things happen. "They were the people who thawed out your frozen water pipes, taught your children how to read or baked the butter tarts for your church socials." They were the people like my own mother, who, while never having done anything a newspaper would consider "newsworthy," was a "pretty fine schoolteacher" and "one special Mom." I offered as another example, without mentioning my father specifically, "the cash-strapped young father who bought a new piano instead of a car so that a musically talented child could develop as a player." "I can't wait to read your next column," said Ken Hull, the city editor who had given me the job. "I think every one of them is going to be a winner."

Hull never gave me any guidelines for the column. "Just write stories," he said when I asked what kind of stuff he expected me to produce. It didn't matter to Ken who I chose to feature in the column. He asked only that I give readers what people in the newspaper business refer to as a "good read."

The column began as an experiment, the first of its kind in Canadian daily journalism. Years later people thought I borrowed the idea for the column's structure from *The Globe and Mail* in Toronto, which carries a similar column called *Lives Lived*. But *Tribute* had been running in the *Herald* for a couple of years before the *Globe* got into the obit-writing business. And *Lives Lived* differs from *Tribute* in one important respect: it is a column written by contributors, usually friends or family of the deceased. I wrote my column.

My columnist colleagues, whose work appeared in the *Herald* three times a week, were shocked when they learned I was going to write *Tribute* five times a week. "You're setting a very bad example," said Tom Keyser. "Claim insanity or mental fatigue. Claim anything that will stop this madness. If you write this thing five days a week, you will end up becoming one of your own subjects."

I was undeterred. I had spent a couple of weeks gathering material for the column before the first one was printed and felt confident I could find five stories weekly to keep the momentum going. These people were not newsmakers, so there was no pressure on me to get their stories into the paper immediately after their deaths. The *Herald* library files had no news stories for me to refer to anyhow, so I had to wait for family members or friends to provide me with the needed information, and that sometimes took several days.

I had no model for this new column. The previous few

years had seen a flowering of obituary writing in the British newspapers, most notably in the *Daily Telegraph*, but these were obituaries of individuals who had achieved the kind of distinction that made them "newsworthy." Nobody was writing about green-space lovers who used their garden hoses to water the shrubs in city parks. The method I developed was to write the column in a chatty, informal style similar to what you would find on a blog nowadays. I wrote as if the deceased had been an acquaintance of mine, which was almost never the case, and included the kinds of anecdotes I would have put in a letter to a friend. The method seemed to work, because the *Herald* editors put my column at the top of the second page in the city news section. All around me were "important" news stories from the courts and from city hall, while I was writing about garden hoses.

For the first couple of months, I stuck to my declared mandate of writing only about unheralded Calgarians, publicly unrecognized individuals who had lived privately important lives. I wrote about an accomplished cook who told her children they wouldn't eat dinner until they had delivered meals from her kitchen to needy neighbourhood shut-ins. I wrote about a ham radio operator who turned into a human helpline during times of crisis and natural disaster, serving as a communications link between earthquake victims without telephones and their worried relatives in Canada. I wrote about a woman who told the government she didn't need her old age security allowance and then donated the pension cheques to charity when the government said she had no choice but to accept the money. "They can make me take it but they can't make me keep it," she said.

I found my subjects through the death notices published daily in the *Herald*. I had always believed in the value of the obits page as a source of potential column material. If a firefighter or former rodeo rider passed away, there had to be a story worth telling. The death notices provided excellent raw material for *Tribute* because Canadians like to give lots of detail when writing about loved ones who have passed away. Whenever I found a death notice that seemed promising, I called up the funeral home and asked that the family be informed of my interest. If a wife or daughter or granddaughter agreed to talk to me, I knew I was in business. Women were the best when it came to talking about their loved ones, because they revealed details that men would never think of mentioning. Would a man ever say that his mother sometimes "forgot" to do the housework? I remember one daughter who told me that about her untidy mother. "If someone can show me something creative about housework," said the mother, "I might get better at it."

I only met face to face with the relatives of the deceased subjects when they specifically requested it. For the most part I did my interviews by phone. That distanced me from their grief and kept me from getting caught up in their emotions. The phone also seemed to help the relatives get comfortable with me. It turned me into a non-threatening presence, a friendly voice in their ear, a person who listened sympathetically and asked gently probing questions like a psychiatrist on the radio. "Hello, I'm listening," said television's fictional Dr. Frasier Crane. I sought basic facts and they gave me golden nuggets. I asked a young woman why her father, a once-promising country singer, had gone back on the road in his late 40s after staying put for 20 years. "Wild horses have to run with the wild horses," she said.

Family members revealed to me the most intimate details about their deceased loved ones. That continually surprised me. Like small children they were, telling their family secrets to a stranger. Weren't they aware of the potential dangers? Didn't they know that reporters, especially when on deadline, often get it wrong? I had seen the damage myself; I would never have entrusted my private family information to a fellow reporter unless I had absolute faith in that reporter's ability to get it right. Yet people who had never met me welcomed me like a long-lost relative when I phoned them up and said I wanted to write in my column about their dearly departed. They were *honoured*, they said, to have me include the story of their loved one in the paper. I tried hard not to betray that trust.

I tried not to be sappy or sentimental in the columns. Some inevitably had to mention illness and death, but I had little interest in writing just about the last part of a deceased's life when a journey truncated by illness moved toward an inevitable conclusion. I wanted it to be a column about the special qualities developed by character and circumstances over the course of an entire lifetime, and I wanted it to be celebratory and life affirming. I wasn't entirely happy with the column heading chosen by editor Hull – *Tribute: People Who Made a Difference* – because it suggested eulogy and I had no desire to sanctify. My aim was to induce readers to look into the middle distance, not lift up their eyes unto the hills. Nor did I want to sanitize. Real people had faults as well as virtues. If they occasionally lost their tempers, drove too fast or refused to suffer fools gladly, I wanted that to be duly noted in my column. That's what made them human. That's what made them real.

I wrote about these previously unsung heroes and heroines from October to December 1992, and then I hit a snag. I had three potential candidates lined up for the next day's column, and all of the relatives said they needed more time before talking to me. What to do now? It was the daily columnist's worst nightmare. The deadline was looming and the well had run dry. In desperation I looked through the *Herald*'s back issues for a possible anniversary subject. The obits page featured a daily in memoriam section next to the current death notices. It seemed to me that I could do an "in memoriam" column and still legitimately put it under the "people who made a difference" heading.

That first in memoriam column, born of desperation, marked another significant departure from my original declared intention of writing only about the recently deceased and writing only about publicly unrecognized individuals.

My chosen subject, "Badger" Bob Johnson, had been a well-known coach with the Calgary Flames hockey team who succumbed to brain cancer a year earlier. His favourite saying, often mentioned by the hockey writers at the paper, was "This is a great day for hockey." "Every day, with Badger Bob Johnson, was a great day for hockey," I wrote. "Every day, except one year ago today."

The *Herald's* widely read opinion columnist Catherine Ford had a twinkle in her eye after she read my Johnson column. "Oh, so now the *Tribute* column can be an anniversary column as well?" she said. "Way to go, Brennan!" I told her I didn't plan to make a habit of mining the pages of history for my material, but a couple of anniversary columns in the bank would give me a good fall-back position should I ever find myself in the same predicament again. The other columnists had their fall-back positions too. You always knew the business guy was having a slow day when his column consisted of a collection of mini-reviews of management books that had landed on his desk recently.

Tribute was sometimes a tough column to write. I had to use the rhetoric of euphemism or ambiguity if there was an aspect of an individual's life or death that the family wanted me to keep private. Thus, "he never married" sometimes became shorthand for homosexuality and "died suddenly" became a euphemism for suicide. I always felt uneasy about using these expressions, because I knew that as a reporter I hadn't told the whole truth. But the family had taken me into their confidence and entrusted me with the telling of their loved one's story, so I could hardly break faith with them by writing something that would cause them additional pain. There were certain things that would always have to go unmentioned.

I did some soul-searching after I had been writing *Tribute* for about a year. Was I still a journalist or had I turned into some kind of peeping Tom? At what point did the telling of a very private story venture into the realm of voyeurism? Did families ever regret having spoken to me after they saw what I put in the paper, especially after I touched on such sensitive subject matter as the details of a terminal illness?

I asked some of these questions in a column I wrote commemorating the first anniversary of *Tribute*, a week after my 50th birthday in October 1993. "Two hundred and twenty people who made a difference," I wrote. "Time to take stock. How am I doing?" The next day, I received more than three dozen phone calls, a handful of faxes (this was before the advent of e-mail) and one letter. I almost didn't get my column written that day.

The answers were gratifying. "You're doing something right, don't change it," said one female caller. "You do dangerous and important work," said another. "*Tribute* is the second thing I read in the paper every day," said a third. *Dare I ask what's the first?* "Why, the sports pages, of course."

Another vote of confidence came from the *Herald*'s ombudsman, Jim Stott. He had received a complaint letter from a reader alleging that too many of my columns were about people who died from cancer. Stott reviewed the columns and acknowledged that many were indeed about cancer victims, but so what? "It is a fact that cancer is an all-too-prevalent illness," wrote Stott. He went on to say that *Tribute* was "one of the best new features this paper has introduced to its pages in a long time." It had reminded readers that there were a lot of extraordinary "ordinary" people in the world. "And in the process, it has defined the real riches and resources of our community: the people all around us."

Not everyone liked *Tribute*, of course. Every time I wrote about someone who had died of AIDS, I could expect to receive at least one unsigned missive filled with hatred, condemnation and Biblical quotations. If I wrote about someone who had left a first marriage to take up with somebody new, I could usually expect to get an angry phone call from a member of the first family. And if I dared to remind readers that a person in the public eye had once fallen from grace and been the subject of negative publicity, I would get an angry call or letter accusing me of irresponsibly dredging up old news. "Why can't you let sleeping dogs lie?"

In my first-anniversary column, I asked readers how they felt about my decision to sometimes obscure or conceal sensitive information about death – especially suicide – to spare further grief to families who had already suffered. One reader told me to leave the sensationalism to the tabloid talk shows on television. "I don't think your column is an appropriate place to try to satisfy the few readers who want to be titillated by others' pain." But two women who had lost loved ones to suicide bravely gave me the names of the deceased and the circumstances of their deaths, and urged me to stop cloaking the subject with euphemisms. Public silence, said one, amounted to tacit acceptance of the societal stigma surrounding suicide. "If you keep it hidden, you're saying to me that my late son did something wrong, something perhaps that I should be ashamed of."

I realized that these two women who had taken a chance by writing letters to me for public consumption were probably typical of many people marginalized and made to feel guilty by society because their loved ones had committed suicide. At a time when more Canadians were taking their own lives than were dying in car crashes, no politician was talking publicly about the need for a government strategy aimed at understanding and prevention. Close to four thousand Canadians annually were dying by their own hands – more than would perish if nine Boeing 747s were to plunge into the Atlantic every year – and yet the deaths could have been occurring in some faraway place like Timbuktu or the Matsu Islands for all the public discussion that was taking place. "Government undecided on suicide prevention program" was a headline that appeared in the *Herald* during that time. The problem was expected to worsen in the future. Researchers were warning that the suicide numbers would increase dramatically when the baby boomers moved into the 21st century, bringing with them a range of social and psychological problems compounded by the negative impact of cuts to public health programs. There had to be more openness, more under-standing, more discussion. I made a mental vow that in the future, if family members were willing to go public with their private pain after a suicide, I would use my column to give dignity and value to that person's life while underlin-ing the need for intervention programs. The time for eu-phemisms was no more.

Although I continued to write mainly about people lit-tle known outside their families, I found myself every few weeks or so during 1993–94 doing a column on someone who had left a mark on the public stage. They included such well-known Canadian individuals as Alberta civil lib-erties activist Sheldon Chumir, popular American blues singer Big Miller, and former Calgary alderman Mary Dover. It was never my idea to write their obits, because I knew the city reporters would already be doing that. But the newsroom managers insisted that I write columns about them as well, which struck me as being excessive. So I wrote the obits just to keep the editors happy. Within a few years, at the behest of one senior editor who had clear-ly forgotten – or never knew – what *Tribute* was supposed to be about, I would be writing about such unlikely sub-jects as Mother Teresa, Roy Rogers and Richard Berry, the guy who wrote the classic pop song "Louie Louie." I even wrote a column about the Scottish poet Robert Burns to coincide with the annual commemorative banquet where the entrance of the haggis is accompanied by the skirling of bagpipes and the drinking of Scotch. *Tribute*, by then, had moved well beyond its original scope of telling the stories of "ordinary" Canadians who had made a difference.

I wrote *Tribute* for seven years, from 1992 to 1999. In the process, I gathered enough life stories to fill a few books. While I was disappointed to see the *Herald* dispense with this regular obituary feature after I left the paper, it still warms my heart to know we blazed a trail. Other Canadian dailies, including the *Edmonton Journal* and the *Globe* with its *Lives Lived* feature, soon followed with obituary columns of their own.

If the choice had been mine, I would have continued writing the *Tribute* column until retirement. But a new generation of newsroom managers came along, looked at my work and saw it as having little more than curiosity value. Instead of writing soft-news obituaries, they said, I should be applying my experience and talents to the more important business of writing about the growth in street crime and the building of big buildings downtown. Clearly, it was time for me to pause and take stock.

LOCKED OUT

I never envisaged it would end the way it did. I had always expected that when my career in Canadian daily newspapering came to a close, I would write a farewell column thanking the readers for taking the time to look at my stuff, and sometimes taking the time to phone or write. I would gather with my colleagues in the centre of the newsroom, the managing editor would make a nice speech about me, and I would respond in kind. I would tell my colleagues that during my time as the *Calgary Herald*'s theatre critic I "gave my best *jeers* to Theatre Calgary." There would be laughter, cards, cake and a chorus of "For He's a Jolly Good Fellow." My colleagues would present me with a framed replica of a dummy front page, filled with photographs of me, and mock news stories about my journalistic achievements. It would be a splendid send-off.

None of this happened, of course. Instead, I found myself, a few weeks after my 56th birthday, scurrying down the back stairs of the *Herald*'s red-brick fortress, clutching my well-thumbed copy of *The Canadian Oxford Dictionary* and the framed photographs of Zelda and Nicole that had been sitting atop my desk, held vertical by little cardboard flaps covered in fake velvet. There had been no fireworks, no marching band, no tickertape parade. This world was ending not with a bang or whimper, but with a step into the unknown. The first strike of newsroom employees in the 116-year history of the *Calgary Herald* was about to begin and I was about to end a 27-year career in Canadian daily journalism.

For more than 20 years at the *Herald* I had looked forward to going to work every day. I had gone from one enjoyable writing assignment to the next and felt appreciated by my bosses. But now I dreaded the thought of entering the red-brick building. I no longer felt appreciated; I no longer felt respected. Why? Maybe it was because I was getting older and the bosses were getting younger.

I told my family doctor about it: "As soon as I get to Memorial and Deerfoot and the *Calgary Herald* building comes into view, I can feel a dull ache rising in my chest." He could tell I was feeling very stressed. He asked me some questions and gave me his assessment. "You're working in a sick building," he said. "Buildings get sick just like people get sick. If you can cure it, great! If not, start working on your exit plan. Give yourself three, five, however many years it takes to get out."

I was 53 years old. Not yet ready for early retirement. But I also didn't have the power to cure whatever sickness plagued the *Herald* building and infected some of us working there. I told a colleague about my dilemma, and she put it to me bluntly. "They just want you to bugger off and die," she said. If that was indeed their desire, I thought, then, damn it, I was going to thwart them. I had no intention of giving them the satisfaction of seeing me leave before I was good and ready.

Then, unexpectedly in the fall of 1998, the promise of

a cure arrived. My fellow editorial staffers and I did what many of us would have considered unthinkable, even laughable, a decade earlier: we voted to bring a union into the *Herald* newsroom. Most of Canada's other major metropolitan dailies already had unionized newsrooms; the *Herald*, the *Edmonton Journal* and the tabloids in the *Sun* chain were among the few exceptions. We had never felt the need for a union. At the *Herald*, we had watched from afar while our unionized colleagues in Vancouver, Ottawa and Montreal weathered strikes and lockouts to win pay increases and better working conditions. Then we held out our hands, asked for the same deal and usually got it.

Up to the mid-1990s most of us had thought the *Herald* was a great place to work, and we enjoyed salaries and benefits comparable to those in unionized newsrooms. Our bosses asked for nothing more than that we get the stories and tell them truthfully, and that we not be dull. They spent the money necessary for us to produce the best journalism possible in a market of our size. When I worked as a theatre critic, my travel budget was the envy of colleagues across the country.

Between 1975 and 1995, you could count on the fingers of one hand the number of people who left the *Herald* newsroom hoping to find a better deal in Vancouver or Toronto. In a newsroom of 160 staffers, that low departure rate suggested most of the employees were generally satisfied with their lot. But eventually, discontent began to simmer.

By the early 1990s, we knew the industry was in trouble.

For the longest time, daily newspapers had been a guaranteed source of profit, a licence to print money as we used to say. Now they were printing in red ink. While the *Herald* continued to generate profits of between $30- and $40-million annually because it is located in one of the most affluent cities in Canada, its sister newspapers in the Southam chain were posting total annual losses of more than $150-million. To alleviate the losses, the Southam bosses began siphoning profits from the *Herald* and ordered the paper to cut costs.

Publisher Kevin Peterson, a former reporter and editor who had worked at the *Herald* since he graduated from the University of Calgary in 1969, tried to develop a business plan to meet Southam targets for spending, circulation and advertising. Peterson's Toronto bosses entrusted him with the task of doubling the *Herald*'s profits: from between 12 and 15 per cent annually to between 25 and 30 per cent. Why? Former *Herald* managing editor Gillian Steward wrote in a *Globe and Mail* article on November 10, 1999, that the aim was to raise the share price, thereby making it more difficult for Conrad Black's Hollinger Inc. to take over Southam. Peterson cut the total *Herald* workforce from 850 to 625 and slashed expense accounts and travel budgets. Then, with the hope that collectively we might find the right way forward, he organized staff into think-tank units known as "visioning groups." To some of the editorial staffers, however, this smacked of desperation, and we viewed the process with a certain cynicism. We had never been consulted or included in management decision-making activities in the past, and we didn't believe our suggestions would be taken seriously now. As it turned out, all efforts aimed at improving the *Herald*'s bottom line came to naught. Peterson never told us what the actual revenue targets were, but it was clear that we were not meeting them. On December 13, 1995, Peterson resigned.

A couple of months later, Ken King, previously the publisher of the rival *Calgary Sun*, took the helm as the *Herald*'s publisher. A few months after that, as feared by the Southam bosses in Toronto, Hollinger Inc. assumed a controlling interest in the company. For some of us editorial staffers, however, this actually seemed like a positive development. Hollinger owned some of the best newspapers in the English-speaking world, including London's *Daily Telegraph* and the *Jerusalem Post*. For as far as we could tell, Conrad Black seemed to care as much about quality journalism as he did about making money, which could only bode well for those of us who worked for the Southam newspapers.

Ken King, a big bear of a man with a successful background in advertising sales and marketing, brought a TV pitchman's approach to the job of fixing the *Herald*. Using the same networking and promotional acumen that had worked well for him at the *Sun*, he set out to raise the *Herald*'s profile in the community through corporate liaisons and marketing partnerships. Editorially, he oversaw the transformation of the *Herald* from a moderately liberal paper into a paper that leaned more to the right. Adding conservative columnists Peter Stockland, Barbara Amiel, Giles Gherson and Andrew Coyne to the editorial pages helped create what King described in a *Herald* article on October 14, 1996, as a "wonderful environment for political and social debate."

The paper became a reflection of King himself, just as Peterson's *Herald* had mirrored his personal style. Peterson, a left-leaning, university-educated intellectual, had worked his way up from political reporter in 1969 to the *Herald*'s publisher from 1989 to 1995. He often went to the theatre, boasted a fine collection of paintings and had a library full of Margaret Atwood and Robertson Davies novels. During his tenure as publisher, the paper exuded intelligence and middle-class values. It revealed a social conscience and told the truth even when it was neither popular nor profitable to do so. It was also clear from the coverage that Peterson's paper considered arts and culture to be a significant part of Calgary's community life. A review of a Theatre Calgary production always occupied a more prominent place in the entertainment section than the reviews of that week's Hollywood movie releases.

King's *Herald*, on the other hand, reflected the values of this street-smart glad-hander from small-town Saskatchewan who smoked Cuban cigars, drank with oilmen and played old-timer's hockey. Taking commercial television as its model, the new *Herald* promoted the interests of corporate Calgary, gave generous space to crime and sports coverage, and sponsored rock concerts. King worked long hours and liked his people to do the same. "He's a dynamo," said one senior *Herald* manager. "I can barely keep up with him." Before King's arrival, newsroom department heads came to work late and left early, ate lunch at the club, spent their summer afternoons on the golf course and were home in time to watch *Seinfeld*. Reporters filed their stories after the bosses left for the day and the night crew of deskers, assistant managers and deputy editors put out the paper. If a senior manager had appeared in the newsroom during the evening when the stories were being edited and the pages were being laid out, the staffers would have wondered what he or she was doing there. The job of the bosses, it seemed to us, was to set editorial policy and decide what should be in the next day's paper. Our job was to take care of the nuts and bolts.

With King's arrival, the newsroom turned into a white-collar sweatshop. Senior managers remained on the job scrutinizing copy, rewriting leads and changing headlines, until the paper went to bed. Reporters had always expected to see some changes made to their stories, especially when a story was chosen for front-page display and the editors wanted to incorporate material from the wire services or from other *Herald* journalists. But increasingly, reporters opened their papers in the morning to find their stories altered beyond recognition. This was top-down interference of a kind never seen in the newsroom before. The "drive-by editing," as we dryly dubbed it, saw changes made without consultation with reporters, without re-interviewing people quoted in the stories and without checking facts. The published results included misquotes and embarrassing inaccuracies that regularly called for corrections, apologies and retractions.

My own stories emerged relatively unscathed from this process, but I too had to deal with some unwelcome editing changes. The most bizarre of these came when I wrote a first-person feature series entitled "Brian Brennan's Canada" and a manager added in such mawkish lines as "Canada had seized my heart and wouldn't let it go." Cardiac arrest, anyone?

At the root of some editing changes, it seemed, was a desire on the part of newsroom managers to advance King's goal of putting out a *Herald* that reflected Calgary with "fairness, accuracy and balance." He elaborated on this concept in an interview with a *Herald* reporter published on October 14, 1996. The relevant questions to be asked by editorial staffers, King said, were: "Are the facts right? Are the quotes in context? And is this story being told fully and not with bias on behalf of the writer, be that either personal or political or with any other agenda?" He added that a policy of fairness, accuracy and balance did not suggest that every story in the paper should have a positive spin. "I'm not talking about boosterism here. I'm not talking about cheerleading. We do, in fact, have roles and obligations in those areas too. The greatest acid test is the response you get from people who are in the news." If that response was positive, King said, the *Herald* was doing its job. If not, the paper was failing in its obligations to its readers. In his view, the *Herald* had become increasingly unpopular in the marketplace and thus disconnected from its readers. "It was not reflective of the city. If Calgary was an entrepreneurial, enthusiastic, upbeat city with a robust economy, the newspaper was not reflecting that."

King professed not to know anything about news gathering and reporting, and declared himself happy to leave that to the professionals in his newsroom. "I'm like the administrator of a hospital," King said. "I know how to run the business, but you wouldn't want me doing open-heart surgery." In King's hospital, however, the triage process seemed to dictate that the only hearts that really mattered were those belonging to the *Herald*'s corporate and political friends. Among the paper's most valued clients were those who occupied the executive offices located within a two-kilometre radius of the Calgary Tower. "It's time we started supporting free markets and entrepreneurship," said one of the editors who had previously worked at King's *Sun*. "It's time we came down off the hill and back into the city." Also favoured were Premier Ralph Klein and his provincial Tory colleagues, who had long complained of unfair treatment at the hands of the *Herald*.

At most newspapers, reporters and editors come to believe there are written and unwritten rules about what stories get ignored, what get covered and how they get covered. At the *Herald*, the unwritten rule after King arrived was that articles critical of big business and big government were out and that civic boosterism – notwithstanding King's public statements to the contrary – was in. The paper would no longer be infected by what one manager cynically referred to as "left-leaning groupthink." If a picture of the Calgary Flames appeared on the *Herald*'s front page after a routine home game during the regular NHL season, it would do so because the paper had formed a marketing relationship with the team's owners. The same held true whenever a big pop star came to town. If the Shania Twain concert was a *Herald* promotion, the country diva would appear prominently on the front page in all her navel-baring glory. If her show was sponsored by the *Sun*, the story would rate little more than a two-paragraph advancer in the back of the entertainment section.

By the spring of 1998, the newsroom staffers had endured about as much of this second-guessing and top-down interference as they could stand. Reporters had come to expect every piece they wrote would be routinely rewritten to make the stories more palatable to the *Herald*'s friends, who now seemed to include just about every business leader and important political figure in the province. Copy editors had been led to believe that they could never get a headline right and that the stories and pictures they chose for front-page display would never be the right ones. Dignity went out the window, along with respect. Some staffers quit in disgust. Others were pushed out the door because they dared to be defiant. What the bosses perceived as a "bad attitude" became grounds for constructive dismissal and firing.

In one instance, a respected left-wing editorial writer and international affairs columnist was encouraged to leave the editorial board to make way for a new right-wing commentator. He was told he could move to the newsroom and become a "senior features writer" with privileges – such as a semi-private office and no weekend shifts – not granted to less favoured writers. Only problem was, the newsroom didn't have such a "star" system in place and wasn't about to create one. After struggling unsuccessfully to satisfy the hard-news demands of an assignment editor who didn't want the former columnist's "point-of-view" feature stories appearing in the paper, the columnist was left to languish as a general reporter until eventually he took a severance package and left.

To add to these frustrations, *Herald* management systematically eliminated all structured means by which newsroom staffers could express their concerns. When the paper's human resources director – a popular manager sympathetic to employee problems – left the *Herald* to seek other employment opportunities, we lost one of our most important allies. When members of the newsroom staff association tried to hold meetings on-site to discuss shared concerns, a manager told us such meetings were now considered an expensive drain on the company's resources and should be ended forthwith. This left the employees with no way to collectively voice worries about such issues as the unfair application of the newsroom salary grid, the rescheduling of holiday shifts to avoid overtime costs, the hiring of contract workers to replace full-time staffers, and the increasing of workloads without additional compensation. If ever there was a workplace ripe for the union picking, this was it.

After months of lunchtime discussions in the *Herald* cafeteria, the journalists made the first move. One employee talked to the Teamsters Union but was told the union had no interest in organizing the *Herald* newsroom without an assurance that at least 40 per cent of the 160 staffers would sign up. Another newsroom staffer talked to a friend who was an executive with the Communications, Energy & Paperworkers Union (CEP) of Canada. CEP is an omnibus union representing 150,000 members from a diverse range of industries including print shops, mines, telephone companies, chemical plants and forestry. In Alberta, the CEP represented sawmill workers in Hinton, Catholic school support staff in Edmonton and television workers in Calgary and Edmonton.

The prospect of organizing the *Herald* newsroom was very appealing to the CEP. The union already represented newspaper workers in Ontario and British Columbia, and was keen to extend its reach into Alberta. During the spring and summer of 1998, organizers for the union made several trips to Calgary to hold secret meetings with unhappy *Herald* employees. Many, including me, agreed to sign membership cards. I was worried that I would be pushed out the door to make room for a younger and cheaper employee. This had already happened to a couple of my contemporaries and I was feeling vulnerable.

The *Tribute* column, once characterized by the *Herald* ombudsman as "one of the best new features this paper has introduced to its pages in a long time," was no longer appearing five times weekly and had been moved from the well-read city news pages to the section of the paper dealing with fashions and food. I still had the satisfaction of writing it once a week, but the rest of the time I was obliged to generate trivial stories about "trends" and "lifestyles" that were of little interest to me.

On the Thanksgiving weekend of 1998, the organizing drive moved into full gear. The CEP organizers set up shop in the Sheraton Cavalier hotel and conducted a certification blitz. They signed up 62 per cent of the 160 newsroom employees before *Herald* managers had a chance to digest their Thanksgiving turkeys. The number of signers came as a surprise to us, and undoubtedly a shock to management. We figured we would be lucky to get 50 per cent. A year earlier, we had doubted we could get 40 per cent of the staff to sign. However, the level of discontent had risen considerably since then. On the Tuesday morning, the union formally applied for a certification vote. Having certification meant that the union, under Alberta law, would be able to officially represent us in negotiations with management for a first collective agreement.

The certification vote, conducted under the auspices of the Alberta Labour Relations Board, took place two weeks later. In the meantime, the managers did everything in their power to try and block the union. They held meetings with employees, singly and in small groups, to find out why we were unhappy. Christmas came early to the *Herald* newsroom, with a flurry of staff upgradings and attendant salary increases. Temporary editorial employees acquired permanent status and all employees were assured that the mistakes of the past would be corrected. "Our goal is to earn a renewed relationship with every staff member," explained one manager. "To do so, we must change and we will." Few believed him. It was going to take more than a few personality makeovers to fix problems that we saw as systemic.

On the afternoon before the certification vote, King held a staff meeting in the newsroom and appealed to us not to vote for the union. "We were guilty of taking our eye off the ball," he said. "Give us a second chance." Asked by one reporter if the presence of a union would stop him from pursuing his stated goal of making the *Herald* a better newspaper, King responded, "You should ask the CEP about that." The die was cast. It was clear that many of us were going to vote for the union.

The newsroom staffers, including those who had not previously signed membership cards, voted more than 75 per cent in favour of certifying the CEP as our bargaining agent. It was a significant majority for a newsroom that had never been unionized. Few of us believed that things would change for the better without a union. Management had said, in effect, "trust us," but offered no blueprint for improvement. The result of the vote came as a bitter disappointment to the *Herald* managers, who had convinced themselves – based on the premise that most of the employees, like the residents of Calgary itself, were moderate conservatives with little appetite for union politics – that the certification application would fail. When the Labour Relations Board ratified the result, the bosses grudgingly accepted that the majority had spoken. But that did not mean they would make it easy for us to proceed.

Bargaining for the newsroom's first collective agreement began in January 1999. King would not grant permission for us to negotiate on company property, so the talks took place at a nearby hotel. We were also refused permission to bargain on company time, so the four of us newsroom-elected staffers – reporters Andy Marshall, Lisa Dempster, Mark Lowey and I – had to work a full shift every day after we had been in negotiations from 4:00 a.m. to noon. At other unionized newspapers, we would have been granted paid leave to participate in the bargaining process. But we didn't have a collective agreement yet, so there was no obligation on the part of management to give us that leave.

The talks proceeded at glacial pace. We argued at length over semantics and contract language. The company's hired gun, a tough human resources pro named Gary Johanson, reminded us repeatedly that a contract was a legal document and could not contain language that was ambiguous or unclear. The fact that such language was common in other North American newspaper contracts was of no matter to Johanson. He was determined, he said, to develop a document that would not repeat the mistakes of past contracts: a flexible agreement that would be a model contract for the ever-changing workplace of the 21st century.

A couple of months into the talks, it was clear to our chief CEP bargainers, the late Joy Langan and current CEP president Dave Coles, that this was more than just a battle over contract language or any particular issue in the collective agreement. This was about something more fundamental: our very right to have a union. The contract we were slowly and painstakingly putting together had plenty of clauses about management rights but very little – aside from a legally mandated grievance procedure – dealing with the concerns that had caused us to unionize. The most significant omission from the union's point of view was a clause providing for protection against indiscriminate firings – the kind of job security employees expect for doing their jobs responsibly. Another sticking point was our demand for a clause allowing reporters to remove their names from stories that had been substantially changed without consultation.

In April 1999, after bargaining for a total of 91 mostly unproductive hours, our CEP team applied for a provincial mediator, hoping this would help us achieve an equitable collective agreement. But the mediator did little more than ferry messages back and forth between the two sides. His shuttle diplomacy brought us no closer to our goal of reaching an agreement.

In May 1999, King's Hollinger bosses transferred him from Calgary to Vancouver to run the company that jointly operates the *Vancouver Sun* and *Province*. Three months later, King resigned and left the newspaper business. He returned to Calgary to run an asset-management firm and two years later became the president of the Calgary Flames hockey team. He said he felt bad about the labour unrest at the *Herald* and "any contribution I may have made, because (a) that was not my intention and (b) my intentions were completely honourable." King also said that the employees should have come to him with their concerns because he would have been their greatest champion. This was being a bit disingenuous, however. The practice at the *Herald*, as at other large workplaces, was for employees to bring their concerns to their immediate superiors, not to do end runs around management to speak directly with the top boss. Hollinger replaced King at the *Herald* with Dan Gaynor, the 43-year-old publisher of the *St. Catharines Standard*. Gaynor had fought unionization at the *Standard* in 1998, when the paper's newsroom staff went on strike for three weeks in a first-contract dispute over wages.

Our negotiations dragged on intermittently through the summer and fall of 1999, while Gaynor and his managers simultaneously developed an elaborate contingency plan for publishing the paper in the event of a work stoppage. By September, it was clear that the paper was actively preparing for such a stoppage. The managers had beefed up security inside the building, installed Plexiglas screens and video monitors in the lobby, and rented a dozen Ryder trucks to move papers out of the building to designated pickup points for the carriers, who previously had driven to the *Herald* building to collect their papers.

On September 16, 1999, the company rejected all of the key proposals we had tabled during the eight months of negotiations. The principal proposal was the clause protecting seniority rights – the cornerstone of every collective agreement – stating that in the event of layoffs the most recent hires would be the first to go. It also rejected a non-harassment clause, which stated that employees should be treated with respect and dignity. Three weeks later, the *Herald's* 160 editorial staff voted 82.5 per cent in favour of strike action, hoping this would be the hammer to forge a first contract. Three more days of bargaining followed, but the company persisted in refusing to deal with any of our key proposals. The talks broke off on October 28.

On November 5, a Friday afternoon, four of us newsroom staffers served 72-hour strike notice on the company, hoping this would aid our quest for a first contract. We did so knowing that publisher Gaynor had hinted ominously at a chamber of commerce dinner that such action would be folly: "I hope these people know that if they go on strike, they will be jumping off a cliff."

I was reluctant at first to take strike action. I saw our attempt to reach an equitable agreement with the local employer now escalating into something much larger: an unwinnable battle against Hollinger boss Conrad Black, a millionaire newspaper tycoon who wrote in his 1993 autobiography, *A Life In Progress*, that he "never had much regard for organized labour, other than when it has taken on heroic proportions as in Poland." However, Hollinger was already facing the possibility of a strike at its profitable Vancouver newspapers, and it was losing millions of dollars on the operations of the *National Post*, so I decided to gamble on the possibility that the management might not want to incur further expense by having a long strike in Calgary.

I wondered if my father would have given his support to our action. He had been dead for three years when we served strike notice on the company, and I often found myself thinking about him as I walked the picket line during the weeks and months afterward. Years previously, his bosses had characterized Dad as a "bit of a Red" when he served as general secretary of the tax officers' in-house staff association. Would he have been proud of his son, the junior Red, for taking the stand that I did? I like to believe he would have been with me in spirit.

Though our strike notice did not expire until the Monday afternoon, something told me on that Friday afternoon that I would not be back at work on Monday morning. I turned off my computer, looked around my office cubicle and briefly considered leaving the photos of Zelda and Nicole on my desk to prick the conscience of the strikebreaker that would be occupying the space during my absence. I quickly thought the better of it and tucked the pictures inside my briefcase. Scabs were mercenary and opportunistic, I thought; why would they even care?

The following afternoon, I received a phone message at my home from a nervous *Herald* editor who was obviously reading from a script. The company had decided, she said, to give me a three-day "holiday" with pay. "I'll see you when it's over," she said with a shaking voice. I tried phoning my office number and heard a recorded voice saying the number was invalid. I encountered the same problem when I tried to access my office voice mail and e-mail. I realized that this was no holiday. It was a lockout. It was a heartless and cynical move aimed at keeping us conveniently out of the way while they brought in their strikebreakers. Later that evening, a group of us set up an impromptu picket line in front of the newspaper building.

Local television and radio reporters gave the lockout plenty of coverage. So did the rival *Calgary Sun*, which distributed an edition of the paper wrapped in what appeared to be a *Herald* front page. "I always pray for opportunity," said *Sun* publisher Les Pyette. The *Herald* opted not to tell its readers that the labour dispute had intensified. Publisher Gaynor later told a television reporter "there was nothing new to report" and described the lockout as nothing more than "a day off with pay."

Reporters for other media organizations, asking the only question that ever seems important to them when covering a labour dispute, wanted to know what kind of salary increases we were seeking. I'm sure we told them at the time, but I can't for the life of me remember the details now because this dispute was never about money. That is what made this an unusual event in Canadian labour movement history. We were not looking for more money and we were not looking for shorter working hours. We were a group of well-paid white-collar workers who wanted nothing more than to be treated with dignity and respect. One of the *Herald* managers said we were naive to think that such subjective demands could ever be written into a union contract. But we were determined to prove him wrong.

The strike officially began at 3:00 p.m. on November 8, 1999, with 107 journalists marching down the hill toward the *Herald* building from our newly rented strike office, hoisting our hand-made signs and waving to passing motorists who honked their horns in support. Our numbers constituted about 70 per cent of the newsroom workforce at that time: 40 editorial employees were philosophically opposed to trade unionism and chose to remain inside the *Herald* building, while another 13 adopted a wait-and-see attitude and stayed at home. The rest of us were on the picket line, accompanied by 67 striking workers from the *Herald* mailroom, loading dock and machine shop, who had also hit a roadblock in their talks with the employer. Journalists who usually reported the news were now making the news, giving interviews and putting on a picket-line, slogan-shouting show for the benefit of the television cameras. This was a strange role for many of us. We had changed from dutiful, rule-abiding employees into unionized rebels. Some of us had even taken to calling one another "brother" and "sister," and making the words "solidarity" and "comrade" a regular part of our vocabulary.

The *Herald* was in full battle mode by this time. The depleted newsroom workforce was augmented by 40 reporters, copy editors, photographers and editorial managers flown in from newspapers in British Columbia, Saskatchewan, Manitoba, Ontario and Quebec. These strikebreakers were housed in an expensive hotel near the *Herald* building, given rental cars and free meal tickets for the *Herald* cafeteria (unlike regular *Herald* staffers, who still had to pay). On top of that, they were paid up to $600 a day for their replacement services, which was more than double what a senior *Herald* reporter earned. Sinister-looking, black-clad, commando-style security guards also patrolled the entrances to the *Herald* building 24 hours a day. Even with the newsroom on strike, a version of the newspaper was published daily with minimal disruption.

The union leaders moved quickly to ensure our battle would not be just a local skirmish like the three-week strike that *St. Catharines Standard* workers staged during the summer of 1998 when publisher Gaynor was running the paper. Money and other support poured in from union locals across the country, letters were written to politicians, and reader and advertiser boycotts were organized. Our story became national news thanks to the Canadian Press news agency, *The Globe and Mail*, *Maclean's* magazine and the CBC radio and television networks. Also contributing to the flow of information about the strike was a cheeky union web page providing background detail unavailable elsewhere in the media, including a "Wall of Shame" featuring biographical snippets and photographs of the strikebreakers.

We told the media that the labour dispute began as a reaction by a group of *Herald* editorial employees to intolerable working conditions in the *Herald* newsroom. Publisher Gaynor begged to differ. He said the labour dispute stemmed from an "immovable core" of senior editorial employees resisting the paper's efforts to shift from "advocacy" journalism to what his predecessor, Ken King, had described acronymically as FAB (fairness, accuracy, balance). "They want an environment in which they can continue their efforts to resist this new direction, free from the responsibilities of basic job expectations," Gaynor wrote in a *Herald* column. None of the striking journalists had ever heard him use this far-fetched argument before, but I decided to respond to it. I published the following open letter to Gaynor on the union's web page:

> Let me tell you about new directions at the Calgary Herald, *Mr. Gaynor. I have seen my share of them during the twenty-five years I have worked in the* Herald *newsroom.*
>
> *I have seen the* Herald *progress from Underwoods to iMacs, switch from afternoon to morning publication, publish on Sundays, launch and subsequently abandon the* Sunday *magazine, embrace colour*

photography, and downplay the task of covering news and sports while actively promoting "line extensions" – otherwise known as advertising-driven special sections. Heck, I can even remember a time when we didn't have rug on the newsroom floor.

Have I resisted any of these new directions? Of course not. I don't make up the rules; I just play by them. Whenever someone brings in a new set of rules, I adjust my game accordingly. Whatever the gig calls for, as my colleagues in the music business used to say.

Because of advocacy journalism – which Mr. Gaynor suggests has no place in today's Herald and which I would characterize as journalism practised selflessly in the public interest – city taxpayers received enough information to know that Calgary did not need a new city hall that would have been the Taj Mahal of Canadian municipal buildings, a lavish structure that would have given new definition to the term "edifice complex." Because of advocacy journalism, Calgary received massive government funding for a performing arts centre that is rated by The New York Times as one of the finest in North America. Because of advocacy journalism, the Herald has won a slew of National Newspaper Awards and been nominated several times for the Michener awards in public service journalism.

What has FAB brought us? Let me count the ways. It has brought us celebrity gossip and turned us into purveyors of printed junk food at the expense of in-depth news and analysis. It has brought us seventeen – count them – front-page stories on Shania Twain, published before and after a concert that just happened to be co-sponsored by the Calgary Herald. It has brought us wall-to-wall coverage of such one-off events as the Rotary International convention, a bus-and-truck version of The Wizard of Oz musical, and the World Police/Fire Games – the kind of blanket coverage that even the participants in the games considered excessive.

We used to be the paper of record. Now we traffic in phony drama driven by the trash mentality of the tabloid press, the hysterical urgencies of commercial television and the blather of local talk-radio shows. We now fill our paper with sensation: Lewinskiana, Diana-itis, O.J. Simpsonitis; front-page rumour (remember the Spice Girls never coming to town?) and bloated Daily Telegraph trivialities, all at the expense of significant fact. We used to be the Calgary Philharmonic Orchestra. Now, we play in a kazoo band.

As for the Herald's supposed abandonment of advocacy journalism, how does one reconcile this with the fact that its current roster of scab writers includes both a former researcher for the right-wing Fraser Institute and a policy advisor to the Progressive Group for Independent Business – a right-wing lobby group that ran candidates in the 1997 Alberta provincial election under the Alberta Social Credit banner. The paper also has a replacement writer who belongs to the racist South African Institute, and a replacement writer with an anti-feminist, anti-gay agenda who pickets the Kensington abortion clinic on weekends.

I had a great job at the Calgary Herald before I went on strike. I wrote the Tribute column and feature stories about people and subjects that engaged me. I was well paid, had a semi-private office and generous company benefits. So why am I walking a picket line?

I am walking because I am one of the people chosen by the tribe to lead them from darkness into light. I am walking because I – together with Andy Marshall, Lisa Dempster and Mark Lowey – was elected by our newsroom colleagues to go to the bargaining table and bring back a collective agreement. I am walking because I believe in the fundamental need for a contract providing a measure of job security for all editorial employees, and protection against exploitation. My colleagues voted 82.5 per cent in favour of strike action supporting our efforts to obtain such a contract. I will not let them down. It would be a betrayal of everything I believe in if I were to do otherwise.

I have worked at the Herald for most of my adult life. I have the gold watch to prove it. I started as a police reporter and progressed through a succession of coveted writing assignments – arts and entertainment

> reporter, theatre critic, Sunday magazine writer, features writer – to my current position.
>
> The Herald has been very good to me. It was a destination newspaper when I came here in 1974, and I have never wanted to work anywhere else. My sincerest hope for the future is that the people who come after me would be given similar recognition for their skills and years of service and be rewarded accordingly.

Mr. Gaynor, needless to say, never responded to my letter. Nor was I ever invited to run it in the newspaper as an opinion piece. As far as the *Herald* was concerned, the people working inside the building were the good guys and those of us on the picket line were the bad guys. If we had anything to say about the labour dispute, it would never be deemed sufficiently important to appear in the pages of the paper. I did, however, receive many congratulatory messages about my letter from union members across the country and around the world.

During the first month of the strike, we enjoyed some of the warmest weather in southern Alberta history, which helped boost spirits on the picket line. On November 11, Remembrance Day, the strikers were wearing shorts and T-shirts when I brought my accordion down to the line to play "The Last Post." We observed two minutes of silence in memory of Canada's war veterans and then sang a few choruses of "Solidarity Forever." It was my 34th Remembrance Day in Canada, one I would always keep pressed in the memory book along with that wonderful day in 1966 when I became a landed immigrant. On other warm days, we tossed footballs and Frisbees around on the picket line, much to the annoyance of the grim-faced managers and replacement workers driving past.

We lost a few people from the picket line during the first weeks of the strike. Four returned to work, mainly for financial reasons, as Christmas was coming and they just couldn't afford to go without their salaries any longer. Some of us were disappointed by this, others were angry. We were hurting too, but we were staying the course. Why couldn't they do the same? The defecting strikers immediately became pariahs in our eyes. Such was the divisive, polarizing nature of this labour dispute. If they weren't with us, they were against us. Friendships were broken as a result. But the defections did serve to cement the bonds between those of us still walking the line. Our numbers remained at a solid 103 for the next few months.

I could never see the point of the picketing. It was a 19th-century strike tactic that served no useful purpose in the late 20th century. We had no ability to shut down the plant, and nobody to give our message to aside from the workers going in and out of the building, the truck drivers who delivered mail and supplies, and the occasional individual who ventured into the building to buy an ad. If the *Herald* had been located in downtown Calgary, we would have had a more visible presence and the ability to remind passing pedestrians that we were the people responsible for giving them something worthwhile to read with their morning coffee. But the *Herald* building was located in an industrial district atop a hill on the outskirts of downtown, where the only passing creatures were rabbits, gophers, field mice and migrating Canada geese. Because we were journalists, we wanted to put out a strike paper to compete with the *Herald*, but the union leaders wouldn't hear of this. Too expensive, they said. So, walking around the building became our daily routine, for hours and hours and hours at a time.

Though we could not stop the paper from coming out, we were able to delay cars and trucks entering and leaving the *Herald* building for the first six weeks. That allowed us to taunt the scabs, tell receptive individuals why we were striking and distribute our information leaflets. We received a sympathetic hearing from friends inside the building – non-unionized sales reps and other workers who brought us coffee and donuts – until senior management ordered them, under threat of termination, to keep their car windows closed and have no further truck with the enemy. The Labour Relations Board then took away our right to delay vehicles after a big labour rally outside the *Herald* building on the night of December 11, when the outgoing paper-delivery trucks were held up for more than the five minutes agreed to under the protocol ratified by the company and the union. That night, to stop the trucks from leaving the plant, several striking workers sat on the ground in front of the vehicles. The police asked us to move away, and when some refused, they were tossed into the back of a paddy wagon. One was CEP bargainer Joy Langan, who phoned fellow bargainer Dave Coles on her cell phone and said, "I have a really serious problem."

"Yeah," said Coles. "I know you have. You've been arrested."

"No, it's not that," said Langan. "I need a cigarette."

After the December 11 rally, the Labour Relations Board ruled we could no longer delay vehicles, so we shifted our focus away from the picket line and took our fight into the community. Though some of us were still walking around the building, despite the fact that we now saw picketing as mainly useless, most of us stood on city street corners with big banners urging people to, "Cancel the *Herald*." We distributed 4,000 leaflets daily in Calgary neighbourhoods, at the stores and offices of *Herald* advertisers and at special events around town.

Our efforts met with some success. A survey conducted for us by Vancouver pollsters Campbell Goodell Traynor showed *Herald* readership down by 24 per cent. Chapters Online stopped advertising in the *Herald* and Ford Canada said it would consider doing the same. Other advertisers demanded rebates from the *Herald*. The paper's daily press run dropped from 140,000 to 116,000, and the *Herald* tried vainly, with offers of free dinners and free subscriptions to the Hollinger-owned *National Post*, to woo back subscribers who cancelled their papers. Publicly, the *Herald* managers disputed our numbers and insisted the strike was having little or no effect on circulation. But among themselves they admitted that readership was declining precipitously and that they were powerless to stop it. By 2002, Audit Bureau of Circulations figures would show that the *Herald*'s weekday circulation had plunged to an all-time low of 112,258 during the strike.

A "cyber picket line" organized by CEP Local 2000 in Vancouver grew rapidly to reach 3,000 subscribers. Support for the striking workers came from people all around the world, including journalists in Britain, Lithuania, Brazil, Sweden and the Commonwealth of Independent States in the former Soviet Union. But for all the moral and financial support we received from other trade unionists, nothing brought us any closer to getting a first collective agreement. The CEP, while nominally a national union with members all across Canada, had little clout when it came to marshalling nationwide support for our cause. Unionized journalists at the *Vancouver Sun* and *Province* could not walk out in support, or refuse to handle copy produced by non-striking *Herald* employees, because they were bound by the terms of a contract signed with their local management. Unionized journalists at other Hollinger papers were in the same situation. A "national day of protest" planned by union leaders from different parts of the country fizzled out before it began.

We went to some lengths to ensure that the strike remained constantly in the public eye. Hundreds of letters went to Calgary's Mayor Al Duerr and Premier Ralph Klein to complain about the mounted police in riot gear who intimidated participants at the labour rally outside the *Herald* building on December 11. A group of about a hundred community leaders, calling themselves Friends of the *Herald*, asked Calgary city council to vote on a motion urging the two sides to get back to the table. Six Christian church leaders did the same. The aldermen voted 13 to 1 in favour of the motion, but Gaynor responded by telling a radio reporter that nobody dictated to him how to run his business.

Throughout the strike, Gaynor insisted in radio, television and print interviews that returning to the table would be a waste of time unless the CEP dropped its demand for seniority protection. "It's important we have an editorial department that encourages initiative and is motivated by pursuit of excellence, and that we have a framework for encouraging that," he told Southam News. "I don't think seniority contracts – last-in, first-out language – do anything to support that." Yet at the same time, Gaynor conceded he did not know of any newspaper contracts that lacked seniority language. In fact, there was even a seniority clause in the first agreement he reached with the *St. Catharines Standard* workers in 1998.

On the picket line, during the weeks leading up to Christmas 1999, we had plenty of social activities – pancake breakfasts, barbecues, carol singing – to keep our spirits high. On Christmas Day, striker Dave Climenhaga served a turkey dinner cooked by his wife, Luanne, to 25 picketing strikers. Dave referred to it as a "union turkey" because the unionized workers at Safeway had donated it to us. "It was a great delight to carve a fine-looking fowl like that on the line and serve it up in a spirit of comradeship and fraternity," said Dave. "Here we were, after several weeks on the picket line, serving up dinner to a happy throng, playing Frisbee and good-naturedly heckling the odd scab that scuttled past us."

We started to become disgruntled, however, as the old year turned into the new. Repeated phone calls to *Herald* management went unanswered as we tried to get them back to the bargaining table. Finally, on February 1, 2000, they agreed to meet with us, but the talks went nowhere. After little more than an hour at the table, they left us with a take-it-or-leave-it contract proposal that would have allowed the company to indiscriminately fire workers without giving a reason or providing an avenue for appeal. Needless to say, we rejected the proposal. No further talks were scheduled after that.

While I hated being in limbo, not knowing when or how this labour dispute was going to end, I did manage to fill my time and preserve my equilibrium with activities unrelated to the strike. Because I was still on the books as a *Herald* employee, I could not freelance for competing publications, but I was able to do some commercial writing that helped to ease the financial strain. I also added some professional music engagements to my calendar, including a week-long concert tour of Saskatchewan with my friend Felix Possak, one of Calgary's top banjo players. Plus, I made a little money appearing as a piano-playing extra in a B movie called *Dead Simple*, a forgettable bit of trash that went straight to video. And I began work on my first two books: a literary biography of my ancestor Mary O'Leary, one of the most celebrated Irish-language poets of the 19th century; and *Building a Province*, a collection of biographical profiles of notable Albertans.

The enduring support of Zelda and Nicole also helped me to stay calm. Zelda knew exactly what I was going through, because she too had been involved in labour disputes, as a teacher with the Calgary Catholic School District. She often joined me on the picket line, as did Nicole, a strong believer in workers' rights. Zelda came down to the line whenever we held a rally or an event, such as a candlelight hymn sing, and Nicole joined me on the line when she wasn't working or rehearsing as lead singer for Calgary jump blues band the Dino Martinis.

In early May 2000, we were joined on the picket line by one hundred pressroom workers, who rejected concession demands that would have seen them working additional shifts for no added compensation. We hoped this would cause the *Herald* to stop production, but the paper continued to publish without significant disruption. The press workers stayed on the line for just six weeks and then ratified an agreement with the company. At that point, the heart went out of our strike. We had been on the line for more than six months and hopes for getting a first collective agreement had all but faded. To drag out the negotiations for as long as possible, the company had taken full advantage of Alberta's labour laws, which are viewed as among the weakest in the country because they allow replacement workers and have no provisions for compulsory first-contract arbitration.

In early June 2000, with our seven-month-old picket line crumbling, our bargaining committee decided to play the one last card that we hoped would win us an agreement: we dropped seniority protection from our list of contract demands. We knew this would draw criticism from people in the labour movement, as well as from some of our own members, but it seemed our only remaining hope. Then, just as we felt we were about to start scoring some points, the company moved the goalposts by saying that seniority was only one of several issues that would have to be resolved before an agreement could be concluded. Among the outstanding issues were the conditions for returning to work, which would involve finding new positions for the striking journalists in a soon to be restructured newsroom. This process, the company said, would be complex and take time. "We'll grind them down," said one of the managers at a staff meeting inside the building.

As a last-ditch effort, the union launched a bad-faith bargaining action against the company in mid-June. Hollinger's chairman and CEO, Conrad Black, had told our local president, Andy Marshall, during a televised confrontation in the lobby of a Calgary hotel that the strike would be resolved "either by coming to an end after two years, by decertification, or by you people coming back to work." Black added, in an interview with *The New York Times*, that he expected the strikers to continue with their job action for a further two years "and then [the company] won't have to keep their jobs anymore" (because a union that goes for that length of time without a first collective agreement automatically becomes subject to decertification). This statement struck union leaders as being actionable, and they filed suit accordingly. However, with the prospect of the Labour Relations Board hearings carrying on through the summer and into the fall, the striking journalists were not consoled by this initiative. We wanted an end to the strike. And we wanted it soon.

The end, when it came, was not pretty. Union bargainer Dave Coles met behind closed doors in June 2000 with senior company executives and came back with two offers from the employer that might have been drafted in Hades. The first involved continuing to bargain until all the outstanding issues, including the bad-faith legal proceedings, were resolved. That would mean us fighting on for many more months for a contract the company clearly did not want to give us, with the prospect of imminent decertification always hanging over us. The other offer was for us to immediately end our job action, disband the union and either return to work with a no-retribution promise from the company or accept buyout packages. We voted 68.5 per cent in favour of the second option. Of the 93 remaining strikers, only eight opted to return to the newsroom. The rest, including me, accepted buyouts. "I wouldn't call it a loss," said Andy Marshall, our courtly, soft-spoken local president. "I'd call it a disengagement with honour."

Why did most of us take the money and leave? In my case, it was because I knew life would be unbearable for me in a non-unionized newsroom run by anti-union managers. This was not the "leaving-on-my-own-terms" exit I had envisaged four years earlier when I vowed I would never give younger managers the satisfaction of seeing me "bugger off and die." But the protracted labour dispute, and the attitude of the managers toward it, left me with no choice. I simply did not believe the company's statement that there would be no retribution. In fact, the reprisals had already started. *Herald* editor-in-chief Peter Menzies had sent us a "without prejudice" letter (meaning he could not later be held legally accountable for its contents) saying that the proposed newsroom restructuring would mean the loss of several full-time positions, including the Edmonton legislature correspondent; the theatre critic; baseball, hockey and golf writers; the chief business columnist; the books editor; the food columnist; and my own job as *Tribune* columnist. Menzies wasn't bluffing. One writer who did decide to return to work, editorial page columnist Naomi Lakritz, had to hire a lawyer get her old job back after the employer invented a new position for her writing "personality profiles" that the editors had no interest in publishing.

A few of the strikers were upset over the way the strike ended. They had walked a picket line in solidarity for close to eight months to get a first collective agreement, only to see the company divide and conquer by offering buyouts in return for decertification. For me, the governing emotions were relief and sadness. This was not the outcome any of us would have wished for, but we had stood by our principles, fought until there was no longer a majority will to continue and ended our struggle with dignity. As my fellow bargainer Mark Lowey said:

> I believe the union was ours to create. I believe it was ours to bring to an end, or continue as we saw fit. I made the choice I made because I don't believe you can plant a seed in barren ground, in a hostile environment, and retain much hope that it will grow. For me, it was either be cleaved now in terms of this union local, or face a thousand tiny cuts and a withering away over the next five years. Either way, our local that we all fought so hard for would bleed to death. This way, at least the choice was ours and it was, in keeping with the principles of trade unionism, a democratic choice. The union will rise again, I am convinced, on more hospitable ground. To everything there is a season.

Which leads to the inevitable question: did we, as Gaynor suggested in November 1999, jump off a cliff when we decided to take strike action against the company? Though I had some reservations at the time, I now believe we took the only course left open to us as a newly certified bargaining unit with fading hopes of getting an equitable first contract. We used the strike option, the last tool at our disposal, to bring the company to the table to deal with our grievances. If the company saw this as an opportunity to rid itself of some journalists that it perceived as trouble-makers, one of whom undoubtedly could have been me, then so be it. There are some battles you fight not because you think you can win, but because you know it's the right thing to do. The defenders of the Alamo, who as legend holds opted to stay and fight, could have gotten on their horses and ridden away. We could have done likewise, but chose not to. This was our hill to die on.

The strike ended on June 30, 2000. Within a matter of weeks, the grass around the red-brick building had lost its trampled-down look, stamped by the feet of a hundred pickets. Our crudely built wooden picket shack was gone, as was the phalanx of black-clad security guards who had patrolled the building 24 hours a day. To all outward appearances, it was back to business as usual at the *Calgary Herald*. Yet, even a cursory glance at any issue of the paper showed that the pre-strike quality was now permanently gone, never to be regained. Missing were the familiar names of dozens of reporters and photographers, many of them national award winners, who had once combined to make the *Herald* one of the best daily newspapers in western Canada. With a new editorial roster of mainly young and inexperienced prospects, the *Herald* had become, as one sports-minded media commentator, John Mather, later observed, a minor-league paper in a major-league city. Management no longer viewed the reporters as writers, in the literary sense. They were now "content providers."

I was sad to see the paper's decline in quality, but hardly surprised. It was no longer the paper I had come to work for in April 1974. It was no longer the paper of my old mentor, Bill Gold, the respected and influential editor who ran the newsroom during the *Herald*'s glory days as the newspaper of record for southern Alberta. Retired early on disability pension, Gold had died during the last month of our strike. He likely would not have approved of our "left-wing" union activities, because he was a dyed-in-the-wool conservative who had once written speeches for Ontario premier William Davis. But then, there wouldn't have been any need for a union when Gold was running the newsroom, because he believed in the importance of good journalism and supported his journalists accordingly.

I paid tribute to Gold in a chapter of my first book, *Building a Province*, completed during my 234 days on the picket line and published in the fall of 2000. After marking time for all those long weeks and months, I was now ready to get on with the rest of my life. I no longer felt a dull ache rising in my chest, and I had no desire to suffer a relapse. I had been in limbo for far too long. I wanted to write more books and experience the freedom and fear associated with being a freelance journalist. I wanted, in some manner, to return to the state of blissful uncertainty that defined those early years in Canada when my father thought I was "unemployed." I had already started writing the next scene in the drama of my life, as an author of books about the social history and colourful characters of western Canada.

—

An Intermezzo

with My Family

IN SEARCH OF A
LITERARY ANCESTOR

When I began to think about writing this book, back in the mid-1990s, I had this notion that I should offer myself to you, the reader, as the spiritual heir to Yeats and Synge. I think every Irishman who puts pen to paper wants to do that. I wanted to be able to say that Brendan Behan's father told me all the stories his son later put into his dramas, that Joyce's Martello Tower in Sandymount was a shrine I visited weekly, and that I regularly made a pilgrimage to the house in Foxrock where Beckett lived before moving to Paris. My rationale was that if I could show you I had moved in the realm of literary greatness, you might think some of it had rubbed off on me.

But, alas, the fact is that as a teenager in Dublin, I knew little about Brendan Behan apart from the fact he was a well-known drunk who once uttered the F-word on a live British television talk show. Joyce I knew only as one of several maverick exiles whose books were banned in Ireland. The Martello Tower was a grubby grey fortress on Sandymount strand. It had a "Tower Café" sign on the bricks and a cheap souvenir shop and tea room on the ground floor. After reading the plaque you would know that the British had built the tower as a defence against a Napoleonic attack that never happened and that Joyce had lived in it for four days with Oliver St. John Gogarty, his prototype for the "stately plump" Buck Mulligan of *Ulysses*.

MY PARENTS' WEDDING AT
S.S. PETER AND PAUL'S CHURCH
IN CORK CITY, 1942. (L TO R)
REV. FR. PATRICK, OFM CAP.
(ASSISTANT CELEBRANT), PETER
BRENNAN (BEST MAN), DAD,
MOTHER, SHEILA TWOMEY
(BRIDESMAID), REV. TERENCE
O'DONOGHUE, OP (CELEBRANT).

PERFORMING EMCEE DUTIES AT
OATLANDS COLLEGE CHRISTMAS
CONCERT, DUBLIN, 1953. THE "CC"
INSIGNIA ON THE BLAZER STANDS
FOR COLÁISTE CAOIMHAÍN (ST.
KEVIN'S COLLEGE). ST. KEVIN WAS
THE PATRON SAINT OF OATLANDS.

MY MOTHER ON THE PIER AT GLENGARIFF,
COUNTY CORK, CIRCA 1940.

Public Body or Employer: *Revenue Commissioners*

Service *Income Tax Department*

Premises *14/15 Upper O'Connell St.*

Dublin

Signature *P. S. Ó Braonáin*

DAD'S CIVIL SERVICE IDENTIFICATION CARD, DUBLIN, 1942.

ROLLING MY HOOP AT OUR MOUNT MERRION, DUBLIN, HOME, 1953.

DOMINION DAY CONCERT, KITIMAT, BRITISH COLUMBIA, 1969.

RED ISLAND HOLIDAY CAMP,
SKERRIES, COUNTY DUBLIN, 1960.

MICHAEL MURPHY, SMITHERS,
BRITISH COLUMBIA, 1969.

THE DUBLIN ROGUES, PALACE GRAND THEATRE,
DAWSON CITY, YUKON, 1967.

OUR WEDDING DAY IN VANCOUVER, 1968.

CJCI RADIO, 1970.

CALGARY HERALD PICKET LINE, REMEMBRANCE DAY, 1999.

CALGARY, 2011.

But I knew nothing of the dreams and visions that haunted this historic building. Nor did I become aware of Beckett until long after the enigmatic *Waiting for Godot* had been translated from the French and first produced at Dublin's tiny Pike Theatre.

I do, however, recall two encounters with literary figures during my childhood. One was with a shy man in a battered fedora and brown gabardine raincoat. My father called him Myles. He lived not too far from us, in a modest red-brick bungalow in Stillorgan. He drank quietly by himself in Boland's Pub. Like my father, he worked (or had worked) for the Irish civil service. His given name was Brian O'Nolan. He wrote novels under the pen name Flann O'Brien and produced humorous columns for the *Irish Times* under the pseudonym Myles na Gopaleen.

I know now that Myles was one of the great comic writers of the century. But I didn't appreciate this at the time. I tried to read his *Times* column when I was 16, but I couldn't understand the humour, with its bilingual puns and wordplay. I also know that Myles was an incorrigible purveyor of the "Irish fact." This can be defined as an attempt to make reality entertaining. Out of such dedication, Myles in 1943 told a *Time* magazine reporter he had once defeated a world champion chess player and had been wed, though tragically, to the violinist daughter of a Cologne basket weaver. Myles's friends in Dublin talked about the article as if it was a complete joke; a hoax by Myles perpetrated on the unsuspecting American. But the author, *Time* senior editor Stanford Lee Cooper, was known to be a stickler for accuracy, so perhaps some of it was true.

The other writer was a remote figure too. This left me thinking, as a child, that all writers must be distant, intensely private people. They were unwilling to make small talk with children, because we hadn't read enough, because we functioned on a lower intellectual plane. His name was Francis J. MacManus, author of such novels as *The Fire in the Dust, Stand and Give Challenge* and *Candle for the Proud*. He was director of talks and features for Radio Éireann. Like other Irish writers of the mid-20th century, he needed a day job because he couldn't make a living from fiction alone. And because he lived in Ireland he couldn't write freely. He couldn't risk being described in the paper as "indecent" or "obscene," because he had a handicapped son, wheelchair bound due to a heart defect, to support. MacManus was one of many Irish writers whose fiction was shackled by the constraints of the Irish Censorship Board. His novel *The Fire in the Dust* actually addressed the issue of Irish censorship in a critical way, but the board never seems to have cottoned on to this fact.

MacManus lived about a five-minute bicycle ride from where I lived in Mount Merrion. His second son was John, my friend at Oatlands College. When I first met MacManus Senior, briefly one afternoon in his book-filled study while John was upstairs getting ready for school, I truly believed I was in the presence of a great man. He had, after all, written novels that were published in hardcover and sat on the shelves of the Stillorgan Public Library next to the poems of Archibald MacLeish and Louis MacNeice. But I never got around to actually reading any of them. Years afterwards, son John – who became a scientist and moved to Canada to work for the National Research Council in Ottawa – told me the novels were rather slight and sentimental. They only survived, said John, because they were required reading in Dublin schools.

When I got into the newspaper business in Canada, while in the process of creating my own mythology, I started to think that these brief early encounters with Irish literary figures might have indirectly influenced my decision to make a living from the pen. I found what I thought was a link to my future destiny when I looked at my baptismal certificate and discovered I had been baptized Catholic on October 7, 1943 – three days after my birth – in the parish Church of St. Andrew on Westland Row in downtown Dublin. Why that particular church? It was located many miles away from my parents' cold-water flat in Rathmines. Why had they chosen it for my baptism? I began to think about this when I was working as a reporter at the *Prince George Citizen*. Then I discovered something interesting: Oscar Wilde was born at 21 Westland Row. Could this be a sign? Could my book-loving father have chosen this church for its association with literary greatness? My father, however, had a more prosaic explanation: St. Andrew's was just a block away from the Holles Street hospital where I was born. "All the babies from Holles Street were baptized in

Westland Row," he said. War babies, it seems, had a short life expectancy and so their baptisms always took place within a few days of birth. Irish-Catholic parents didn't want to risk having their babies go to limbo with original sin staining their tiny souls.

I did, however, find a legitimate connection with Irish literary greatness when I discovered that one of my maternal ancestors was a famous 19th-century folk poet in rural West Cork. Her name, in Irish, was Máire Bhuí Ní Laoire. Phonetically: *Moy-rah Vwee Nee Lay-rah*. It translates literally as Yellow Mary O'Leary. My grandmother had told me about her when I was a small boy in short pants with scabby knees.

"She is your great-great-great grandmother," she told me during one of those long summers of my early childhood when I and my siblings, Michael, Mary and John, travelled down from Dublin on the steam-engine train and spent the months between the end of school in June and the beginning of school in September staying at my grandmother's farm in Ballyvourney. My mother used to say she had done her duty by looking after us children during the school year, and so she packed us off to Ballyvourney as soon as the end-of-term bell rang.

I couldn't imagine what a great-great-great grandmother would look like. My grandmother, though only 67 (my age now), looked older than anyone I knew. I used to sleep in a cot in her bedroom, and I still remember that white shrivelled body with the drooping shrunken breasts when she was putting on her nightshirt. Her long-ago voice still resonates in my memory. She gave the orders and the children complied. There never seemed to be an end to the work that had to be done on this small farm where Grandma lived with her second-oldest son, John Pat. Her oldest son, Mikey, abandoned his birthright when he took off for England during the Second World War.

"Go down the boreen (lane) and bring back another galleen (gallon can) of water from the well."

"When you finish cutting the thistles in the meadow, go over to the shed and bring back some turf for the kitchen fire."

"Peel the poppies (potatoes), dust the settle (kitchen bench) and bring in the eggs from the henhouse."

We did these chores and my grandmother was happy.

Grandma told me about Máire Bhuí during one of those rainy afternoons in Ballyvourney when there was nothing to do but sit at the kitchen table, looking out the window across the Sullane River valley to where St. Gobnait's old churchyard held the grassed-over graves of my Twomey ancestors. The fields rising up on the other side of the valley looked like a patchwork quilt of green squares. *Forty shades of green.* I would think of those fields, years later, when the Johnny Cash song came wafting across the airwaves from America.

"She wrote the poem 'Cath Chéim an Fhia' ('The Battle of Keimaneigh')," said my grandmother. Then she would sing the poem to me. I never knew that poems could be sung. I thought poems were given out in class like the multiplication tables and then had to be memorized with your eyes clenched tight. If you stumbled or forgot the words, the Brother would slap you across the back of the neck and call you an eejit.

They didn't teach "*Cath Chéim an Fhia*" at my school in Dublin, so I never learned the words. Though I had a famous poet in my family, I could never tell my classmates about her. There was no opportunity for the subject to come up. Máire Bhuí Ní Laoire, Yellow Mary O'Leary, what an unusual name. My grandmother thought the yellow reference might have something to do with the colour of her hair, but it was in fact the dynastic name given to the branch of the O'Leary clan into which Máire Bhuí was born. If she had been born into one of the other branches, we would have known her as Dark Mary O'Leary or Secretive Mary O'Leary or Pallid Mary O'Leary. I stowed her name away somewhere in the back of my mind and turned my attention to other things.

I must have told Nicole about Máire Bhuí at some point during her growing-up years because when she was living in Ireland for a year in 1992–93, she remembered the name. She returned to Canada with a wonderful gift for me: a rare copy of a 95-page, red-covered book, *Filíocht Mháire Bhuidhe Ní Laoghaire* (*The Poetry of Yellow Mary O'Leary*) by An tAthair Donncha Ó Donnchú (Father Denis O'Donahue), MA. I hadn't known about the existence of this book. A gem from the dusty stacks, it was first published in 1931, 82 years after Máire Bhuí's death. Its third and last printing was in 1950 by the Irish government's Oifig an tSoláthair (Stationery Office), Baile Átha Cliath (Dublin). The author, who served as assistant parish priest in the West Cork village of Ballingeary during the First World War, didn't know Máire Bhuí, of course, but he did know some of the grandchildren. They told him some of what they knew about their grandmother, and he wrote it down. They did not give him – or perhaps he did not ask for – any of the anecdotal material that would have given her form and substance and helped bring her to life. Instead, the priest concentrated on tracing her genealogical links back to her 12th-century O'Leary ancestors, dutifully recording their births, marriages and deaths, and then giving a general sense – without much descriptive detail – of the fate that befell Máire Bhuí's family and the other tenant farming families of West Cork during the years leading up to the famine and afterwards.

As I leafed through the little red-backed book, I wished I could remember more of my Irish. I struggled with the old cumbersome spelling used in Ireland until 1948, when the government introduced a cleaner spelling to get rid of silent consonants. *Rugadh Máire Bhuidhe Ní Laoghaire ar Thúirín na nÉan i mbliain a 1774, agus is ann a chaith sí a saoghal le linn a hóige go dtí gur phós sí Séamas de Búrca timcheall na bliana 1792.* "Máire Bhuí Ní Laoire was born in Tooreennanean in the year 1774, and it was there she spent her early life until she married Seamus Burke around

1792." Would that the rest of the words could come to me so easily.

My work on the Máire Bhuí story sometimes seemed like an extension of the biographical profiling I was doing in the *Tribute* column at the *Herald* in 1994, but much more difficult because of the language barrier. I tried translating more of the red-backed book with a tattered old copy of *Dinneen's Irish–English Dictionary* sitting on the desk next to my computer. I particularly wanted to clear the hurdles in Máire Bhuí's epic poem "The Battle of Keimaneigh," about an armed clash in 1822 between British militia troops and a secret society of Catholic tenant farmers. But I stumbled badly. Every Irish word that brought me down seemed to have three or four possible meanings in English. Plus, it had some references – to "pulverizing porks" and a villain named Barry, for example – that mystified me. If I had managed to gain some momentum in the translating— even while missing the occasional word—I likely could have gotten a sense of what the poet was saying, in much the same way that you can get the general drift of *Hamlet* when it is performed in Russian, or understand *Finnegan's Wake* when the Irish actor Niall Tóibín reads excerpts on the radio. But I couldn't get beyond the first fence with Father O'Donahue's manuscript. I put the little red book away and again turned my mind to other things.

Not for long, though. Something kept drawing me back to this book that this long-ago priest had been moved to write about my ancestor. I needed to know more. How did a farmer's wife, a busy mother of nine and an apparent illiterate, become one of Munster's most celebrated folk poets of the 19th century? I needed to know more about this ancestor of mine.

I faxed off pages from the little red book to cousins and friends in Ireland whose grasp of the Gaeilge was surer than mine. I thought I would fashion their translations into a manuscript that I would circulate privately among family members. The translations came back in bits and pieces, and I started to put together a text that – like the O'Donahue original – was part genealogical exploration, part social history, part anecdotal biography, part literary preservation and analysis and part tribute to a woman who clearly was the poet of her people and the voice of West Cork's dispossessed. These were the Irish-speaking peasants forced to go underground with their language, culture, religion and Gaelic literature after the infamous Penal Laws were imposed on the population in the early 1700s.

I had assumed initially that Máire Bhuí must have been illiterate because she came from an oral tradition and never put her poems in writing. They were passed secretly and orally from generation to generation like amulets, until a couple of folklore collectors from West Cork eventually gathered and transcribed them, phonetically, crediting them to "Mary Burke of Keimaneigh." However, the more I learned about her story from Father O'Donahue's book, the more I realized she was only illiterate in the sense of being unable to read or write. She was far from being illiterate when it came to knowledge and education. But educated Irish-speaking peasants were not the favourite subjects of the British authorities who ran Ireland as a colonial fief during the 19th century, so Máire Bhuí kept her head down and the authorities were none the wiser.

You can tell from her poetry that she was well versed in Irish history and mythology, as well as the legends of Greece and Rome. The poems abound with references to Phoebus, Achilles and the mythical hunter-warrior Finn McCool. Where did her learning come from? Most likely from the illegal hedge schools operated in the rural areas in defiance of laws aimed at proselytizing and anglicizing the Irish. The children who attended these unchartered schools were always referred to as "scholars," and I can think of no better word to apply to them. The scribes and historians may have been stretching things a bit in terms of the holiness of the Irish when they dubbed Ireland "the island of saints and scholars" back in the sixth century. But they got it right as far as the learning part was concerned. Without access to a writing system, these hedge-school students received a very good education indeed.

As it turned out, I didn't include any of Máire Bhuí's poems in the first draft of the manuscript I created with the help of Father O'Donahue's book. My translators in Ireland and I were not entirely happy with some of our renditions, and I worried about going into print with weak or hackneyed versions of the poems that would do her a disservice. So I concentrated instead on getting the historical and the biographical bits right and then looked around for an Irish printing firm that would turn the manuscript into a booklet. Good fortune brought me in 1999 to the doorstep of The Collins Press in Cork, which undertook not only to print the manuscript but also to publish it as a paperback book – if I could come up with some money to subsidize the venture. A generous first cousin in Ireland, Dermot Desmond, offered to provide the needed funds, and I was on my way to seeing my first book in print.

Before sending the manuscript off for publishing, I took a quick research trip to Ireland to ensure that I wasn't missing out on some important aspect of Máire Bhuí's story. I scoured the archives at University College Cork, took photographs of the poet's gravestone in the old churchyard in Inchigeelagh and made a pilgrimage to the Pass of Keimaneigh, where the famous battle was fought. The pass, according to local legend, had received its name (Keimaneigh – *Chéim an Fhia* – Jump of the Deer) after a deer successfully evaded a group of hunters on horseback by leaping across the gap like a daredevil motorcyclist. Centuries later, in 1822, the pass became the lookout point for four hundred Catholic rebel tenant farmers who had taken up arms to protest the payment of tithe rents for the upkeep of the Protestant church. When they heard that a British militia unit was on its way to arrest and disarm them, the rebels lay in waiting behind the rocks and then leaped out with muskets blazing. Máire Bhuí's poem is about the ensuing conflict. Three of her sons participated in the fighting, and – while there are no government reports available to confirm this – one appears to have been subsequently executed by the British for murder and treason. So the poet believed, at any rate, because she composed two laments for her dead son.

I found one important document when I was in Ireland completing my research. Two Irish-born priests in the United States, Richard Burke and Seán Sweeney, had done an excellent translation of the entire Father O'Donahue book – poems and explanatory notes included – and I was lucky enough to acquire a copy. It was the piece of the puzzle that I had been missing. The Irish-American translators had effectively preserved the rhythms of the original Gaelic while rendering the poems into English. With their permission granted, it now became possible for me to include the entire canon of Máire Bhuí's poetry in my book, thus making it a richer work.

The poems gave me a strong sense of Máire Bhuí as a person, what her concerns were and what motivated her to compose poetry. Many of her poems were nationalistic polemics against British imperialism, filled with brimstone, energy and passion. The "porks" in "The Battle of Keimaneigh," I discovered, were the much-hated tithe collectors, whom Máire Bhuí also referred to variously as "swine" and "boors." The villainous "Barry" was one of these tithe collectors, a powerful landlord and a determined oppressor of the poor. There was a lot of anger in "The Battle of Keimaneigh." She talked about the landlords and the tithe collectors joining forces with the militia and "coming viciously like a pack of venomous hounds" to put to rout "the heroes of Ireland at a mountain recess." The soldiers were a "wicked, perverse horde of big-bellied butchers" who should be "cast down into fires of hell without remission for all eternity." I could see why Máire Bhuí would not have wanted her poems to be written down. If they had fallen into the wrong hands, some would have been grounds for a charge of treason.

Not all of her poems were as angry as "The Battle of Keimaneigh." Some were tributes to loved ones who had died. Others were gentle love songs. She also composed religious meditations, humorous pieces reflecting the life of her community and nationalistic wish-fulfillment poems in which Ireland was depicted as a beautiful and sorrowful maiden who could never be happy until released from captivity. As I read through them I found myself wishing I could hear them performed. What kind of artistry did Máire Bhuí bring to the singing of these songs when she was urging one of her sons to get married or lamenting the death of another son?

I received an answer when I returned to Ireland in the summer of 2000, shortly after the *Calgary Herald* strike ended, to launch the book that is now titled *Songs of an Irish Poet: The Mary O'Leary Story*. In the bar of Creedon's Hotel in Inchigeelagh, I was fortunate to hear a folksinger from the village performing "The Battle of Keimaneigh" in the original Irish. She gave a spirited rendition. Though I couldn't understand the words, I could feel the power of Máire Bhuí's language. The performance was bold and brave and stirring. It sent chills down my spine.

My book was very well received in that region of West Cork, where everyone still knows the name of Máire Bhuí Ní Laoire. I was grateful for that. I was an exile writing about a local subject from afar, and I wanted to get it right.

MOVING TO THE FRONT OF
THE GENERATIONAL TRAIN

The first important person in my life, my mother, died of colon cancer in 1977 at age 62. I knew it was inevitable – 18 months of chemo and radiation had brought neither cure nor remission – but still I had hoped for a miracle. When my father phoned with the news, I found it difficult to accept that this flame that burned so brightly in our lives had been snuffed out. She was much too young. I wept for weeks.

She had struggled with the disease for seven years. I call it a struggle, but she would never have termed it such. She would have called it a cross to be borne, with prayers and acceptance, along with all the other tribulations in this vale of tears. She was first diagnosed in 1970, four years after I left for Canada. She didn't use the word cancer, and my father didn't use it either, so I never knew that her situation was serious. People of my parents' generation never revealed too much information about medical problems that hit below the belt. When Zelda, one-year-old Nicole and I visited with the family that summer, my mother told me she had to undergo surgery to correct a small "plumbing" problem, and that she would only have to wear the bag for a few weeks.

If I had known her illness was serious, I would have made an effort to visit her frequently after that. But in the early 1970s I was more interested in spending my holidays in parts of the world – including parts of Canada – where I had never been before. Staying with family in Ireland was not my idea of a good time. I wanted to stay in hotels, eat in restaurants and see new and interesting places.

When I finally visited Ireland again, in the summer of 1975, my mother's cancer was in remission and still she was not talking about it. But she was talking about her brother, Jerome, who had died earlier that year at age 57. "We wanted to have an autopsy done," she said. "He fell off a ladder and hurt his back, and we didn't think that would be serious enough to kill him. But the doctor said no autopsy was necessary because he knew the cause of death: cancer. We told the doctor there must be some mistake because we never knew he had cancer. 'Well, Jerome knew,' said the doctor." The reticence of the Irish.

My mother's cancer returned in the spring of 1976. My father waited until the end of the year – when he sent his annual Christmas letter – to tell me about her condition. He explained that she had sworn him to secrecy because she didn't want me to be over in Canada worrying about her. She was being well looked after by the doctors, he said, and the prognosis was good. A couple of months later, he telephoned me long distance – something he had never done during the 10 years I had been in Canada – and told me I should probably plan on coming home that summer. The treatment was not working, he said, and my mother was expected to live little more than a few months.

I wrote a letter to Dad and asked him for specific details

about the type of cancer, the treatment my mother was receiving, her state of mind and so on. My father responded with another phone call. "What were you thinking of?" he asked angrily. "What if your mother had opened that letter, how do you think it would have made her feel?"

I visited my mother for the last time that August. It still saddens me to remember that she got out of her sick bed, came downstairs in her dressing gown and cooked me fried eggs and rashers for my breakfast. It was the first time she had been down to the kitchen in months. My father told me he was now cooking all her meals, coming home from the office every day to make lunch for her and trying to make her life as comfortable as possible. "It's the least I can do," he said. "Your mammy and I have been together for a long time."

My parents seemed closer at that time than I ever remembered them being during my growing-up years. My mother had never seemed to depend on my father for anything – aside from housekeeping money – when he was putting in 12-hour days at the office and she was looking after the four kids. Now, for the first time in her life, this fiercely independent woman needed him to bring her soup and help her down the stairs. As I watched him tenderly caring for her, I realized for the first time that perhaps there was more warmth and love in this relationship than I had ever suspected.

Her world became smaller as the disease pursued its homicidal voyage of destruction. Friends who had once dropped in to sip tea, chat and listen, were asked to leave their gifts of home baking outside the front door. She did not want to receive visitors because she could not bear the thought of them seeing the damage the cancer treatments were doing to her body. "The radiation is the worst part," she told me. "I feel so sick afterwards." She spent her waking hours praying with her rosary, reading detective novels and writing in her diary. In it, she expressed her appreciation for the way my father was looking after her, and said she worried that she might never see her Canadian grandchildren again. She had visited Canada on a couple of occasions during the early 1970s, after my sister Mary moved to Ontario with her husband and two sons.

I didn't go back to Ireland for Mammy's funeral. She had told me not to because of the cost involved. I kissed her goodbye on a Monday morning and flew from Dublin to London, where I spent a night at the Strand Palace Hotel before flying back to Canada. That evening, I went to see a West End hit, a right-to-die play at the Mermaid Theatre called *Whose Life Is It Anyway?* Bad choice. I sobbed all through the first act and left during the intermission.

The day after I left Dublin, my mother was taken by ambulance to the Mount Carmel Hospital in Churchtown, where she died 10 days later. By odd coincidence, I had spent six months in the same hospital 24 years previously, when I was nine. I went in to have my appendix out and then developed some kind of acute gastroenteritic condition that kept me in bed for the duration. My father visited me every day, bringing me a bunch of grapes, a bottle of Lucozade "liquid energy" and a *Classics Illustrated* comic book. My mother never came to visit. I still wonder why. Just one of the many unanswered questions I never got around to asking.

I grieved her loss at home at the piano, playing endless choruses of "I'll Take You Home Again, Kathleen" with the tears streaming down my face. It was my mother's favourite song, the one song she had always recognized when she was cooking dinner and I was doing my practice. I had first played it for her as a 10-year-old and felt very proud of myself because I worked out the arrangement by ear.

My father supplied the touching words that captured her final days. "Our thirty-fifth wedding anniversary was on Friday, September 2," he wrote in a tear-stained letter to me five days after her death. "Although she was just starting to slip away then, she mustered sufficient strength and concentration to wish me many happy returns. The sadness of it . . ."

Dad went on to describe his visit to the hospital the day after her death, and how he was spellbound by the sight of her lying in peace in the mortuary chapel. "She looked breathtakingly beautiful," he wrote. "A stranger would have taken her for a girl of twenty. She was smiling, and I am positive that she had glimpsed the face of God. I think, Brian, that we have a powerful friend in Heaven."

My father was right when he said a stranger would have taken her for a 20-year-old. At a time when adults looked older than they did in the Peter-Pan 1970s, my mother was the exception. Tall and fair-haired with big blue eyes and a Pepsodent smile, she was a 60-year-old who looked like a 40-year-old.

I grieved the loss of my mother for a long time. I found it hard to accept that this beautiful light, this bright candle would never burn again. What had happened to that energy, that spirit, that warm breath of air? I shuddered at the thought of her body being lowered into that cold earth, never to rise again. What was the point of it all? What was the point of creation if, at the end of the day, every earthly body was to be dumped like trash into a landfill site? For the first time in my life, my Christian faith was being tested, and I was having doubts. I used to believe in the immortality of the human soul, but now I wasn't sure. My father could see my mother entering the Kingdom of Heaven. I could only see a door closing and then blackness.

I wept for my mother on my 34th birthday when she would have sent me a cassette tape with a recorded message of greetings. Eight-year-old Nicole was devastated too; she had only met her Irish grandmother twice in her young life. I wept for her on St. Patrick's Day when she would have sent me a sprig of shamrock and a little packet of seeds so that we could grow shamrock in Canada. (I did try a few times but it never worked.) And I wept for her on Mother's Day. I thought about her when I saw the kids dressed up in their Sunday best, carrying flowers and balloons, heading off to buffet brunch with their parents. I thought about her when I played the organ at St. Pius X Church, where Zelda and Nicole and I had been part of the music ministry since our arrival in Calgary. The choir sang a Marian song in Spanish called "Madre del Desaparecido – Mother of the Disappeared Son."

I was the disappeared son too. I was the son who went off to Canada to become part of what the poet Robert Bly called the sibling society – eternal half-adults, Peter Pans in jeans, who abandoned their kids to daycare centres and their elders to old folks' homes – when I might have stayed home and learned from observation how to be an elder, how to be a person who understood that the world belonged to the dead, to the people who made the poetry and the songs.

I realized that I had never phoned home or sent her a card on Mother's Day. That May holiday hadn't been observed in Ireland when I was growing up, and I didn't think my mother would understand this North American custom of setting aside a special day for children to tell their mothers they loved them. Foolish, she would have called it. If her son loved her so much, why did he go away to Canada?

I realized that I had never told my mother I loved her. She had never told me she loved me. Parents and children didn't talk like that when I was a kid. The first time I ever remembered her hugging me was on the day I left for Canada. "Look after yourself," she had said. I was surprised to see she had tears in her eyes.

Choosing to emigrate was the first big decision I had ever

made without her advance approval. My mother had stage-managed my life since the day I was born. But I hadn't left home for that reason. I had left because I felt all grown-up and wanted to see the world. Her stage-managing had given me the maximum possibility for growth. My mother had given me a great gift. At the time when I was ready to leave the nest she had given me wings to fly. So even though I knew she would have called me foolish, I should have been sending her Mother's Day cards.

And I should have been phoning her more often.

I invited Dad to spend the summer of 1978 with us in Calgary. I thought he should get away from painful reminders of his life's companion. He was grateful for the chance to escape. "It will be good therapy," he said. "A chance for me to come to terms with life."

With the local theatres closed until after Labour Day, I switched my focus to reviewing jazz concerts while my father was in Calgary and invited him to accompany me to some of them. He was a perceptive spectator. He should have been a critic himself. In fact, you might say he was a critic, albeit one whose critical writings were confined to those he put in his book review journal. We attended one concert that was supposed to feature Ella Fitzgerald, Oscar Peterson and Joe Pass together on the same bill. However, Peterson was a no-show due to illness. Afterwards my father commented, "It was like seeing *Hamlet* without the prince." I used that line in my review.

My father came back to Calgary the following summer,

this time when the annual Stampede had us all – residents and visitors alike – playing urban cowboy for the week. He drank vodka-laced orange juice at the outdoor pancake breakfasts, watched the Young Canadians singing and dancing on the grandstand stage and bought himself a cowboy hat that he would likely never wear in Dublin. He camped with us in the mountains, had his picture taken standing next to a bear-warning sign and toasted marshmallows under the stars. For the first time in my adult life I felt very close to him.

Within a few years, however, our relationship changed. My father never came back to Calgary after that second visit. He stopped writing letters to me, except for the obligatory annual Christmas greeting, despite the fact that I continued to write to him several times a year. What had gone wrong? I determined, in September of 1990, to find out.

I flew to Dublin and spent a week with him. He seemed surprised when I said I was there just to see him. He had come to expect that all my trips to Dublin were somehow connected with theatre junkets to London and thus didn't really count as family visits. If I was going to the West End to write about theatre, then any visit with him had to be a secondary consideration. It never seemed to have occurred to him that I applied for these business trips with the express purpose of being able to visit with him at the same time.

Dad did his best to make things comfortable for me in Dublin. He generously took time away from his regular routine, drove me to see the houses where we had lived during my childhood and sought out restaurants he would not normally have frequented but thought I might enjoy. I dearly wanted to ask him why he had distanced himself from me after 1978, but somehow I could not muster up the courage to say the words. At the same time, I did learn some important things about myself and about the place my father still occupied in my life.

I realized that when I left my father's house to move to Canada in 1966, I had abandoned him forever. I might have thought occasionally about moving back – in fact, I did think about this seriously for a while after my mother died – but the reality was that I was writing in Canada the second act of my life's script, and the second act was better than the first. I had a beautiful Canadian family, a loving wife and daughter, and a great Canadian newspaper job that suited my temperament and satisfied my desire for creative expression. I had a life filled with good music, good food, good wine and good conversation. I did not want to give any of that up. The physical separation from my father had brought an inevitable emotional distancing, and that could never be bridged as long as I chose to remain in Canada.

Another reason I went to visit my father in 1990 was because I had a guilt complex. I felt ashamed that I had not been around much during my mother's last years, so now I was determined to be the prodigal son who maintained a steady connection with the surviving parent even if he never reciprocated. This would be the first in a series of annual visits to spend time with him.

My father, I discovered in 1990, was still a product of the environment that created him. At age 73, he still held the same pre–Vatican II views on matters of Church and State. Ireland had changed; my father had not. I felt a certain envy. He maintained a rock-hard consistency, an unwavering sense of right and wrong. I struggled with doubts and the nagging feeling that the new answers might be no more satisfying than the old.

He still loved to vent. When he sat at the kitchen table denouncing the Irish and English governments for their failure to achieve a settlement in Northern Ireland, I was transported back to a time when it was my lot in life to be seen and not heard. With the assured conviction of a cabinet minister with a new portfolio, my father could offer a ready opinion on everything from the escalation of world oil prices to the French fact in Canada. No subject was beyond his purview. He would have made a splendid editorial page commentator.

If I offered a dissenting opinion, it was usually tentative and unconvincing. He looked at the world through unblinking Irish eyes. I was the overseas visitor in his house, the Yankee at the Court of King Arthur, the expatriate who had traded my birthright for a mess of Canadian pottage. It was not my place to challenge him. He was clearly disappointed by my failure to engage him in robust debate.

There was one time during my 1990 visit when I saw

my father in a different light, not as a dispenser of ready opinions, but as the long-ago parent who sang "I'm an Old Cowhand from the Rio Grande" to me on bath nights. It happened on a day when he had to go to the Bray Golf Club to pick up some tournament scorecards for processing in his capacity as club handicapping secretary. When he finished his business at the golf club, he invited me to accompany him over to the nearby lawn bowling club, where he was a member. I don't bowl, but he offered to show me, in one quick and easy lesson.

The sun was bright on this late September day when we walked out onto the bowling green. I was uncomfortable in a borrowed pair of too-small galoshes. He was proudly in charge with his customized bowling woods, regulation shoes and floppy sun hat. He explained the rules, demonstrated the techniques and invited me to have a go. I stumbled initially, a child taking his uncertain first steps. Then, slowly, shakily, I began to get the hang of it. He was solicitous, encouraging, complimentary, a father beaming at the unsteady child who would soon be running around in the garden, giggling and chasing after butterflies. The bond was complete. It was a magical moment. *I know all the trails in the Lone Star State. Yippee-yi-yo-ki-ay.*

But it was a fleeting moment. Later that evening we went for dinner at Éamonn's Restaurant on the Bray Esplanade. I started to tell Dad about some problems I was having at work, hoping this might bring us to a deeper level of mutual understanding. He listened without comment for several minutes and then said, "Eat up the rest of your vegetables." So much for baring my soul.

Dad acknowledged that his golf club and bowling club friendships were little more than casual connections. "Frothy," he called them. Yet he didn't seem to want anything more. He showed no desire to fill the emotional void left after my mother's death, perhaps to protect himself from further pain. Instead he filled his life with things to keep his body active and his mind occupied: golf, bowling, bridge and reading the great works of world literature, which he borrowed from the library in alphabetical order according to the surnames of the authors. He had his family in Ireland that he met with on a weekly basis, and his family in Canada that he connected with once or twice a year, and that seemed to be enough to satisfy his emotional needs.

On the day of my departure, Dad drove me to the airport, waited for my boarding gate to be posted and said how much he had enjoyed his visits to Calgary. When it was time to go, I hugged him, thanked him for putting his life on hold for me and asked him if he might come to Calgary the following summer. He was non-committal.

He never did come back to Calgary. But I did go back to Ireland, in 1992 when Nicole was living over there, and I went every year after that until he died in 1996. By that time, I was no longer trying to forge a stronger link with him. I was just happy to spend a week in Dublin with him every year and receive a letter from him occasionally. We also talked on the phone from time to time. More I could not have asked for.

I received the long-distance phone call we all dread at 4:00 a.m. on Sunday, September 8, 1996, after trying unsuccessfully for three days to reach him. I wanted to tell Dad I was making plans to visit in a couple of weeks. My brother Michael had been trying to reach him at the same time, to reschedule a bridge date my father had cancelled. They played together once a week at a bridge club near my father's home. My sister Mary too had been trying to reach him. She wanted to tell him his children were planning to help him celebrate his 80th birthday the following March. But, alas, too late for all of us. After phoning for a couple of days, Michael went over to the house on the Saturday evening and found my father dead in his bed with his hands clutched tightly around his Redemptorist Mission prayer book. Over the previous nine months, he had been seeing a specialist for treatment of chronic obstructive pulmonary disease, a bronchial condition that produced a racking cough and caused him great distress. He was also being treated for cardiac arrhythmia. He died in his sleep, presumably after a bout of coughing that proved too much for his weakening heart. I hope he went quickly and without too much pain.

I flew to Dublin for the funeral, booked a tenor to sing "Panis Angelicus," the Schubert "Ave Maria," "How Great Thou Art" and "The Lord Is My Shepherd," and played the organ to accompany him. I was very pleased that

Monsignor Rogers, the priest who gave me the chance 39 years previously to play the organ at Mount Merrion, was a co-celebrant of the funeral Mass. When I saw him in the sacristy after Mass, I reminded Monsignor Rogers of that long-ago church gig he had given me. It seemed right that he should be there at the funeral while I gave some of my music back to my father. I also gave some of my words back, when I delivered the eulogy.

"Melancholic thoughts abound," I said, quoting from a letter my father had sent me in September 1984 about the arrival of autumn in Ireland. "Melancholic thoughts abound because, at this time of year, the summer ends and the days grow shorter."

I told the congregation that my father was a wonderfully evocative letter writer. "Latterly, he only wrote to me once or twice a year, his rationale being that because nothing much changed in his life from year to year, there wasn't much point in trying to make more soup out of the same old bone. But when he did put pen to paper, he could weave a vivid tapestry of anecdote, image and philosophical observation. My own love of storytelling could only have come from one place. My father was a man of letters in every sense of the phrase."

I recalled that when my father came to Calgary on a visit in 1978 I had encouraged him to review a book about the two peace activists in Northern Ireland, Mairéad Corrigan and Betty Williams, who won the 1976 Nobel Peace Prize. I offered the review to the books editor at the *Calgary Herald*, who was pleased to publish it. I added that my father was so proud of his one-time professional literary achievement that he kept as a souvenir the uncashed *Herald* cheque.

I went on to say that when my father retired from the civil service in 1982, he made it his personal mission to supplement his daily diet of newspaper reading by borrowing from the library – by surname in alphabetical order – the works of all the great authors of history. "By his mid-70s he was up to the letter D, discovering the joys of Dickens and Dostoevsky."

My father's final ambition, I said, was to complete "in my eightieth year" the Leaving Certificate English course he had abandoned during the 1930s when he seized the opportunity to drop out of secondary school and begin an entry-level job with the Irish government. He never achieved that goal of finally completing his secondary school education. But he did make it all the way to the letter W in his alphabetical reading program. On his reading table, I had noticed when I arrived from Canada, was an anthology of writings by Oscar Wilde, opened to *The Picture of Dorian Gray*. Another month on his alphabetical journey through the great works of literature and he would have been savouring the writings of Yeats and Zola.

I noted, with a catch in my voice, that my father was being buried on the 19th anniversary of my mother's death. Melancholic thoughts abounded that day.

While sorting through my father's personal effects I found an old ledger of his that provided me with a rare insight into the way he managed his finances when money was tight. He had used it to keep track of his household expenses between 1960 and 1962, when he was being transferred from Dublin to Cork and back again. It didn't include everything he would have paid for in those three years. There were no references, for example, to money spent on clothing, doctor's visits, school fees for the four children, movie tickets or house insurance. But his record of expenditures on groceries and public transportation painted a vivid picture of a man making do with very little. From the lined pages of this government-issue, green-covered book sprang a fascinating and often affecting tale.

The ledger showed that my father earned £675 in 1960. I don't know what the exchange rate was back then, but I would guess that in dollar terms, his yearly salary amounted to no more than $1,000. Although that was about $7,700 in 2011 dollars, and things were seven times cheaper then, it still would not have been a princely sum. On that income, he had to support my mother and the four children.

On his first trip from Dublin to Cork, a distance of 260 kilometres, my father had travelled on a one-way, third-class train ticket that cost him approximately $3. Third-class travel on that milk run meant he had sat on a wooden seat for close to four hours. He noted he had left Dublin at 8:04 a.m. and arrived in Cork at eight minutes past noon. Attention to such detail was one of my father's defining characteristics. Breakfast on the train had cost him about 38 cents, lunch at Cork's Windsor Hotel about 42 cents.

Accommodation and meals at a Cork boarding house cost my father the equivalent of about $6 a week. His government bosses balked at this expenditure and suggested he move to a cheaper, "self-catering" flat, costing about $2.50 My father did so and allowed himself a food budget of $3 a week. His bosses also quibbled with other expenses he turned in. They docked him 95 cents from a $5.50 claim he made for return train fare to visit with his family in Dublin. They said he should have taken advantage of the lower weekend rate.

When my father advertised for a house to buy in Cork, his bosses allowed him the 12¢ cost of the newspaper ad, but they refused to cover the $79 in legal costs related to the actual house purchase. Nor would they compensate him for the cost of altering the drapes and carpets he brought down from our house in Dublin. My father recorded all these unreimbursed expenses and subsequently lodged an appeal.

The appeal took five years to resolve. My father patiently wrote memos to the various levels of authority, submitting his receipts and citing the legal circulars supporting his claim. When one level of government turned him down, he gathered up his documents and sent them on to the next level. For him, it was a matter of principle. He was simply asking for what he felt he was rightfully owed.

The story had a happy ending. At the back of the ledger, an accountant-general's memo listed the government's final judgment on his five-year quest for transfer expenses.

My father figured the government owed him a total of £129.12 ($255) – the equivalent of about two months' salary. The government calculated that, in fact, it owed him £130.12 – one pound, or $1.50 more. He came out ahead!

When I look in the mirror today, I see an image of my father. I see the same big nose, the same serious expression and the same lank hair, thinning and grey. I often wonder what he would think of me now. Would he have told his buddies at the golf club about the books I have written? Would he have read this book and understood that some part of me still longs for his approval?

There are no answers, only more questions.

Coda

FOR THOSE I MIGHT
HAVE MISSED

Who did I leave out? I look over my shoulder as I pen this tribute to the people who made a difference in my life, and I see the room filling up with ghosts.

I see the ghost of Brother Nolan, my grade 4 teacher, who told us on the first day of school that he would only allow us to speak Irish in his class. "But we hardly know any Irish," we protested. "You will know plenty if you do it my way," he said. Brother Nolan knew that if we failed the Irish-language exam in our last year of high school, we wouldn't be allowed to graduate, so he wanted to grab us early. Because Irish was the country's second official language, we would need it for everything from university entrance to civil service employment.

Brother Nolan's only concession in class was to let us substitute an English word if we didn't know the Irish equivalent. "*Tá mé* (I am) feeling happy *an lá inniu* (today)." We struggled, but we learned. At the end of the year, we were fluent.

I see the ghost of Mr. Courtney, my grade 7 English teacher, who got me so excited about the writings of P.G. Wodehouse that I spent months borrowing from the Mount Merrion library the author's wonderfully entertaining books about the idle Bertie Wooster and his butler, Jeeves. "The funniest writer in the English language," said Mr. Courtney, and I could not disagree.

I see the ghost of my uncle John Pat Twomey, who took over the family farm in Ballyvourney after one brother left for England and two others left for the United States. I got to know him better than some of my other uncles because I spent the summers of my childhood on the farm, watching Uncle John at work and play. He was a very fine button accordionist, and he had a dry sense of humour that I seem to have inherited. An American tourist drove by the farm one day when Uncle John was in the meadow cutting thistles. "Say, buddy," said the Yank, "does this road take you to Killarney?" My uncle paused for the longest moment and then slowly replied, "And what would be stopping it?"

I never met Winifred Atwell, the Jamaican-born pianist who shot to the top of the British bestselling pop charts in 1952 with a tune called "Black and White Rag." But I listened to her on the radio every week and tried hard to convince my mother we should attach thumbtacks to the hammers of our piano keys so that the instrument would have the same tinny sound as what Winnie called her "other piano." My mother would not hear of blemishing our valuable piano like that, but I did learn to play "Black and White Rag."

As with Winifred Atwell, I only knew the Clancy Brothers and Tommy Makem from their performances on the radio, but these guys had a profound influence on me when I was in my late teens. The Irish traditional songs that had been largely forgotten were suddenly alive again. The Clancys took them out of the closet, set them to the accompaniment of guitar, banjo and pennywhistle, sang them on *The Ed Sullivan Show* and brought them home to Ireland, where they became more popular than the songs of The Beatles. I came to Canada with my head full of Clancy songs and found a receptive audience in pubs and nightclubs from Vancouver to Halifax.

I see the ghost of Rick McNair, the red-haired theatrical maverick who defied the odds and proved to the skeptics that new Canadian plays could do just as well on the big stages of Calgary and Winnipeg as the hits of Broadway or the West End. Because of Rick, I developed an appreciation for the works of Sharon Pollock and John Murrell that I would not have otherwise known about. A fun-loving Peter Pan who never seemed entirely at home in the world of adults, Rick would have enjoyed knowing that his pals left empty beer glasses on his casket after he died in 2007.

"Make the words sing," said Reg Vickers, an editor for whom I spent a rewarding three years writing stories for the *Calgary Herald*'s old *Sunday* magazine. When Reg died in 1994, I lamented the loss of a rare newspaperman who cared as much about literary style as he did about informational content. A story didn't become a story in Reg's mind until it was endowed with the felicities of fine writing. Otherwise, it was nothing more than facts and figures.

I knew almost nothing about magazine writing when I moved out of the *Herald*'s entertainment department and landed on Reg's doorstep in 1988. But like Gary White, my first boss when I started in the newspaper business in 1968,

Reg was gracious and supportive and did not complain if I sometimes tried to reach beyond my grasp. I'm still trying to make the words sing, Reg. It's the best advice I can think of for those who want to make writing their life's work.

My two trusty keyboards are still close at hand. I don't play music professionally any more, but I still like to noodle. As long as I have tunes in my head, I will continue to play. And as long as the words continue to flow, I will pay tribute to those who have touched me, inspired me and made the journey easier. Thus will the strands of my life continue to intertwine. Thus will the stories continue to unfold.

ACKNOWLEDGEMENTS

Most of the people I want to thank are named in the pages of this book. In particular, I want to thank my wife Zelda and daughter Nicole for allowing me to invade their privacy, and the Club of 93 for providing friendship and support during our eight lonely months on the picket line. My sister, Mary, shared some great stories about our family that I happily included. I want to express my gratitude to Don Gorman of RMB for taking on this book as a publishing project, and to Shauna Rusnak and Meaghan Craven for whipping the manuscript into shape. An abbreviated version of my coming-to-Canada story appeared in *The Story That Brought Me Here: To Alberta From Everywhere* (Brindle & Glass, 2008), and I would like to thank the editor of that book, my good friend Linda Goyette, for encouraging me to set aside my journalistic detachment and expose some of myself for all the world to see.

INDEX

57
6

ABOUT THE AUTHOR

Irish-born Brian Brennan has written seven non-fiction books about the colourful characters of Canada's past and one book, *Songs of an Irish Poet: The Mary O'Leary Story* (Bowness Press, 2007), about a celebrated Irish-language folk poet of the 19th century who also happened to be Brennan's ancestor. He lives in Calgary, Alberta. For more information, visit www.brianbrennan.ca.

Collector's

Guide to Easton

Press Books

Collector's Guide
to Easton Press Books:
A Compendium

———

by Kimberly Blaker

Green Grove Press
Farmington Hills, Michigan

Collector's Guide to Easton Press Books

Published by Green Grove Press
P.O. Box 48333
Farmington Hills, Michigan 48333

Printed in the United States of America

1 2 3 4 5 6 7 8 9 10

Cover design by Kimberly Blaker
Interior design by Kimberly Blaker

Collector's Guide to Easton Press Books

Contents

Collector's Guide to Easton Press Books

Collector's Guide to Easton Press Books

Introduction

For approximately 30 years, collectors of modern leather bound books have enjoyed adding Easton Press editions to their collections. Based out of Norwalk, Connecticut, Easton Press publishes a broad array of titles ranging from reprints of classic books to modern fiction, science fiction, and non-fiction. What draws collectors to these books is their elegant beauty. Easton Press books are bound in high quality leather with 22kt gold stamped spines. Pages are Smyth-sewn and the page edges are gilded. Most volumes also have moiré silk endsheets and sewn-in ribbon page markers.

Easton Press has also long been known for it's signed and first editions. In recent years, the publisher also started adding limited facsimile editions, many of which are housed in sleeves or clam shell boxes.

A guide for Easton Press collectors

As a former bookseller of rare and collectible books as well as Easton Press editions, I decided a collector's guide to Easton Press books would be a welcome addition to the library of Easton Press collectors. Easton Press has had so many wonderful titles over the years, which many collectors would surely love to locate and add to their collections.

The purpose of this guide, therefore, is to provide collectors an exhaustive list of Easton Press titles and the names of the series under which the titles were published.

The 'Easton Press as Collectible' Debate

For years booksellers have hotly debated whether Easton Press books are truly 'collectible' or not. Some dealers, particularly those dealing in antiquarian books, have a strong distaste for Easton

Press books. Their argument is Easton Press books dull in comparison to the binding quality of the better 19th century and earlier bindings.

Some booksellers also point out that just because a publisher calls their books 'collector editions' doesn't make them collectible. This is a great point and very true.

Another issue booksellers point to is that Easton Press books are commodity books. In other words, the books are printed by Easton Press in unlimited quantities sufficient to supply the ongoing demand for the titles. This argument is valid for the bulk of Easton Press books. Titles from the 100 Greatest Books Ever Written collection, in particular, are periodically reprinted by Easton Press. So while prices on used copies from the 100 Greatest Books will fluctuate upwards for a short period while they're out of stock at Easton Press, the prices of used copies eventually plummet when Easton Press does a reprint.

Despite these points, Easton Press books are, in fact, collectible. First, the definition of 'collectible' is something that is collected by a number of people. Many people do in fact collect Easton Press books. Therefore, the books are collectible. But 'collectible' and 'valuable' are not one in the same. Just because books are collectible doesn't make them valuable. This is the case with many collected Easton Press books as well as countless other types of collectibles on the market.

But are some Easton Press books 'valuable'? You bet. While many Easton Press books are routinely reprinted leaving too great a supply, Easton Press also publishes signed editions, signed first editions, and limited editions. Though not every signed or limited edition will hold its value, let alone increase in value, many do hold and even increase in value.

To be sure, a signed Easton Press copy of *One Flew Over the Cuckoo's Nest* recently sold on ebay for $1,300. A pair of signed

Michael Crichton books, *Jurassic Park* and *The Lost World,* sold for $1020. There are numerous other examples of Easton Press titles that have proven to be not only collectible but valuable.

So the truth is Easton Press books are collectible in the true sense of the word 'collectible' – and some are also valuable.

As a collector of Easton Press books, you might ask yourself why you are collecting these books to help guide you in your collecting pursuit. Is it because you enjoy the ambiance of a luxurious library? If so, there's nothing wrong with that! So long as you aren't collecting with the idea of getting a good return on your investment, collect the titles you like and enjoy them for years to come.

On the other hand, if what you're really hoping for is a nice profit on your library someday, be selective. Focus on titles that are either signed or limited. That's where you'll have better odds of them increasing in value. Just realize that Easton Press or not, even signed books don't always hold let alone increase in value. So consider whether the author or the particular title is likely to become or remain highly sought after.

Easton Press edition values

Now to tell you what this compendium is not. *The Collector's Guide to Easton Press Books* isn't a values guide. I decided against turning this into a values guide because it would be outdated nearly as soon as soon as it came off the press. Because Easton Press routinely (and unpredictably) reprints many of its titles, values constantly fluctuate up and down. The exception to this is for certain sets and titles, particularly signed, limited, and first editions.

The best way for you to determine the current value of a title is to visit www.used.addall.com. For each title you search, include "Easton Press" in the keyword search box. You'll likely see a broad range of prices. Eliminate the highest and lowest priced copies. Then average out what's left. Keep in mind those copies in better condition will likely be worth much more than copies in poor condition.

Grading Easton Press editions

In the world of book collecting, the condition of a book is an important factor in determining its value. This is especially true with Easton Press editions. In fact, unlike many other collectible books which may still be valuable even if they're graded as only Good+ or Very Good, that isn't the case with Easton Press editions. If there's even a faint scuff to the leather or hairline scratch to the gilt page edges of an Easton Press book, it decreases significantly in value. So keep this in mind when buying and also in how you store and handle your books if you hope to sell them down the road.

Dating Easton Press books

Unlike books by most publishers, Easton Press does not provide the publication dates in its books. The date you typically see in Easton Press books is the copyright date, usually on the copyright page. That date has nothing to do with the date Easton Press actually published (printed) the book. For example, Easton Press might reprint the same title multiple times over a period of 10 years while the copyright date remains unchanged. The exception is periodically Easton Press might change the copyright date when the copyright for the title is renewed. But again, that has nothing to do with the publication date. For this reason, I haven't included dates for most titles because such dates aren't precise and would only add confusion. The exception I made is for signed first editions.

100 Greatest Books Ever Written

The 100 Greatest Books Ever Written is actually well-over 100 titles. That's because over the years Easton Press has altered its title list for this series. So you can collect them all or choose your favorite 100. Easton Press never has all 100 titles in stock at one time, so if you want to collect this series, you'll either need to be patient or buy quite a few used copies.

Aeschylus. *Oresteia.*
Aesop. *Aesop's Fables.*
Alcott, Louisa May. *Little Women.*
Alighieri, Dante. *The Divine Comedy.*
Aristophanes. *The Birds and The Frogs.*
Aristotle. *Politics.*
Augustine, Saint. *The Confessions of St. Augustine.*
Austen, Jane. *Pride and Prejudice.*
Baudelaire, Charles. *Les Fleurs du mal (The Flowers Of Evil).*
Beowulf.
Boccaccio, Giovanni. *The Decameron.*
Bronte, Charlotte. *Jane Eyre.*
Brontë, Emily. *Wuthering Heights.*
Browning, Robert. *Collected Poems.*
Bunyan, John. *The Pilgrim's Progress.*
Burton, Richard. *Tales from the Arabian Nights.*
Butler, Samuel. *The Way of All Flesh.*
Carroll, Lewis. *Alice in Wonderland.*
Cervantes, Miguel de. *Don Quixote.*
Chaucer, Geoffrey. *The Canterbury Tales.*
Chekhov, Anton. *The Cherry Orchard/Three Sisters.*
Confucius. *The Analects of Confucius.*
Conrad, Joseph. *Heart of Darkness.*
Conrad, Joseph. *Lord Jim.*

Cooper, James Fenimore. *The Last of the Mohicans.*
Crane, Stephen. *The Red Badge of Courage.*
Darwin, Charles. *Descent of Man.*
Darwin, Charles. *On the Origin of Species.*
Defoe, Daniel. *A Journal of the Plague Year.*
Defoe, Daniel. *Robinson Crusoe.*
Dickens, Charles. *David Copperfield.*
Dickens, Charles. *Great Expectations.*
Dickens, Charles. *Short Stories.*
Dickens, Charles. *A Tale of Two Cities.*
Dickinson, Emily. *Collected Poems.*
Donne, John. *Poems.*
Dostoevsky, Fyodor. *The Brothers Karamazov.*
Doyle, Sir Arthur Conan. *Adventures of Sherlock Holmes.*
Dumas, Alexandre. *The Count of Monte Cristo.*
Dumas, Alexandre. *Crime and Punishment.*
Dumas, Alexandre. *The Three Musketeers.*
Elios, George. *The Mill on the Floss.*
Eliot, George. *Middlemarch.*
Eliot, George. *Silas Marner.*
Emerson, Ralph Waldo. *Essays.*
Euripides. *Medea - Hippolytus - The Bacchae.*
Faulkner, William. *The Sound and the Fury.*
Fielding, Henry. *Tom Jones.*
Flaubert, Gustave. *Madame Bovary.*
Franklin, Benjamin. *The Autobiography of Benjamin Franklin.*
Frost, Robert. *Collected Poems.*
Goethe, Johann Wolfgang von. *Faust.*
Goldsmith, Oliver. *She Stoops to Conquer.*
Grimm, Jacob and Wilhelm. *Grimm's Fairy Tales.*
Hamilton, Alexander; James Madison; John Jay. *Federalist Papers.*
Harding, Thomas. *Return of the Native.*

Hardy, Thomas. *Jude the Obscure.*

Hardy, Thomas. *Tess of the d'Urbervilles.*

Hawthorne, Nathaniel. *The Scarlet Letter.*

Hemingway, Ernest. *A Farewell to Arms.*

Holy Bible.

Homer. *Iliad.*

Homer. *Odyssey.*

Hugo, Victor. *The Hunchback of Notre Dame.*

Hugo, Victor. *Les Misérables.*

Huxley, Aldous. *Brave New World.*

Ibsen, Henrik. *Three Plays.*

Irving, Washington. *Tales of the Alhambra.*

James, Henry. *The Portrait of a Lady.*

Joyce, James. *A Portrait of the Artist as a Young Man.*

Keats, John. *Collected Poems.*

Khayyam, Omar. *Rubaiyat of Omar Khayyam.*

Kipling, Rudyard. *The Jungle Book and The Second Jungle Book.*

Lawrence, D.H. *Lady Chatterley's Lover.*

The Legend of Sleepy Hollow & Other Stories.

Livy (Titus Livius Patavinus). *History of Early Rome.*

London, Jack. *The Sea Wolf.*

Machiavelli, Niccolò. *The Prince.*

Maupassant, Guy de. *The Necklace and Other Tales.*

Melville, Herman. *Billy Budd.*

Melville, Herman. *Moby-Dick or, The Whale.*

Milton, John. *Paradise Lost.*

Moliere. *Two Plays.*

Orwell, George. *Animal Farm.*

Paine, Thomas. *Rights of Man.*

Plato. *The Republic.*

Plato. *The Symposium.*

Poe, Edgar Allan. *Tales of Mystery and Imagination.*

Rostand, Edmond. *Cyrano de Bergerac.*
Rousseau, Jean-Jacques. *The Confessions.*
Scott, Walter. *Ivanhoe.*
Scott, Walter. *The Talisman.*
Shakespeare, William. *The Comedies.*
Shakespeare, William. *Hamlet.*
Shakespeare, William. *The Histories.*
Shakespeare, William. *A Midsummer Night's Dream.*
Shakespeare, William. *Romeo and Juliet.*
Shakespeare, William. *The Tragedies.*
Shaw, George Bernard. *Pygmalion/Candida.*
Shaw, George Bernard. *Two Plays.*
Shelley, Mary. *Frankenstein.*
Sophocles. *Oedipus the King.*
Steinbeck, John. *Of Mice and Men.*
Stendhal. *The Red and the Black.*
Sterne, Laurence. *Tristram Shandy.*
Stevenson, Robert Louis. *Dr. Jekyll and Mr. Hyde.*
Stevenson, Robert Louis. *Treasure Island.*
Stoker, Bram. *Dracula.*
Stowe, Harriet Beecher. *Uncle Tom's Cabin.*
Swift, Jonathan. *Gulliver's Travels.*
Thackeray, William Makepeace. *Vanity Fair.*
Thoreau, Henry David. *Walden.*
Tolstoy, Leo. *Anna Karenina.*
Tolstoy, Leo. *War and Peace.*
Turgenev, Ivan. *Fathers and Sons.*
Twain, Mark. *Adventures of Huckleberry Finn.*
Verne, Jules. *Twenty Thousand Leagues Under the Sea.*
Virgil. *The Aeneid.*
Voltaire. *Candide.*
Wells, H.G. *The Time Machine.*
Whitman, Walt. *Leaves of Grass.*

Wilde, Oscar. *The Picture of Dorian Gray.*
Wilde, Oscar. *Short Stories.*
Yeats, William Butler. *Collected Poems by W. B. Yeats.*

Baseball Hall of Fame

This series has been out of print for quite some time.

Allen, Maury. *Jackie Robinson: A Life Remembered.*
Angell, Roger. *The Summer Game.*
Appel, Marty. *Slide, Kelly, Slide.*
Barber, Red. *1947: When all Hell Broke Loose in Baseball.*
Creamer, Robert. *Babe: The Legend Comes to Life.*
Gallico, Paul. *Lou Gehrig: Pride of the Yankees.*
Greenberg, Eric Rolfe. *The Celebrant.*
Greenberg, Hank. *The Story of My Life.*
Harris, Mark. *Bang the Drum Slowly.*
Harris, Mark. *The Southpaw.*
Halberstam, David. *Summer of '49.*
Helyar, John. *Lords of the Realm.*
Kahn, Roger. *Boys of Summer.*
Kinsella, W.P. *Shoeless Joe.*
Lardner, Ring. *Ring Around the Bases: Baseball Stories.*
Malamud, Bernard. *The Natural.*
Mantle, Mickey. *The Mick by Mantle.*
Mays, Willie. *Say Hey: Autobiography of Willie Mays.*
Oh, Sadaharu; David Falkner. *Sadaharu Oh.*
Paige, Reggie. *I'll Pitch Forever.*
Peterson, Robert. *Only the Ball Was White.*
Ritter, Lawrence S. *The Glory of Their Times.*
Seymour, Harold. *Baseball The Early Years.*
Seymour, Harold. *Baseball The Golden Age.*
Seymour, Harold. *Baseball The People's Game.*
Will, George F. *Men at Work.*
Williams, Ted. *My Turn at Bat.*

Books That Changed the World

Easton Press discontinued this series a few years back.

Addams, Jane. *Twenty Years at Hull-House.*
Aldrin, Buzz; Neil Armstrong; Michael Collins. *First on the Moon.*
Alger Jr., Horatio. *Ragged Dick.* 1993 Bellamy, Edward. *Looking Backward.*
Aquinas, Saint Thomas. *Selected Writings of Saint Thomas Aquinas.*
Aristotle. *Politics & Poetics.*
Aurelius, Marcus. *The Meditations.*
Beard, Charles A. *An Economic Interpretation of The Constitution.*
The Bhagavad Gita.
Carson, Rachel. *Silent Spring.*
Churchill, Winston. *While England Slept.*
Clausewitz, Carl Von. *On War.* 2 volumes.
Copernicus, Nicolaus. *Revolutionbus.*
Curie, Marie; William Harvey; Edward Jenner; Joseph Lister; Louis Pasteur. *Milestones in Medicine.*
Darwin, Charles. *On The Origin of Species.*
Descartes, René. *Discourse on Method and Related Writings.*
Dewey, John. *The School and Society.*
The Dhammapada.
Douglass, Frederick. *Narrative of the Life of Frederick Douglass: An American Slave.*
Einstein, Albert. *The Meaning of Relativity.*
Euclid. *Euclid's Elements of Geometry.*
Five Books of Moses.
Flexner, Abraham. *Medical Education in The United States and Canada.*

Frank, Anne. *The Diary of a Young Girl.*
Freud, Sigmund. *The Interpretation of Dreams.*
Friedan, Betty. *The Feminine Mystique.*
Galbraith, John Kenneth. *The Affluent Society.*
Gompers, Samuel. *Seventy Years of Life and Labor.*
Gorbachev, Mikhail. *Perestroika.*
The Gospels.
Hamilton, Alexander; James Madison; John Jay. *Federalist
      Papers.*
Hegel, Georg W. F. *Phenomenology of Spirit.*
Herzl, Theodor. *The Jewish State.*
Hippocrates. *The Genuine Works of Hippocrates.*
Hitler, Adolf. *Mein Kampf.*
Hobbes, Thomas. *Leviathan or the Matter, Form and Power of a
      Commonwealth.*
Jung, Carl G. *Psychology of the Unconscious.*
Kant, Immanuel. *Critique of Pure Reason.*
Keynes, John Maynard. *The General Theory of Employment,
      Interest, and Money.*
The Koran.
Lenin, Vladimir. *The State and Revolution.*
Leopold, Aldo. *Sand County Almanac and Sketches Here and
      There.*
Lewis and Clark Journals. 2 volumes.
Locke, John. *Two Treatises of Government.*
Luther, Martin. *The Ninety-Five Theses and Other Treatises.*
Machiavelli, Niccolò. *The Prince.*
Mahan, Alfred Thayer. *The Influence of Sea Power Upon   History.*
Malthus, Thomas R. *An Essay on the Principle of Population.*
Marx, Karl *Das Kapital.* 2 volumes.
Mill, John Stuart. *On Liberty.*
Montesquieu, Charles de. *The Spirit of Laws.*
More, Sir Thomas. *Utopia.*

Morison, Samuel Elio. *Journals of Christopher Columbus.*

Myrdal, Gunnar. *An American Dilemma.* 2 volumes.

The New Testament Bible.

Newton, Isaac. *Principia.*

Nietzsche, Friedrich. *Beyond Good and Evil.*

Paine, Thomas. *Common Sense.*

Pallister, Anne. *Magna Carta.*

Plato. *The Republic.*

Polo, Marco. *The Travels of Marco Polo.*

Rousseau, Jean Jacques. *The Social Contract and Discourses.*

Sartre, Jean Paul. *Being and Nothingness: An Essay on Phenomological Ontology.*

Sinclair, Upton *The Jungle.*

Skinner, B. F. *Walden Two.*

Stowe, Harriet Beecher. *Uncle Tom's Cabin.*

Taylor, Frederick Winslow. *The Principles of Scientific Management.*

Thoreau, Henry David. *Resistance to Civil Government.*

Thoreau, Henry David. *Walden.*

Smith, Adam. *The Wealth of Nations.*

Thoreau, Henry David. *On the Duty of Civil Disobedience.*

Tocqueville, Alexis De. *Democracy in America.* 2 volumes.

The Torah.

Tse-Tung, Mao. *Quotations from Chairman Mao Tse-Tung.*

Tzu, Sun. *The Art of War.*

Tzu, Lao. *Tao Te Ching.*

Veblen, Thorstein. *The Theory of the Leisure Class.*

Watson, James D. *The Double Helix.*

Wollstonecraft, Mary. *A Vindication of the Rights of Woman.*

Collector's Library of Famous Editions

This series has been discontinued.

Aristophanes. *Lysistrata.*
Aurelius, Marcus. *Meditations of Marcus Aurelius.*
Austen, Jane. *Emma.*
Austen, Jane. *Persuasion.*
Austen, Jane. *Sense and Sensibility.*
Balzac, Honore De. *Eugenie Grandet.*
Balzac, Honore De. *Old Goriot.*
Barrie, J.M. *Peter Pan and Wendy.*
Benet, Stephen Vincent. *John Brown's Body.*
Beowulf .
Blackmore, Richard D. *Lorna Doone.*
Blake, William. T*he Poems of William Blake.*
The Book of Job.
Book of Psalms.
Brecht, Bertolt. *The Threepenny Opera.*
Browning, Robert. *The Ring and the Book.*
Buck, Pearl S. *All Men are Brothers.*
Bulfinch, Thomas. *The Age of Fable or Stories of Gods and Heroes.*
Burton, Sir Richard F. *Sinbad the Sailor.*
Butler, Samuel. *Erewhon.*
Byron, Lord. *Don Juan: A Satiric Epic of Modern Life.*
Camus, Albert. *The Stranger.*
Carlyle, Thomas. *The French Revolution.*
Carroll, Lewis. *Through the Looking Glass.*
Coleridge, Samuel Taylor. *The Rime of The Ancient Mariner.*
Collins, Wilkie. *The Moonstone.*
Collins, Wilkie. *The Woman in White.*
Conrad, Joseph. *The Nigger of The Narcissus.*

Conrad, Joseph. *Nostromo: A Tale of the Seaboard.*

Conrad, Joseph. *Three Tales of The Sea : Youth, Typhoon and The End of The Tether.*

Cook, James. *The Explorations of Captain James Cook in the Pacific.*

Cooper, James Fenimore. *The Deerslayer or The First War-Path.*

Cooper, James Fenimore. *The Pilot.*

Creasey, Sir Edward S. *The Fifteen Decisive Battles of the World.*

Dana, Richard Henry. *Two Years Before Mast : A Personal Narrative of Life at Sea.*

Darwin, Charles. *Voyage of HMS Beagle.*

Defoe, Daniel. *Moll Flanders.*

Dickens, Charles. *The Chimes.*

Dickens, Charles. *Hard Times.*

Dickens, Charles. *Life and Adventures of Nicholas Nickleby.*

Dickens, Charles. *The Old Curiosity Shop.*

Dickens, Charles. *The Pickwick Papers.*

Dostoevsky, Fyodor. *The Gambler; Notes from the Underground.*

Dostoevsky, Fyodor. *The House of the Dead.*

Dostoevsky, Fyodor. *The Idiot.*

Dostoevsky, Fyodor. *The Possessed.*

Doyle, Sir Arthur Conan. *Later Adventures of Sherlock Holmes.*

Dumas, Alexandre. *The Black Tulip.*

Dumas, Alexandre. *Camille La Dame Aux Camelias.*

Dumas, Alexandre. *The Count of Monte Cristo.* 2 volumes.

Dumas, Alexandre. *Man in Iron Mask.*

Du Maurier, George. *Peter Ibbetson.*

The Education of Henry Adams.

Edwards, Amelia; Ann Blanford. *A Thousand miles up the Nile.*

Eliot, George. *Silas Marner: The Weaver of Raveloe.*

Fayette, Madame de La. *The Princess of Cleves.*

Flaubert, Gustave. *Salammbo.*

Flaubert, Gustave. *Three Tales : A Simple Heart, The Legend of*

Saint Julian and Herodias.

Foque, De La Motte. *Undine.*

Franklin, Benjamin. *Poor Richard's Almanack : The Almanacks for the Years 1733-1758.*

Galsworthy, John. *The Man of Property.*

Goethe, Johann Wolfgang Von. *Faust.*

Gogol, Nikolai. *Dead souls Chichikov's Journeys; Or, Home Life in Old Russia.*

Goldsmith, Oliver. *Vicar of Wakefield.*

Grahame, Kenneth. *The Wind in the Willows.*

Hardy, Thomas. *Far From the Madding Crowd.*

Hardy, Thomas. *Mayor of Casterbridge.*

Hardy, Thomas. *Tess of The D'Urbervilles : A Pure Woman Faithfully Presented.*

Hawthorne, Nathaniel. *A Wonder Book and Tanglewood Tales.*

Hemingway, Ernest. *Torrents of Spring.*

Henry, O. (William Sydney Porter). *The Voice of the City and Other Short Stories.*

Hesse, Hermann. *Steppenwolf.*

Hoffmann, E.T.A. *Tales of Hoffmann.*

Hope, Anthony. *The Prisoner of Zenda.*

Hudson, W.H. *Green Mansions : A Romance of the Tropical Forest.*

Hugo, Victor. *Les Miserables.* 2 volumes.

Hugo, Victor. *Toilers of the Sea.*

Hugo, Victor. *Notre-Dame De Paris (The Hunchback of Notre-Dame).*

Ibsen, Henrik. *Peer Gynt.*

James, Henry. *Daisy Miller: a Study.*

Kafka, Franz. *The Trial.*

Kingsley, Charles. *The Water Babies.*

Kingsley, Charles. *Westward Ho!.*

Kipling, Rudyard. *Just So Stories.*

Kipling, Rudyard. *Kim.*
Kipling, Rudyard. *Tales of East and West.*
Laclos, Choderlos De. *Dangerous Acquaintances.*
Lamb, Charles and Mary. *Tales From Shakespeare.*
Lewis, Sinclair. *Main Street.*
Lord, Albert B. *Russian Folk Tales.*
Mann, Thomas. *Death in Venice.*
Masters, Edgar Lee. *Spoon River Anthology.*
Maugham, W. Somerset. *The Moon and Sixpence.*
Maugham, W. Somerset. *Of Human Bondage.*
Maupassant, Guy De. *Bel Ami.*
Maupassant, Guy De. *A Woman's Life.*
Melville, Herman. *Billy Budd and Benito Cereno.*
Milton, John. *The Masque of Comus.*
Moncrief, Charles Scott. *The Song of Roland.*
More, Sir Thomas. *Utopia.*
Morier, J.J. *The Adventure of Hajji Baba.*
The Nibelungenlied.
Ovid (Publius Ovidius Naso). *The Art of Love* .
Passos, John Dos. *The 42nd Parallel.*
Pater, Walter. *The Marriage of Cupid and Psyche.*
Perrault, Charles. *The Fairy Tales of Charles Perrault.*
Plutarch. *Lives of Greeks and Romans.* 2 volumes.
Poe, Edgar Allan. *The Bells And Other Poems.*
Poe, Edgar Allan. *Tales of Mystery and Imagination.*
Proust, Marcel. *Swann's Way.*
Pushkin, Alexander. *Eugene Onegin.*
Pushkin, Alexander. *Golden Cockerel.*
Pyle, Howard. *The Merry Adventures of Robin Hood.*
Quincey, Thomas de. *Confessions English Opium Eater.*
Raspe, Rudolph Erich. *The Singular Adventures of Baron
        Munchausen.*
Rawlings, Kinnan. *The Yearling.*

Remarque, Erich Maria. *All Quiet on the Western Front.*

Rhodius, Apollonius. *Argonautica: Jason and the Golden Fleece.*

Riggs, Lynn. *Green Grow The Lilacs.*

The Romance of Leonardo da Vinci.

Rostand, Edmond. *Cyrano De Bergerac.*

Schiller, Johann Christoph Friedrich Von. *William Tell.*

Scott, Sir Walter. *Kenilworth.*

Second Day of the Trilogy.

Seingalt, Jacques Casanova De. *The Memoirs of Jacques Casanova De Seingalt.*

The Seven Voyages of Sinbad the Sailor.

Sewell, Anna. *Black Beauty.*

Shakespeare, William. *Hamlet.*

Shakespeare, William. *A Midsummer Night's Dream.*

Shakespeare, William. *Romeo and Juliet.*

Shakespeare, William. *The Tempest.*

Shaw, George Bernard. *Man and Superman.*

Shaw, George Bernard. *Pygmalion and Candida.*

Shelley, Mary. *Frankenstein.*

Shelley, Percy Bysshe. *Poems of Percy Bysshe Shelley.*

Sienkiewicz, Henryk. *Quo Vadis?.*

Southey, Robert. *Chronicle of The Cid.*

Stanley, Sir Henry Morton. *How I Found Livingstone.*

Steinbeck, John. *The Grapes of Wrath.*

Stendhal. *The Charterhouse of Parma.*

Stevenson, Robert Louis. *A Child's Garden of Verses.*

Stevenson, Robert Louis. *The Master of Ballantrae.*

Stoker, Bram. *Dracula.*

Tennyson, Alfred Lord. *Idylls of the King.*

Thackeray, William Makepeace. *The Rose and the Ring.*

Tolstoy, Leo. *Resurrection.*

Tranquillus, Gaius Suetonius. *The Lives of the Twelve Caesars: Emperors of Rome.*

The Travels of Marco Polo.
Trollope, Anthony. *Barchester Towers.*
Twain, Mark. *Adventures of Tom Sawyer.*
Twain, Mark . *A Connecticut Yankee in King Arthur's Court.*
Twain, Mark. *The Prince and the Pauper.*
Twain, Mark. *Pudd'nhead Wilson.*
Twain, Mark. *Roughing It.*
Verne, Jules. *Around the World in 80 Days.*
Verne, Jules. *From Earth to Moon.*
Verne, Jules. *Journey to the Center of the Earth.*
Verne, Jules. *The Mysterious Island.*
Wagner, Richard. *The Ring of the Niblung: The Rhinegold First Day of the Trilogy / The Valkyrie.*
Wagner, Richard. *Siegfried & the Twilight of the Gods.*
Walton, Izaak. *Compleat Angler.*
Wells, H.G. *Invisible Man.*
Wells, H.G. *Tono-Bungay.*
Wharton, Edith. *Age of Innocence.*
Wharton, Edith. *Ethan Frome.*
Wilde, Oscar. *Lady Windermere's Fan & the Importance Of Being Earnest.*
Wilde, Oscar. *The Picture of Dorian Gray.*
Wilde, Oscar. *Salome: A Tragedy in One Act.*
Wilde, Oscar. *The Short Stories of Oscar Wilde.*
Wilder, Thornton. *Our Town : A Play in Three Acts.*
Williams, Tennessee. *The Glass Menagerie.*
Wordsworth, William. *The Poems of William Wordsworth.*
Wyss, Johann David. *The Swiss Family Robinson.*
Zola, Emile. *Germinal.*
Zola, Emile. *Nana.*

Complete Novels of Charles Dickens

This set is out-of-print at the time of writing this book.

American Notes.
Barnaby Rudge.
Bleak House.
A Christmas Carol.
Christmas Novels.
Christmas Stories.
David Copperfield.
Dombey & Sons.
Edwin Drood.
Great Expectations.
Hard Times.
Little Dorrit.
Martin Chuzzlewit.
Master Humphrey's Clock.
Nicolas Nickleby.
Old Curiosity Shop.
Oliver Twist.
Our Mutual Friend.
Papers, Plays, Poems.
The Pickwick Papers.
Sketches by Boz.
A Tale of Two Cities.

Complete Works of Ernest Hemingway

Most of these titles are not in stock at Easton Press. However, five of the titles are available from Easton Press under 'The Masterpieces'.

Across the River.
By Line.
Dangerous Summer.
Death in the Afternoon.
Farewell to Arms.
Fifth Column.
For Whom the Bell Tolls.
Garden of Eden.
Green Hills Africa.
In Our Time.
Island in the Stream.
Men Without Woman.
Moveable Feast.
Old Man and the Sea.
Snow of Kilimanjaro.
Sun Also Rises.
To Have and Have Not.
Torrents of Spring.
True at First Light.
Winner Take Nothing.

Deluxe Limited Editions

The titles below have been labeled 'sold out' if no longer available through Easton Press. Though because of the limited quantities many more may be sold out at the time you're reading this. Where possible, the year in which Easton Press first published the edition is noted. That isn't necessarily the year that'll be shown on the copyright page of the deluxe editions.

The 1717 Book of Common Prayer. Limited edition of 800. 2014. Publisher's price $296.00. Sold Out.

Aesop. *The Fables of Aesop.* Limited edition of 300. 2011. Publisher's price $500.00. Sold Out.

Albee, Edward. *Who's Afraid of Virginia Woolf.* Limited edition of 600. 2013. Publisher's price $237.00. Sold Out.

Alighieri, Dante. *Inferno.* Limited edition of 1,200. Publisher's price $356.00.

Alighieri, Dante. *The Divine Comedy.* Limited edition of 400. 2011. Publisher's price $396.00. Sold Out.

Andersen, Hans Christian. *Hans Christian Andersen.* Limited edition of 400. 2012. Publisher's price $460.00. Sold Out.

Andersen, Hans Christian. *Stories from Hans Andersen.* Limited edition of 600. Publisher's price $445.00.

Angelou, Maya. *I Know Why the Caged Bird Sings.* Limited edition of 800. 2013. Publisher's price $237.00. Sold Out.

Audubon, John James. *Birds of America.* Limited edition of 2,000. Publisher's price $1,393.00.

Aurelius, Marcus. *The Meditations of Marcus Aurelius.* Limited edition of 500. 2010. Publisher's price $199.80. Sold Out.

Baum, L. Frank. *The Wonderful Wizard of Oz.* Limited edition of 1,900. Publisher's price $220.00.

The Book of Common Prayer. Limited edition of 800. Publisher's price $396.00.

The Book of Kells. Limited edition of 1,000. 2015. Publisher's price $460.00. Sold Out.

Bradbury, Ray. *Fahrenheit 451.* Limited edition of 700. 2011. Publisher's price $195.00. Sold Out.

Bryant, William Cullen. *Picturesque America.* Limited edition of 400. 2012. Publisher's price $580.00. Sold Out.

Bulfinch, Thomas. *Bulfinch's Mythology.* Limited edition of 800. 2014. Publisher's price $450.00.

Bunyan, John. *The Pilgrim's Progress.* Limited edition of 800. 2014. Publisher's price $270.00.

Burke, Edmund. *An Impartial History of the War in America Between Great Britain and Her Colonies.* Limited edition of 800. Publisher's price $295.00.

Burroughs, Edgar Rice. *Tarzan of the Apes.* Limited edition of 800. 2012. Publisher's price $267.00. Sold Out.

Burton, Sir Richard Francis. *Vikram and the Vampire.* Limited edition of 800. Publisher's price $236.00.

Carroll, Lewis. *Alice in Wonderland.* Limited edition of 800. Publisher's price $396.00.

Catlin, George. *The North American Indians.* Limited edition of 400. 2013. Publisher's price $540.00. Sold Out.

Caxton, William. *The History of Reynard the Foxe.* Limited edition of 600. Publisher's price $360.00.

Cervantes Saavedra, Miguel De; Dore, Gustave. *Don Quixote.* Limited edition of 600. 2013. Publisher's price $375.00.

Chaucer, Geoffrey. *The Canterbury Tales.* Limited edition of 300. 2011. Publisher's price $750.00. Sold Out.

Chaucer, Geoffrey. *The Kelmscott Press's The Works of Geoffrey Chaucer.* Limited edition of 425. 2009. Publisher's price $594.00. Sold Out.

Chaucer, Geoffrey. *Works of Geoffrey Chaucer.* Limited edition of 1,100. Publisher's price $$495.00.

Cook, Captain James. *Captain Cook's Voyages.* Limited edition of 400. Publisher's price $580.00.

Curtin, Jeremiah. *Quo Vadis.* Limited edition of 700. $356.00.

Da Vinci, Leonardo. *Leonardo Da Vinci: The Notebooks.* Limited edition of 600. 2010. Publisher's price $450.00. Sold Out.

Defoe, Daniel. *Robinson Crusoe.* Limited edition of 400. 2014. Publisher's price $240.00.

Detmold, Edward. *Aesop's Fables.* Limited edition of 800. Publisher's price $300.00.

De Witt, Robert M. *The Life, Trial and Execution of Captain John Brown.* Limited edition of 600. Publisher's price $176.00.

Dickens, Charles. *The Adventures of Oliver Twist.* Limited edition of 600. Publisher's price $296.00.

Dickens, Charles. *A Christmas Carol.* Limited edition of 800. 2013. Publisher's price $267.00.

Dickens, Charles. *David Copperfield.* Limited edition of 400. 2011. Publisher's price $340.00. Sold Out.

Dickens, Charles. *A Tale of Two Cities.* Limited edition of 800. 2013. Publisher's price $300.00.

Dore, Gustave; Blanchard Jerrold. *London.* 2012. Limited edition of 400. Publisher's price $496.00. Sold Out.

Dore, Gustave. *The Holy Bible.* Limited edition of 800. 2012. Publisher's price $996.00. Sold Out.

Doyle, Arthur Conan. *The Hound of the Baskervilles.* Limited edition of 1200. 2013. Publisher's price $356.00.

Dumas, Alexandre. *The Count of Monte Cristo.* Limited edition of 800. Publisher's price $675.00.

Dumas, Alexandre. *The Three Musketeers.* Limited edition of 400. 2011. Publisher's price $500.00. Sold Out.

Duyckinck, Evert A. *The War for the Union.* Limited edition. Publisher's price $507.00.

Ebers, Prof. G. *Egypt: Descriptive, Historical and Picturesque.* Limited edition of 800. Publisher's price $534.00.

Engels, Robert. *The Romance of Tristan and Iseult.* Limited
   edition of 500. Publisher's price $336.00.
Erasmus. *In Praise of Folly.* Limited edition of 800. Publisher's
   price $196.00.
Froissart, Sir John. *Froissart's Chronicles.* Limited edition of
   500. 2015. Publisher's price $596.00.
Gibbon, Edward. *The Decline and Fall of the Roman Empire.*
   Limited edition of 600. Publisher's price $500.00.
Goldin, Judah. *The Living Talmud.* Limited edition of 600.
   Publisher's price $356.00.
Grimm, Brothers; Arthur Rackham. *Grimm's Fairy Tales.*   Limited
   edition of 800. Publisher's price $396.00.
Grimm, Brothers; George Cruikshank. *Grimm's German
   Popular Stories.* Limited edition of 800. Publisher's price
   $360.00.
The Gutenberg Bible. Limited edition of 2,500. Publisher's price
   $894.00.
Henry. O. *Stories.* Limited edition of 1,200. Publisher's price
   $375.00.
History of the United States. Centennial Edition. Limited edition
   of 1,776. Publisher's price $796.00.
The Holy Bible Antiquarian 1873. Limited edition of 800.
   Publisher's price $594.00.
The Holy Bible Cassell's Illustrated Family Edition. Limited
   edition of 600. 2011. Publisher's price $396.00. Sold Out.
Homer. *The Iliad & The Odyssey.* Limited edition of 400. 2013.
   Publisher's price $356.00. Sold Out.
Homer. *The Odyssey.* Limited edition of 600. Publisher's price
   $350.00.
Hugo, Victor. *The Hunchback of Notre Dame.* Limited edition of
   400. 2013. Publisher's price $396.00. Sold Out.
Hugo, Victor. *Toilers of the Sea.* Limited edition of 1,000.
   $316.00.
Ireland, William Henry; George Cruikshank. *The Life of*

Napoleon Bonaparte. Limited edition of 400. 2012. Publisher's price $596.00. Sold Out.

Irving, Washington. *Rip Van Winkle.* Limited edition of 400. 2012. Publisher's price $396.00. Sold Out.

James, Grace. *Green Willow & Other Japanese Fairy Tales.* Limited edition of 1,200. Publisher's price $380.00.

Johnson, W. Fletcher. *Life of Siting Bull and History of the Indian War of 1890-91.* Limited edition of 600. Publisher's price $276.00.

Jones, Owen. *The Victoria Psalter.* Limited edition of 800. Publisher's price $475.00.

Kafka, Franz. *The Metamorphoses.* Limited edition of 1,200. Publisher's price $395.00.

Keyes, Daniel. *Flowers for Algernon.* Limited edition of 600. 2013. Publisher's price $225.00. Sold Out.

The King James Bible The Classic 1611 Edition. Limited edition of 400. 2010. Publisher's price $596.00. Sold Out.

Leroux, Gaston. *The Phantom of the Opera.* Limited edition of 1200. Signed. Publisher's price $375.00.

Leslie, Frank. *The Solider in Our Civil War: A Pictorial History of Conflict 1861-1865.* Limited edition. Publisher's price $660.00.

Lossing, Benson J.; Matthew Brady. *A History of the Civil War.* Limited edition of 1,865. 2012. Publisher's price $225.00. Sold Out.

Machiavelli, Nicolo. *The Prince.* Limited edition. Signed by artist. Publisher's price $340.00.

Mackay, Charles. *Memoirs of Extraordinary Popular Delusions.* Limited edition of 800. Publisher's price $300.00.

Malory, Sir Thomas. *The Romance of King Arthur*: Limited edition of 400. 2011. Publisher's price $356.00. Sold Out.

McKenney, Thomas L; James Hall. *History of the Indian Tribes of North America.* Limited edition of 400. 2010. Publisher's price $597.00. Sold Out.

Michaud, Joseph-Francois. *History of the Crusades.* Limited edition of 600. 2010. Publisher's price $500.00. Sold Out.

Milton, John. *Paradise Lost.* Limited edition. Publisher's price $300.00.

Mitchell, Stephen. Rebecca Yanovskaya. *Gilgamesh.* Limited edition of 1,200. Signed by artist. Publisher's price $296.00.

Montgomery, Lucy Maud. *Anne of Green Gables.* Limited edition of 1,908. Publisher's price $147.00.

More, Sir Thomas. *Utopia.* Limited edition of 1,200. Publisher's price $295.00.

Murasaki, Lady. *The Tale of Genji.* Limited edition. Publisher's price $315.00.

Nicolay, John G.; John Hay. *Lincoln: A History.* Limited edition of 400. 2011. Publisher's price $999.00. Sold Out.

Orwell, George. *Animal Farm.* Limited edition of 1,200. Publisher's price $336.00.

Ovid. *Metamorphoses.* Limited edition of 400. 2011. Publisher's price $500.00. Sold Out.

Perry, Commodore Matthew. *Narrative of the Expedition of an American Squadron to the South China Seas and Japan.* Limited edition of 400. 2013. Publisher's price $396.00.

Plutarch. *Plutarch's Lives of the Noble Greeks and Romans.* Limited edition of 400. Publisher's price $495.00.

Poe, Edgar Allan. *Stories & Poems.* Limited edition of 1,200. Publisher's price $236.00.

Porter, Robert F.; Carroll D. Wright. *Report on Indians in the United States.* Limited edition of 600. Publisher's price $525.00.

Pyle, Howard. *The Illustrated Legends of King Arthur.* Limited edition of 1,000. Publisher's price $396.00.

Rand, Ayn. *The Fountainhead.* Limited edition of 1,943. Publisher's price $156.00.

Roberts, David. *The Holy Land.* Limited edition of 800. 2014.

Publisher's price $837.00.

Schoolcraft, Henry. *The Indian Tribes of the United States.* Limited edition of 600. Publisher's price $1,194.00.

Scott, Sir Walter. *Ivanhoe.* Limited edition of 800. Publisher's price $260.00.

Shakespeare, William. *The First Folio.* Limited edition of 1,623. Publisher's price $450.00.

Shakespeare, William. *A Midsummer Night's Dream.* Limited edition of 250. 2010. Publisher's price $495.00. Sold Out.

Shakespeare, William. *Macbeth.* Limited edition of 1,200. Publisher's price $396.00.

Shakespeare, William. *The Tempest.* Limited edition of 400. 2013. Publisher's price $396.00.

Shakespeare, William. *The Works of Shakespeare.* Limited edition of 800. Publisher's price $447.00.

Stevenson, Robert Louis. *The Strange Case of Dr. Jekyll and Mr. Hyde.* Limited edition of 1,200. Publisher's price $375.00.

Stevenson, Robert Louis. *Treasure Island.* Limited edition of 800. Publisher's price $207.00.

Stoker, Bram. *Dracula.* Limited edition of 1,200. Publisher's price $276.00.

Stowe, Harriet Beecher. *Uncle Tom's Cabin.* Limited edition of 1,200. Publisher's price $199.00.

Swift, Jonathan. *Gulliver's Travels.* Limited edition of 500 2011. Publisher's price $199.80. Sold Out.

Tennyson, Alfred Lord. *Idylls of the King.* Limited edition of 600. Publisher's price $399.80.

Timlin, William M. *The Ship That Sailed to Mars.* Limited edition of 600. Publisher's price $396.00.

Twain, Mark. *The Adventures of Tom Sawyer.* Limited edition of 800. Publisher's price $207.00.

Twain, Mark. *A Connecticut Yankee In King Arthurs Court.* Limited edition of 300. 2012. Publisher's price $297.00.

Sold Out.

Twain, Mark. *The Prince and the Pauper.* 2011. Limited edition of 600. Publisher's price $285.00. Sold Out.

Twain, Mark. *Pudd'nhead.* Limited edition of 300. Publisher's price $276.00.

Verne, Jules. *Around the World in 80 Days.* Limited edition of ,000. Publisher's price $254.00.

Verne, Jules. *Hector Servadac or the Career of a Comet.* Limited edition of 800. Publisher's price $316.00.

Verne, Jules. *A Journey to the Centre of the Earth.* Limited edition of 300. 2013. Publisher's price $267.00. Sold Out.

Verne, Jules. *Twenty Thousand Leagues Under the Sea.* Limited edition of 400. 2012. Publisher's price $267.00. Sold Out.

Vesalius, Andreas. *De Humani Corporis Fabrica.* Limited edition of 400. 2013. Publisher's price $496.00.

Virgil; John Dryden. *The Works of Virgil.* Limited edition. Publisher's price $316.00.

Vonnegut Jr., Kurt. *Cat's Cradle.* Limited edition of 500. 2013. Publisher's price $276.00. Sold Out.

Vonnegut Jr., Kurt. *The Masterpieces.* Limited edition of 1,000. Publisher's price $395.00.

Vonnegut Jr., Kurt. *Slaughterhouse-Five.* Limited edition of 850. 2011. Publisher's price $267.00. Sold Out.

Wagner, Richard. *Wagner's Ring Cycle.* Limited edition of 800. Publisher's price $845.00.

Watson, James D. *Double Helix: The Annotated and Illustrated Edition.* Limited edition of 1,962. Publisher's price $177.00.

Wells, H.G. *The Island of Doctor Moreau.* Limited edition of 1,200. 2017. Publisher's price $395.00.

Wells, H.G. *The Outline of History.* Limited edition of 400. 2012. Publisher's price $476.00. Sold Out.

Werner, E.T. Chalmers. *Myths and Legends of China.* Limited edition. $319.80.

Wiesel, Elie. *Night.* Limited edition of 850. 2012. Publisher's price $267.00. Sold Out.

Wilde, Oscar. *Salome.* Limited edition of 600. Publisher's price $380.00.

Wyss, Johann David. *Swiss Family Robinson.* Limited edition of 600. Publisher's price $256.00.

F. Scott Fitzgerald

At the time of writing, this series is not in stock at Easton Press.

Babylon Revisited.
The Beautiful and Damned.
The Great Gatsby.
The Last Tycoon.
This Side of Paradise.
Tales Of The Jazz Age.
Tender Is The Night.

First Edition Library

These books are not true first editions. Rather, they are hardcover non-leather bound facsimile editions of the first editions of the titles. This series is now out-of-print.

Baldwin, James. *Go Tell It On The Mountain.*
Burroughs, Edgar Rice. *Tarzan of the Apes.*
Caldwell, Erskine. *Tobacco Road.*
Cather, Willa. *My Antonia.*
Chandler, Raymond. *Farewell, My Lovely.*
Crane, Stephen. *The Red Badge of Courage.*
Ellison, Ralph. *Invisible Man.*
Faulkner, William. *Absalom, Absalom!.*
Faulkner, William. *As I Lay Dying.*
Faulkner, William. *The Sound and the Fury.*
Fitzgerald, F. Scott. *The Great Gatsby.*
Fitzgerald, F. Scott. *Tender is the Night.*
Fitzgerald, F. Scott. *This Side of Paradise.*
Heller, Joseph. *Catch-22.*
Hemingway, Ernest. *Farewell to Arms.*
Hemingway, Ernest. *For Whom The Bell Tolls.*
Hemingway, Ernest. *The Sun Also Rises.*
Kerouac, Jack. *On the Road.*
Kesey, Ken. *One Flew Over the Cuckoos Nest.*
Lee, Harper. *To Kill A Mockingbird.*
Lewis, Sinclair. *Babbitt.*
Lewis, Sinclair. *Main Street.*
Mailer, Norman. *The Naked and the Dead.*
Mitchell, Margaret. *Gone with the Wind.*
Penn, Robert Warren. *All the King's Men.*
Rand, Ayn. *The Fountainhead.*
Steinbeck, John. *East of Eden.*
Steinbeck, John. *The Grapes of Wrath.*

Steinbeck, John. *Of Mice and Men.*
Steinbeck, John. *Old Man and the Sea.*
Twain, Mark. *Adventures of Huck Finn.*
Twain, Mark. *Adventures of Tom Sawyer.*
Vonnegut, Kurt. *Slaughterhouse Five.*
Wharton, Edith. *The Age of Innocence.*
Wolfe, Tom. *Look Homeward, Angel.*
Wright, Richard. *Native Son.*

Glorious Art

This series has long been out-of-print at Easton Press.

Bajard, Sophie; Raffaello Bencini. *Rome: Palaces and Gardens.*

Bajard, Sophie; Raffaello Bencini. *Villa and Gardens of Tuscany.*

Blanc, Olivier; Joachim Bonnemaison. *Mansions of Paris.*

Boissiere, Olivier. *Twentieth-Century Houses -Europe.*

Bougault, Valerie. *Paris-Montparnasse.*

Buisson, Sylvie; Christian Parisot. *Paris-Montmartre.*

Cabanne, Pierre. *Cubism.*

Cabanne, Pierre. *Van Gogh.*

Caubet, Annie; Patrick Pouyssegur. *The Ancient Near East.*

Cros, Philippe. *Renoir.*

Dubost, Jean-Claude; Jean Francois Gunther. *Architecture of the Future.*

Durand, Jannic. *Byzantine Art.*

Ellridge, Arthur. *Gauguin and the Nabis.*

Ellridge, Arthur. *Mucha: The Triumph of Art Nouveau.*

Ferrier, Jean-Louis. *The Fauves: The Reign of Color.*

Ferrier, Jean-Louis. *Paul Klee.*

Ferrier, Jean-Louis. *Picasso.*

Frere, Jean Claude. *Early Flemish Paintings.*

Frere, Jean-Claude. *Leonardo.*

Huguenin, Daniel; Erich Lessing. *The Glory of Venice.*

Jarrasse, Dominique. *Eighteenth-Century French Painting.*

Jarrasse, Dominique. *Rodin: A Passion for Movement.*

Laisne, Claude. *The Art of Ancient Greece.*

Lemaitre, Alain J.; Erich Lessing. *Florence and the Renaissance.*

Lessing, Erich; Antonio Varone. *Pompei.*

Lista, Giovanni. Futurism.

Metalsi, Mohamed; Cecil Treal; Jean-Michel Ruiz. *The Imperial Cities of Morocco.*

Meyer, Laure. *Art and Craft in Africa.*

Meyer, Laure. *Black Africa: Masks, Sculpture, Jewelry.*

Meyer, Laure. *Masters of English Landscape.*

Monneret, Sophie. *David and Neo-Classicism.*

Morvan, Berenice. *Impressionists.*

Papadakis, Andres; James Steele. *Architecture of Today.*

Papadakis, Andres. *Classical Modern Architecture.*

Parisot, Christian. *Modigliani.*

Passeron, Rene. *Surrealism.*

Penney, David W. *Native Arts of North America.*

Sala, Charles. *Caspar David Friedrich.*

Sala, Charles. *Michelangelo.*

Stierlin, Henri. *The Gold of the Pharaohs.*

Stierlin, Henri. *The Pharaohs: Master Builders.*

Taillandier, Yvon. *Cezanne.*

Vezin, Annette; Luc Vezin. *Kandinsky and the Blue Rider.*

Great Books of the 20th Century

Great Books of the 20th Century is no longer in print.

Baldwin, James. *Go Tell It on the Mountain.*
Borges, Jorge Luis. *Ficciones.*
Bradbury, Ray. *Fahrenheit 451.*
Burgess, Anthony. *A Clockwork Orange.*
Camus, Albert. *The Stranger.*
Capote, Truman. *In Cold Blood.*
Cather, Willa. *Death Comes for the Archbishop.*
Elison, Ralph. *The Invisible Man.*
Faulkner, William. *Light in August.*
Fitzgerald, F. Scott. *The Great Gatsby.*
Forster, E.M. *A Passage to India.*
Greene, Graham. *The Power and the Glory.*
Heller, Joseph. *Catch-22.*
Hemingway, Ernest. *The Sun Also Rises.*
Huxley, Aldous. *Brave New World.*
James, Henry. *The Ambassadors.*
Joyce, James. *Ulysses.*
Kafka, Franz. *The Trial.*
Kerouac, Jack. *On the Road.*
Kesey, Ken. *One Flew Over the Cuckoo's Nest.*
Koestler, Arthur. *Darkness at Noon.*
Lawrence, D.H. *Women in Love.*
Lee, Harper. *To Kill a Mockingbird.*
Lewis, Sinclair. *Babbitt.*
London, Jack. *The Call of the Wild.*
Mann, Thomas. *The Magic Mountain.*
Marquez, Gabriel Garcia. *One Hundred Years of Solitude.*
Maugham, W. Somerset. *Of Human Bondage.*
McCullers, Carson. *The Heart Is a Lonely Hunter.*

Mitchell, Margaret. *Gone with the Wind.*
Morrison, Toni. *Beloved.*
Nabokov, Vladimir. *Lolita.*
Orwell, George. *Nineteen Eighty-Four.*
Pasternak, Boris. *Dr. Zhivago.*
Plath, Sylvia. *The Bell Jar.*
Proust, Marcel. *Swann's Way.*
Rand, Ayn. *The Fountainhead.*
Remarque, Erich Maria. *All Quiet On The Western Front.*
Roth, Philip. *Portnoy's Complaint.*
Solzhenitsyn, Aleksandr. *One Day in the Life of Ivan Denisovich.*
Steinbeck, John. *The Grapes of Wrath.*
Updike, John. *Rabbit Run.*
Vonnegut, Kurt. *Slaughterhouse Five.*
Walker, Alice. *The Color Purple.*
Warren, Robert Penn. *All the King's Men.*
Waugh, Evelyn. *Brideshead Revisited.*
Wharton, Edith. *The Age of Innocence.*
Wiesel, Elie. *Night.*
Woolf, Virginia. *To The Lighthouse.*
Wright, Richard A. *Native Son.*

Greatest Adventure Books of All Time

This set is not currently available through Easton Press.

Burton, Richard F. *First Footsteps in East Africa.*
Cherry-Garrard, Aspley. *The Worst Journey in the World.*
Herzon, Maurice. *Annapurna.*
Lewis and Clark. *The Journals of the Expedition.* 2 volumes.
Markham, Beryl. *West with the Night.*
Nansen, Fridtjof. *Farthest North.*
Powell, John Wesley. *The Exploration of the Colorado River.*
Saint-Exupery, Antoine De. *Wind, Sand, and Stars.*
Scott, Robert Falcon. *Journals of Captain Scott's Last
        Expedition.*
Shackelton, Ernest. *South: A Memoir of the Endurance Voyage.*
Simpson, Joe. *Touching the Void.*
Thesiger, Wilfred. *Arabian Sands.*

Greatest Shakespeare Library Ever Written

The name 'Greatest Shakespeare Library Ever Written' was changed a few years ago and a new Shakespeare series came out. A few of the titles are currently available from Easton Press.

All's Well That Ends Well.
Anthony and Cleopatra.
As You Like It.
Comedy of Errors.
Coriolanus.
Cymbeline.
Hamlet.
Henry the Eighth.
Henry the Fifth.
Henry the Fourth Volume 1.
Henry the Fourth Volume 2.
Henry the Sixth Volume 1.
Henry the Sixth Volume 2.
Henry the Sixth Volume 3.
Julius Caesar.
King John.
King Lear.
Love's Labour's.
Macbeth.
Measure for Measure.
Merchant of Venice.
Merry Wives of Windsor.
A Midsummer Night.
Much Ado About Nothing.
Othello.
Pericles.
Poems Volume 1.

Poems Volume 2.
Richard the Second.
Richard the Third.
Romeo and Juliet.
Taming of the Shrew.
The Tempest.
Timon of Athens.
Titus Andronicus.
Troilus and Cressida.
Twelfth Night.
Two Gentleman of Verona.
The Winter's Tale.

Harvard Classics

The Easton Press produced two versions of The Harvard Classics both of which are out of stock:

> Millennium Edition, Publication Dated 1993 to 1994
> Standard Edition, Publication Dated 2001

Volume 1. *Plutarch's Lives.*
Volume 2. *Plato, Epictetus, Marcus Aurelius.*
Volume 3. *Bacon, Milton's Prose, Thomas Browne.*
Volume 4. *Milton's Complete Poems in English.*
Volume 5. *Emerson's Essays and English Traits.*
Volume 6. *Robert Burns' Poems and Songs.*
Volume 7. *St. Augustine – Confessions and The Imitation of Christ.*
Volume 8. *Nine Greek Dramas.*
Volume 9. *Letters and Treatises of Cicero and Pliny.*
Volume 10. *Adam Smith – The Wealth of Nations.*
Volume 11. *Darwin – The Origin of Species.*
Volume 12. *Benjamin Franklin, John Woolman, William Penn.*
Volume 13. *Virgil's Aeneid 14. Cervantes – Don Quixote.*
Volume 14. *Don Quixote Part I.*
Volume 15. *Bunyan's Pilgrim's Progress; Walton's Life of Donne and Herbert.*
Volume 16. *The Thousand and One Nights (Arabian Nights).*
Volume 17. *Folk-lore and Fable of Aesop, Grimm, Andersen.*
Volume 18. *Modern English Drama.*
Volume 19. *Goethe's Faust and Egmont; Marlowe's Dr. Faustus.*
Volume 20. *Dante – The Divine Comedy.*
Volume 21. *Manzoni – I Promessi Sposi.*
Volume 22. *Homer – The Odyssey.*
Volume 23. *Dana – Two Years Before the Mast.*
Volume 24. *Burke – On the Sublime, The French Revolution.*
Volume 25. *John Stuart Mill and Thomas Carlyle.*

Volume 26. *Continental Drama.*

Volume 27. *English Essays, Sidney to Macaulay.*

Volume 28. *Essays, English and American.*

Volume 29. *Darwin – Voyage of the Beagle.*

Volume 30. *Scientific Papers of Faraday, Helmholtz, Kelvin and Others.*

Volume 31. *Cellini – Autobiography.*

Volume 32. *Montaigne, Sainte-Beuve, Renan – Essays.*

Volume 33. *Voyages and Travels.*

Volume 34. *Descartes, Voltaire, Rousseau, Hobbes.*

Volume 35. *Froissart, Malory, Holinshed – Chronicles and Legends.*

Volume 36. *Machiavelli, More, Luther.*

Volume 37. *Locke, Berkeley, Hume.*

Volume 38. *Scientific Papers of Harvey, Jenner, Lister, Pasteur.*

Volume 39. *Famous Prefaces.*

Volume 40. *English Poetry Volume I.*

Volume 41. *English Poetry Volume II.*

Volume 42. *English Poetry Volume III.*

Volume 43. *American Historical Documents.*

Volume 44. *Sacred Writings Volume I.*

Volume 45. *Sacred Writings Volume II.*

Volume 46. *Elizabethan Drama Volume I.*

Volume 47. *Elizabethan Drama Volume II.*

Volume 48. *Pascal – Thoughts.*

Volume 49. *Epic and Saga.*

Volume 50. *Introduction, Reader's Guide, Indexes.*

Volume 51. *Lectures.*

Horror Classics

This series is no longer available at Easton Press.

Bierce, Ambrose. *Tales of Soldiers and Civilians.*
Jackson, Shirley. *The Haunting of Hill House.*
Jacobs, W.W. *The Monkey's Paw & Other Tales of Mystery and The Macabre.*
James, M.R. *Ghost Stories of an Antiquary.*
Fanu, Sheridan Le. *In A Glass Darkly.*
LeRoux, Gaston. *Phantom of The Opera.*
Lovecraft, H.P. *At The Mountains Of Madness.*
Maurier, Daphne Du. *The Birds and Other Stories.*
Poe, Edgar Allan. *Tales of Mystery and Imagination.*
Shelley, Mary. *Frankenstein.*
Stevenson, Robert Louis. *The Strange Case of Dr. Jekyll and Mr. Hyde.*
Stoker, Bram. *Dracula.*
Wells, H.G. *The Island of Dr. Moreau.*

Ian Fleming's *James Bond*

This set is not currently in stock.

Casino Royale.
Diamonds are Forever.
Dr. No.
For Your Eyes Only.
From Russia with Love.
Goldfinger.
Live and Let Die.
The Man With The Golden Gun.
Moonraker.
Octopussy / The Living Daylights.
On Her Majesty's Secret Service.
The Spy Who Loved Me.
Thunderball.
You Only Live Twice.

Kurt Vonnegut

Easton Press is sold-out of all signed Vonnegut editions. Many of these titles have increased in value as a result.

Bamboo Snuff Box. Signed. First Edition.
Bluebeard. Signed.
Breakfast of Champions. Signed.
Cat's Cradle. Signed.
Fates Worse Than Death. Signed. First Edition.
Galapagos. Signed.
God Bless You Dr. Kevorkian. Signed. First Edition.
God Bless You, Mr. Rosewater. Signed.
Look at the Birdie. Signed. First Edition.
A Man Without A Country. Signed.
Mother Night. Signed.
Piano Player. Signed.
The Sirens of Titan. Signed.
Slapstick. Signed.
Slaughterhouse Five. Signed.
Slaughterhouse Five.
Timequake. Signed. First Edition.
Welcome to Monkeyhouse. Signed.

Library of American History

This series has long been out-of-print.

Anthony, Katharine. *Dolly Madison.*

Barbour, Philip L. *Pocahontas and Her World.*

Bartlett, Irving H. *Daniel Webster.*

Bernstein, Carl; Bob Woodward. *All the President's Men.*

Bill, Alfred Hoyt. *Valley Forge.*

Boorstin, Daniel. *The Americans: the Colonial Experience.*

Boorstin, Daniel. *The Americans: the Democratic Experience.*

Boorstin, Daniel. *The Americans: the National Experience.*

Bowen, Catherine Drinker. *Yankee from Olympus: Justice Holmes and His Family.*

Brown, Dee. *Bury My Heart at Wounded Knee.*

Bruce, Robert. *Alexander Graham Bell and the Conquest of Solitude.*

Burns, James MacGregor. *Roosevelt.* 2 Volumes.

Caffrey, Kate. *The Mayflower.*

Callow Jr., Alexander B. *The Tweed Ring.*

Carter, Dan T. *Scottsboro: A Tragedy of the American South.*

Chidsey, Donald Barr. *The Great Separation.*

Coffman, Edward M. *The War to End All Wars.*

Coit, Margaret L. *John C. Calhoun.*

Coleman, Terry. *Passage to America.*

Dangerfield, George. *The Era of Good Feelings.*

Day, Donald. *Will Rogers.*

Devoto, Bernard. *The Course of Empire.*

Devoto, Bernard. *The Year of Decision.*

Donald, David. *Charles Sumner and the Coming of the Civil War.*

Eisenhower, John S.D. *So Far from God: The U. S. War with Mexico.*

Faragher, John Mack. *Daniel Boone.*

Fischer, David Hackett. *Paul Revere's Ride.*

Garrow, David J. *Bearing the Cross.*

Gilbert, Bil. *God Gave Us This Country.*

Halberstam, David. *The Best and the Brightest.*

Halberstam, David. *The Fifties.* 2 volumes.

Hamilton, Edward P. *The French and Indian Wars.*

Harwell, Richard. *Lee* (Abridged)

Holliday, J.S. *The World Rushed In.*

Howard, Fred. *Wilbur and Orville.*

James, Marquis. *The Raven.*

Josephson, Matthew. *Edison.*

Josephson, Matthew. *The Robber Barons.*

Kennedy, Robert. *Thirteen Days.*

Lamont, Lansing. *Day of Trinity.*

Lash, Joseph. *Eleanor and Franklin.* 2 volumes.

Lewis and Clark Journals. 2 volumes.

Link, Arthur S. *Woodrow Wilson and the Progressive Era.*

Livesay, Harold C. *Andrew Carnegie and the Rise of Big
        Business.*

Lord, Walter. *Day of Infamy.*

Lorenz, Lincoln. *John Paul Jones.* 2 volumes.

McCague, James. *Moguls and Iron Men.*

McCullough, David. *The Johnstown Flood.*

McCullough, David. *Morning on Horseback.*

McCullough, David. *The Path between the Seas.*

McDonald, Forrest. *Alexander Hamilton.*

McDougall, Walter A. *The Heavens and the Earth.*

McFeeley, William S. *Frederick Douglas.*

McPherson, James M. *Abraham Lincoln and the Second
        American Revolution.*

Monaghan, Jay. *Custer.*

Morison, Samuel Eliot. *Old Bruin Commodore Matthew C.*

Perry.

Morison, Samuel Eliot. *The Two Ocean War.*

Myrdal, Gunnar. *An American Dilemma: The Negro Problem and Modern Democracy.* 2 volumes.

Nevins, Alan. *The Emergence of Lincoln.* 2 volumes.

Olson, James S. *Where the Dominos Fell.*

Oshinsky, David M. A *Conspiracy So Immense: the World of Joe McCarthy.*

Parkman, Francis. *The Oregon Trail.*

Passos, John Dos. *The Shackles of Power.*

Ryan, Cornelius. *The Longest Day.*

Schlesinger, Arthur. *The Age of Roosevelt: the Coming of the New Deal.*

Schlesinger, Arthur. *The Imperial Presidency.*

Silverman, Kenneth. *The Life and Times of Cotton Mather.*

Sinclair, Andrew. *Prohibition: the Era of Excess.*

Stampp, Kenneth. *The Peculiar Institution: Slavery in the Antebellum South.*

Swanberg, W.A. *Citizen Hearst.*

Taylor, Emerson. *Paul Revere.*

Thomas, Bob. *Walt Disney an American Original.*

Thomas, Gordon. *The San Francisco Earthquake.*

Tinkle, Lon. *Thirteen Days to Glory.*

Tyler, Moses Coit. *Patrick Henry.*

Vanderbilt II, Arthur T. *Fortune's Children.*

Wallace, Anthony. *Rockdale.*

Weems, John Edward. *The Fate of the Maine.*

Wik, Reynold M. *Henry Ford and Grass-roots America.*

Williams, T. Harry. *Huey Long.*

Zobel, Hiller. *The Boston Massacre.*

Library of the Civil War

This series has been out-of-print for many years.

Catton, Bruce. *Glory Road.*

Catton, Bruce. *Mr. Lincoln's Army.*

Catton, Bruce. *A Stillness at Appomattox.*

Chestnut, Mary; Vann Woodward. *Mary Chesnut's Civil War.* 2 volumes.

Coddington, Edwin B. *The Gettysburg Campaign.* 2 volumes.

Cooling, Benjamin Franklin. *Forts Henry and Donelson.*

Cozzens, Peter. *This Terrible Sound: The Battle of Chickamauga.*

Davis, Jefferson. *Rise and Fall Confederate Government.* 2 volumes.

Davis, William. *Battle at Bull Run.*

Davis, William C. *Jefferson Davis.*

Foote, Shelby. *The Civil War.* 3 volumes.

Freeman, Douglas Southall. *R.E. Lee.* 4 volumes.

Furguson, Ernest B. *Chancellorsville: 1863.*

Gabor, Boritt S. *Why the Confederacy Lost.*

Glatthaar, Joseph. *Partners in Command.*

Grant, Ulysses S. *Personal Memoirs of U.S. Grant.*

McPherson, James M. *Battle Cry of Freedom.* 2 volumes.

Miers, Earl Schenck. *The Web of Victory: Grant at Vicksburg.*

Murfin, James. *The Gleam of Bayonets.*

Sears, Stephen W. *To the Gates of Richmond.*

Sherman, General William T. *Memoirs of General William T. Sherman.*

Stackpole, Edward J. *Sheridan in the Shenandoah.*

Vandiver, Frank E. *Mighty Stonewall.*

Whan Jr., Vorin E. *Fiasco at Fredericksburg.*

Wiley, Bell Irvin. *The Life of Billy Yank.*

Wiley, Bell Irvin. *The Life of Johnny Reb.*

Library of Fly Fishing Classics

This series has been out-of-print for many years.

Branche, George M.L. La. *Dry Fly & Fast Water.*
Brooks, Charles E. *Nymph Fishing for Larger Trout.*
Caucci, Al; Bob Nastasi. *Hatches II.*
Fedden, Romilly. *Golden Days.*
Fontaine, Gary La. *Caddisflies.*
Gierach, John. *Trout Bum.*
Gill, Emlyn M. *Practical Dry Fly Fishing.*
Gingrich, Arnold. *The Well-Tempered Angler.*
Greene, Harry Plunket. *Where the Bright Waters Meet.*
Hackle, Sparse. *Fishless Days, Angling Nights.*
Haig-Brown, Roderick L. *A River Never Sleeps.*
Halford, Frederic M. *Dry-Fly Fishing.*
Hewitt, Edward. *Trout and Salmon Fisherman for Seventy-Five Years.* .
Hill, John Waller. *History of Fly-Fishing.* .
Leeson, Ted. *The Habit of Rivers.*
Lyons, Nick. *Bright Rivers.*
Marinaro, Vincent C. *Modern Dry Fly Code.* .
Marinaro, Vincent; Pearce Bates. *The Ring of the Rise.*
McDonald, John. *Origins of Angling.*
Proper, Datus C. *What the Trout Said.*
Ronalds, Alfred. *A Fly-Fisher's Entomology.* .
Rosenbauer, Tom. *Reading Trout Streams.*
Schullery, Paul. *American Fly Fishing.*
Schwiebert, Ernest G. *Matching the Hatch.*
Skues, G.E.M. *Minor Tactics.*
Skues, G.E.M. *The Way of a Trout With a Fly.* .
Steward, W.C. *The Practical Angler.*
Swisher, Doug; Carl Richards. *Selective Trout.*

Voelker, John. *Trout Madness*.
Voelker, John. *Trout Magic*.
Walton, Izaak. *The Complete Angler*.
Wulff, Leo. *Atlantic Salmon*.

Library of Great Lives

This early Easton Press series has been out-of-print for a long while.

Alden, John R. *George Washington: A Biography.*

Alexander, John T. *Catherine the Great: Life and Legend.*

Baker, Carlos. *Ernest Hemingway: A Life Story.* 2 volumes.

Baker, Leonard. *John Marshall: A Life in Law.* 2 volumes.

Bar-Zohar, Michael. *Ben-Gurion: A Biography.*

Benson, E.F. *Ferdinand Magellan.*

Bonner, Gerald. *St. Augustine of Hippo: Life and Controversies.*

Callow, Phillip. *Vincent Van Gogh.*

Castelot, Andre. *Napoleon.*

Christianson, Gale E. *In the Presence of the Creator: Isaac Newton and His Times.*

Chute, Marchette. *Shakespeare of London.*

Clark, Kenneth. *An Introduction to Rembrandt.*

Clark, Ronald W. *Benjamin Franklin: A Biography.*

Clark, Ronald W. *Freud: The Man and the Cause.*

Clark, Ronald W. *The Survival of Charles Darwin: A Biography of a Man and an Idea.*

Conot, Robert. A *Streak of Luck: The Life and Legend of Thomas Alva Edison.*

Creel, H.G. *Confucius: The Man and the Myth.*

Crozier, Brian. *De Gaulle.*

Cunningham Jr., Noble E. *In Pursuit of Reason: The Life of Thomas Jefferson.*

Curie, Eve. *Madame Curie: A Biography.*

Dubos, Rene J. *Louis Pasteur: Freelance of Science.*

Erickson, Carolly. *The First Elizabeth.*

Erlanger, Philippe. *Louis XIV.*

Fischer, Louis. *The Life of Lenin.* 2 volumes.

Fischer, Louis. *The Life of Mahatma Gandhi*.

Ford, Alice. *John James Audubon: A Biography*.

Forrest, McDonald. *Alexander Hamilton: A Biography*.

Fox, Robin Lane. *Alexander the Great*.

Frank, Phillip. *Einstein: His Life and Times*.

Freeman, Douglas Southall; Richard Harwell. *Lee: An Abridgement*.

Garrow, David J. *Bearing the Cross: Martin Luther King, Jr. and the Southern Christian Leadership Conference*.

Geymonat, Ludovico. *Galileo Galilei: A Biography and Inquiry Into His Philosophy of Science*.

Gilbert, Bill. *God Gave Us This Country: Tekamthi and the First American Civil War*.

Green, F.C. *Jean Jacques Rousseau: A Critical Study of His Life and Writings*.

Harrod, R.F. *The Life of John Maynard Keynes*.

Hart, Henry H. *Marco Polo: Venetian Adventurer*.

Hibbard, Howard. *Michelangelo: A Biography*.

Hildesheimer, Wolfgang. *Mozart*.

Jacobs, Herbert. *Frank Lloyd Wright: America's Greatest Architect*.

Kahn, Arthur D. *The Education of Julius Caesar: A Biography, A Reconstruction*.

Kaplan, Fred. *Dickens: A Biography*.

Keller, Helen. *The Story of My Life with Her Letters 1887 to 1901: An Autobiography*.

Lamb, Harold. *Charlemagne: The Legend and the Man*.

Lauber, John. *The Inventions of Mark Twain*.

Mabee, Carleton. *The American Leonardo: A Life of Samuel F.B. Morse*.

MacKenzie, Catherine. *Alexander Graham Bell: The Man Who Contracted Space*.

Magarshack, David. *Dostoevsky*.

Marconi, Degna. *My Father, Marconi*.

Maurois, Andre. *Disraeli: A Picture of the Victorian Age.*
McFeely, William S. *Frederick Douglass.*
McLelland, David. *Karl Marx: His Life and Thought.*
McMurry, Linda O. *George Washington Carver: Scientist and Symbol.*
Morison, Samuel Eliot. *Christopher Columbus: Mariner.*
Nevins, Allan. *A Study in Power: John D Rockefeller Industrialist and Philanthropist.* 2 volumes.
Nock, Arthur Darby. *Saint Paul.*
Oates, Stephen B. *With Malice Toward None: The Life of Abraham Lincoln.*
Pelling, Henry. *Winston Churchill.* 2 volumes.
Randall Jr., John Herman. *Aristotle: A Biography.*
Ricciotti, Giuseppe. *Life of Christ.*
Robinson, Maxine. *Muhammad.*
Rusk, Ralph L. *The Life of Ralph Waldo Emerson.*
Sackville, V. *Saint Joan of Arc.*
Sadat, Anwar El. *In Search of Identity: An Autobiography of Anwar El Sadat.*
Schlesinger Jr., Arthur M. *A Thousand Days: John F. Kennedy in the White House.* 2 volumes.
Schweitzer, Albert. *Out of My Life and Thought: An Autobiography.*
Solomon, Maynard. *Beethoven.*
Strachey, Lytton. *Queen Victoria.*
Swanberg, W.A. *Luce and His Empire.*
Sward, Keith. *The Legend of Henry Ford.*
Taylor, A.E. Plato: *The Man and His Work.*
Taylor, A.E. *Socrates: A Biography.*
Taylor, A.J.P. *Bismarck: The Man and the Statesman.*
Taylor, Rachael Annand. *Leonardo The Florentine: A Study in Personality.*
Terrill, Ross. *Mao: A Biography.*
Terry, Charles. *Sanford. Bach: A Biography.*

Troyat, Henri. *Peter the Great.*
Troyat, Henri. *Tolstoy.* 2 volumes.
Tse-Tung, Mao. *Quotations From Chairman.*
Vrooman, Jack Rochford. *Rene Descartes: A Biography.*
Ybarra, T.R. *Caruso: The Man of Naples and the Voice of Gold.*

Library of Great Poetry

This series is out-of-print.

Blake, William.
Bronte, Emily
Browning, Elizabeth Barrett.
Browning, Robert.
Burns, Robert.
Byron, Lord.
Coleridge, Samuel Taylor.
Cummings, E.E.
Dickinson, Emily.
Donne, John.
Eliot, T.S.
Frost, Robert.
Hopkins, Gerard Manley.
Hughes, Langston.
Keats, John.
Longfellow, Henry Wadsworth.
Millay, Edna.
Plath, Sylvia.
Poe, Edgar Allan.
Shakespeare, William.
Shelley, Percy Bysshe.
Tennyson, Alfred Lord.
Whitman, Walt.
Wordsworth, William.
Yeats, William E.

Library of Military History

Another early series, this has been out-of-print for quite some time.

Alexander, Bevin. *Korea: the First War We Lost.*

Ambrose, Stephen E. *D-Day, June 6, 1944: The Climactic Battle of World War II.*

Bauer, K. Jack. *The Mexican War 1846 to 1848.*

Bigelow Jr., John. *The Campaign of Chancellorsville.*

Blumenson, Martin. *Anzio: The Gamble That Failed.*

Blumenson, Martin. *Mark Clark.*

Blumenson, Martin; James L. Stokesbury. *Masters of the Art of Command.*

Blumenson, Martin. *Patton: The Man Behind The Legend 1885 to 1945.*

Bonaparte, Napoleon. *The Military Maxims of Napoleon.*

Bowden, Mark. *Black Hawk Down: A Story of Modern War.*

Bradley, James. *Flags of Our Fathers: Heroes of Iwo Jima.*

Bradley, Omar N. *A General's Life: An Autobiography by General of the Army.*

Bradley, Omar N. *A Soldier's Story.*

Brickhill, Paul. *The Great Escape.*

Burne, Alfred H. *The Crecy War: A Military History of the Hundred Years War from 1337 to the Peace of Bretigny 1360.*

Caesar, Julius. *The Gallic Wars.*

Cartledge, Paul. *Thermopylae: The Battle That Changed the World.*

Carver, Michael. *The War Lords: Military Commanders of the Twentieth Century.*

Catton, Bruce. *A Stillness At Appomattox: The Army of the Potomac.*

Chambers, James. *The Devil's Horsemen: The Mongol Invasion of Europe.*

Chandler, David G. *The Campaigns of Napoleon. 2 volumes.*

Chandler, David. *Waterloo: The Hundred Days.*

Churchill, Winston S. *The Boer War.*

Churchill, Winston S. *Memoirs of World War II.*

Churchill, Winston S. *The River War: An Account of the Reconquest of the Sudan.*

Churchill, Winston S. *The Story of the Malakand Field Force.*

Clausewitz, Carl von. *On War.* 2 volumes.

Coddington, Edwin B. *The Gettysburg Campaign: A Study in Command.* 2 volumes.

Collins, J. Lawton. *War In Peacetime: The History and Lessons of Korea.*

Connell, Evan S. *Son of the Morning Star.*

Creasy, Edward S. *The Fifteen Decisive Battles of the World.*

Davis, Burke. *To Appomattox: Nine April Days 1865.*

Dayan, Moshe. *Diary of the Sinai Campaign.*

D'Este, Carlo. *Patton: A Genius for War.*

Donovan, James. *A Terrible Glory.*

Douhet, Guilio. *The Command of the Air.*

Duffy, Christopher. *The Military Life of Frederick the Great.*

Eisenhower, John S.D. *The Bitter Woods: The Dramatic Story, Told at All Echelons.*

Eisenhower, Dwight D. *Crusade in Europe.*

Falk, Stanley L. *Bataan: The March of Death.*

Falk, Stanley L. *Decision at Leyte.*

Fall, Bernard B. *Street Without Joy: Indochina at War, 1946 to 1954.*

Falls, Cyril. *The Great War.*

Fischer, David Hackett. *Paul Revere's Ride.*

Fischer, David Hackett. *Washington's Crossing.*

Fox, Robin Lane. *Alexander the Great.*

Fraser, David. *And We Shall Shock Them: The British Army in the Second World War.*

Freeman, Douglas Southall. *Lee's Lieutenants*. 3 volumes.

Garland, Albert N.; Howard McGraw Smyth. *Sicily and the Surrender of Italy.*

Gilbert, Adrian D. *Voices of the Foreign Legion.*

Graham, Dominick; Shelford Bidwell. *Tug of War: The Battle for Italy 1943 to 1945.*

Grant, Ulysses S. *Personal Memoirs of Ulysses S. Grant.*

Guderian, Heinz. *Panzer Leader.*

Halberstam, David. *Coldest Winter: America and the Korean War.*

Hamley, Edward. *The War in the Crimea.*

Hart, B.H. Liddell. *The Real War 1914 to 1918.*

Hart, B.H. Liddell. *Strategy.*

Hastings, Max. *The Korean War.*

Hastings, Max. *Overlord : D-Day and the Battle for Normandy.*

Hattaway, Herman; Archer Jones. *How the North Won: A Military History of the Civil War.* 2 volumes.

Hechler, Ken. *The Bridge at Remagen.*

Henderson, Bruce. *Hero Found.*

Herodotus. *The Histories of Herodotus.*

Hibbert, Christopher. *Agincourt.*

Hibbert, Christopher. *The Great Mutiny: India 1857.*

Higginbotham, Don. *The War of American Independence: Military Attitudes, Policies, and Practice, 1763 to 1789.*

Horne, Alistair. *The Fall of Paris: The Siege and The Commune 1870 to 1871.*

Horne, Alistair. *The Price of Glory: Verdun 1916.*

Horne, Alistair. *A Savage War of Peace: Algeria 1954 to 1962.*

Howard, Michael. *The Franco Prussian War: The German Invasion of France 1870 to 1871.*

Howe, George F. *Northwest Africa: Seizing the Initiative in the West.*

Hurley, Alfred F. *Billy Mitchell: Crusader for Air Power.*

Jones, Virgil Carrington. *Roosevelt's Rough Riders.*

Karnow, Stanley. *Vietnam: A History.* 2 volumes.

Keegan, John. *The Face of Battle.*

Keegan, John. *The First World War and The Second World War.*
    2 volumes.

Keegan, John. *The Mask of Command.*

Kelly, Christopher. *End of Empire: Attila The Hun and The Fall*
    of Rome.

Kesselring, Albert. *Kesselring: a Soldier's Record.*

Ketchum, Richard M. *Decisive Day: The Battle for Bunker Hill.*

Ketchum, Richard M. *Saratoga: Turning Point of America's*
    Revolutionary War.

Ketchum, Richard M. *The Winter Soldiers.*

Kohli, M.S.; Kenneth Conboy. *Spies in the Himalayas: Secret*
    Missions and Perilous Climbs.

Lamb, Harold. *Genghis Khan: The Emperor of All Men.*

Lawrence, T.E. *Seven Pillars of Wisdom.*

Lawson, Eric; Jane Lawson. *The First Air Campaign: August*
    1914 to November 1918.

Lewin, Ronald. *Ultra Goes to War: The First Account of World*
    War II's Greatest Secret Based on Official Documents.

Lengel, Edward G. *To Conquer Hell: The Meuse-Argonne, 1918.*

Lewis, Lloyd. *Sherman: Fighting Prophet.* 2 volumes.

Livy. *The War With Hannibal.*

Longstreet, James. *From Manassas To Appomattox: Memoirs of*
    the Civil War in America.

Lorch, Netanel. *The Edge of the Sword: Israel's War of*
    Independence, 1947 to 1949.

Lord, Walter. *Day in Infamy.*

Lukacs, John. *Five Days in London: May 1940.*

MacDonald, Charles B. *Company Commander.*

MacDonald, Charles B. *The Mighty Endeavor: American Armed*

Forces in the European Theater in World War II.

Machiavelli, Niccolo. *The Art of War.*

MacIntyre, Donald. *Jutland.*

Mahan, A.T. *The Influence of Sea Power Upon History 1660 to 1783.*

Marshall, S.L.A. *Pork Chop Hill: The American Fighting Man in Action, Korea, Spring, 1953.*

Mattingly, Garrett. *The Armada.*

McClellan, George Brinton. *McClellan's Own Story.*

Moore, Harold G.; Joseph L. Galloway. *We Were Soldiers Once and Young: Ia Drang the Battle That Changed the War in Vietnam.*

Moorehead, Alan. *Gallipoli.*

Morison, Samuel Eliot. *John Paul Jones: A Sailor's Biography.*

Morison, Samuel Eliot. *The Two Ocean War: A Short History of the United States Navy in the Second World.*

Morris, Donald R. *The Washing of the Spears.*

Musashi, Miyamoto. *The Book of Five Rings.*

O'Connell, Robert L. *The Ghosts of Cannae.*

Oren, Michael B. *Six Days of War.*

Pakenham, Thomas. *The Boer War.*

Palmer, Dave. *George Washington and Benedict Arnold: A Tale of Two Patriots.*

Parkman, Francis. *The Battle for North America.*

Picq, Ardant Du. *Battle Studies: Ancient and Modern Battle.*

Pope, Dudley. *Decision at Trafalgar.*

Potter, E.B. *Nimitz.*

Prange, Gordon W. *At Dawn We Slept: The Untold Story of Pearl Harbor.* 2 volumes.

Prange, Gordon William. *Miracle at Midway.*

Reilly, Robin. *The British at the Gates.*

Rhodes, Richard. *The Making of the Atomic Bomb.*

Rodgers, William Ledyard. *Greek and Roman Naval Warfare.*

Rodgers, William Ledyard. *Naval Warfare Under Oars: 4th to 16th Centuries a Study of Strategy, Tactics and Ship Design.*

Rommel, Erwin. *The Rommel Papers.*

Roosevelt, Theodore. *The Naval War of 1812.*

Rothenberg, Gunther. *The Art of Warfare in the Age of Napoleon.*

Ryan, Cornelius. *A Bridge Too Far.*

Sajer, Guy. *The Forgotten Soldier.*

Salisbury, Harrison Evans. *The 900 Days: The Siege of Leningrad.*

Sears, Stephen W. *Landscape Turned Red: The Battle of Antietam.*

Smith, Gene. *Lee and Grant.*

Smythe, Donald. *Pershing: General of the Armies.*

Sontag, Sherry; Christopher Drew. *Blind Man's Bluff.*

Spector, Ronald H. *Eagle Against the Sun: The American War with Japan.*

Steere, Edward. *The Wilderness Campaign.*

Stoneberger, Brett A. *Combat Leader's Field Guide.*

Symonds, Craig L. *Decision at Sea: Five Naval Battles That Shaped American History.*

Thomas, Evan. *Sea of Thunder: Four Commanders and the Last Great Naval Campaign 1941-1945.*

Thucydides. *History of the Peloponnesian War.*

Toland, John. *The Last 100 Days.*

Toland, John. *No Man's Land.*

Toland, John. *The Rising Sun: The Decline and Fall of the Japanese Empire 1936 to 1946.* 2 volumes.

Tourtellot, Arthur B. *Lexington and Concord: The Beginning of the War of the American Revolution.*

Tuchman, Barbara W. *The Guns of August.*

Tuchman, Barbara Wertheim. *Stilwell and the American Experience in China, 1911 to 1945.*

Tregaskis, Richard. *Guadalcanal Diary.*

Trevelyan, Raleigh. *Rome '44: The Battle for The Eternal City.*

Tse-Tung, Mao. *On Guerrilla Warfare.*

Tyerman, Christopher. *Fighting for Christendom : Holy War and the Crusaders.*

Tzu, Sun. *The Art of War.*

Wedgwood, C.V. *The Thirty Years War.*

Weigley, Russell F. *The American Way of War: A History of United States Military Strategy and Policy.*

Westmoreland, William C. *A Soldier Reports.*

Williams, T. Harry. *Lincoln and His Generals.*

Williamson, Murray. *Luftwaffe.*

Xenophon. *The March Up Country : A Translation of Xenophon's Anabasis.*

Zacks, Richard. *The Pirate Coast: Thomas Jefferson, the First Marines, and the Secret Mission of 1805.*

Zucchio, David. *Thunder Run: The Armored Strike to Capture Baghdad.*

Library of the Presidents

This series has been discontinued though a few of the titles may still be available through Easton Press. I've included all titles related to the presidents here even if not officially part of the 'Library of the Presidents' as that's the most logical place to include the titles.

John Adams
Adams, John *The works of John Adams.* 2 volumes.
Ferling, John *John Adams: A Life.*
McCullough, David *President John Adams.*
Smith, Page *John Adams Biography.* 2 volumes.

John Quincy Adams
Bemis, Samuel Flagg. *John Quincy Adams Biography.* 2
      volumes.
Volume 1 - The foundation of American foreign policy.
Volume 2 - The Union.
Nagel, Paul C. *John Quincy Adams A public Life.*

James Buchanan
Klein, Philip Shriver. *President James Buchanan.*

George H.W. Bush
Bush, Barbara. *A Memoir: Barbara Bush.* Signed. First Edition.
Bush, Barbara. *Reflections: Life After The White House.* Signed.
      First Edition.
Bush, George H.W. *All The Best: Autobiography of George
      Bush.* Signed, First Edition, in blue leather. Signed, in red
      leather.
Bush, George H.W. *Speaking of Freedom.* Signed.
Parmet, Herbert S. *George Bush The life of a Lone Star Yankee.*

George W. Bush
Bush, George W. *A Charge to Keep.* Signed. First Edition.

Jimmy Carter
Carter, Jimmy. 7 volumes.
   Volume 1 - Always a Reckoning. Signed
   Volume 2 - Turning Point.
   Volume 3 - Everything to Gain.
   Volume 4 - A Government as Good as Its People.
   Volume 5 - Why Not the Best.
   Volume 6 - An Outdoor Journal.
   Volume 7 - The Blood of Abraham.
Carter, Jimmy. 2 volumes.
   Volume 1 - Living Faith. Signed.
   Volume 2 - Sources of Strength.
Carter, Jimmy. *A Full Life.* Signed.
Carter, Jimmy. *Beyond the White House: Waging Peace, Fighting Disease, Building Hope.* Signed.
Carter, Jimmy. *Christmas In Plains.* Signed.
Carter, Jimmy. *The Hornet's Nest.* Signed.
Carter, Jimmy. *An Hour Before Daylight: Memoirs of a Rural Boyhood.* Signed. First Edition.
Carter, Jimmy. *Keeping Faith: Memoirs of a President.* Signed.
Carter, Jimmy. *Our Endangered Values: America's Moral Crisis.* Signed.
Carter, Jimmy. *Palestine: Peace Not Apartheid.* Signed.
Carter, Jimmy. *A Remarkable Mother.* Signed.
Carter, Jimmy. *Sharing Good Times.* Signed.
Carter, Jimmy. *Turning Point : A Candidate, a State, and a Nation Come of Age.* Signed. First Edition.

Arthur Chester
Howe, George Frederick. *Chester Arthur A quarter Century of Machine Politics.*

Grover Cleveland

Nevins, Allan. *Grover Cleveland: A Study in Courage.* 2 volumes.

Tugwell, Rexford G. *Grover Cleveland a Biography.*

Bill Clinton

Harris, John F. *The Survivor: Bill Clinton in the White House.*

Calvin Coolidge

White, William Allen. *A Puritan in Babylon The story of Calvin Coolidge.*

Dwight D. Eisenhower

Ambrose, Stephen. *Dwight Eisenhower.* 2 volumes.
> *Volume 1 - Soldier, General of the Army, President Elect 1890 – 1952.*
> *Volume 2 - The President 1952 – 1960.*

Eisenhower, John S.D. *General Ike.* Signed. First Edition.

Eisenhower, Dwight D. *Crusade in Europe.*

Ferrell, Robert H. *The Eisenhower Diaries.*

Millard Fillmore

Rayback, Robert J. *Millard Fillmore: Biography of a President.*

Gerald Ford

Ford, Gerald. *A Time to Heal - Autobiography of Gerald Ford.* Signed.

Ford, Gerald. *Humor and the Presidency.* Signed.

James Garfield

Peskin, Allan. *Garfield: A Biography.*

Ulysses S. Grant

Grant, President Ulysses. *Personal Memoirs of President Ulysses Grant.*

McFeely, William S. *Grant: A Biography.*

Miers, Earl Schenck. *Web of Victory: Grant at Vicksburg.*

Smith, Gene. *Lee and Grant a Dual Biography.*

Warren Harding

Russell, Francis. *The Shadow of Blooming Grove: Warren Harding and His Times.*

Benjamin Harrison

Sievers, Harry J. *Benjamin Harrison.* 2 volumes.
    Volume 1 - Hoosier Warrior.
    Volume 2 - Hoosier Statesman, Hoosier President.

Socolofsky, Homer E. *The Presidency of Benjamin Harrison.*

William Harrison

Cleaves, Freeman. *Old Tippecanoe, William Henry Harrison and His Time.*

Rutherford Hayes

Eckenrode, H.J. *Rutherford Hayes: Statesman of Reunion.*

Hoogenbook, Ari. *Rutherford Hayes: Warrior and President.*

Herbert Hoover

Burner, David. *Herbert Hoover: A Public Life.*

Lyons, Eugene. *Herbert Hoover: A Biography.*

Andrew Jackson

Frost, John. *A Pictorial Biography of Andrew Jackson.*

Marguis, James. *Andrew Jackson.* 2 volumes.
    Volume 1 - The Border Captain.

Volume 1 - Portrait of a President.
Remini, Robert V. *The life of Andrew Jackson.*

Thomas Jefferson

Ambrose, Stephen. *Undaunted Courage: Meriwether Lewis, William Clark, Thomas Jefferson, and the Opening of the American West.* Signed.
Cunningham, Noble E. *The Pursuit of Reason: The Life of Thomas Jefferson.*
Dumas, Malone. *Thomas Jefferson and His Time.* 6 volumes.
    Volume 1 - The Virginian.
    Volume 2 - Jefferson and the rights of Man.
    Volume 3 - Jefferson and the ordeal of Liberty.
    Volume 4 - The President (first term 1801 – 1805).
    Volume 5 - The President (second term 1805 – 1809).
    Volume 6 - The Sage of Monticello.
Ellis, Joseph Jay. *American Sphinx: The charter of Thomas Jefferson.*
Jefferson, Thomas. *The Writings of Thomas Jefferson.* 2 volumes.
Peterson, Merrell D. *Thomas Jefferson and the New Nation.*
Passos, John Dos. *The Shackles of Power: Three Jeffersonian Decades.*

Andrew Johnson

Trefousse, Hans L. *Andrew Johnson a Biography.*
Winston, Robert W. *Andrew Johnson Plebeian and Patriot.*

Lyndon B. Johnson

Caro, Robert A. *The Years of Lyndon Johnson.* 4 volumes.
Dallek, Robert. *Lyndon B. Johnson and His Times.* 2 volumes.
    Volume 1 - Lone Star Rising 1908 – 1960.
    Volume 2 - Flawed Giant 1961 – 1973.
Goodwin, Doris Kearns. *Lyndon B. Johnson and The American*

Dream.

John F. Kennedy

Anderson, Thomas. *Ask Not: Daily Celebrations of the Legacy of John F. Kennedy.*

Halberstam, David. *The Best and the Brightest.* Signed. First Edition.

Kennedy, John. *The Burden and the Glory.*

Kennedy, John. *A Nation of Immigrants.*

Kennedy, John. *Profiles in Courage.*

Lowe, Jacques. *Remembering Jack: Intimate And Unseen Photographs of the Kennedys.*

Parmet, Herbert S. *2 volumes.*
> *Volume 1 - JACK: The Struggles of John Kennedy.*
> *Volume 2 - JFK: The Presidency of John Kennedy.*

Reeves, Richard. *President Kennedy: Profile of Power.*

Schlesinger, Arthur M. *A Thousand Days: John F. Kennedy in the White House.* 2 volumes.

The Warren Commission Report.

Abraham Lincoln

Donald, David Herbert. *Abraham Lincoln His Life and Speeches.* 2 volumes.

Lincoln, Abraham. *Collected works of Abraham Lincoln.* 10 volumes.

Lincoln: An Intimate Portrait.

Lincoln, Abraham. *The Gettysburg Address and Other Writings.*

Lincoln, Abraham. *Literary works of Abraham Lincoln.*

Sandburg, Carl. *Abraham Lincoln the Prairie years and the War years.* One volume edition & two volume edition.

James Madison

Brant, Irving. *The Fourth President: A Life of James Madison.*

Hamilton, Alexander; James Madison. *The Federalist.*
Madison, James. *The Complete Madison: His Basic Writings.*

James Monroe
Cresson, William P. *James Monroe.*

William McKinley
Leech, Margaret. *In the days of McKinley.*
Rove, Karl. *The Triumph of William McKinley.* Signed.

Richard Nixon
Ambrose, Stephen. *Nixon: Ruin and Recovery 1973-1990.* Signed.
  First Edition.
Buchanan, Patrick J. *Nixon's White House Wars.* Signed. First
  Edition.
Nixon, Richard. *Beyond Peace.*
Nixon, Richard. *In the Arena: a Memoir of Victory, Defeat, and
  Renewal.*
Nixon, Richard. *The Memoirs of Richard Nixon.* 2 volumes.
  Signed in Volume 1.
Nixon, Richard. *Richard Nixon.* 6 volumes.
  Volume 1 - Six Crises.
  Volume 2 - The Real War.
  Volume 3 – Leaders.
  Volume 4 - Real Peace/No More Vietnams.
  Volume 5 - Victory without War.
  Volume 6 - Seize The Moment. Signed.

Barack Obama
The New York Times Obama : The Historic Journey.
Obama: The Historic Front Pages.
Greenberg, Mark. *Obama: The Historic Presidency.*
The Obamas: The White House Years.

President Obama : The Path to The White House.

Franklin Pierce
Nichols, Roy Franklin *Franklin Pierce: Young Hickory of the
        Granite Hills*

James K. Polk
Bergeron, Paul. *The Presidency of James K. Polk.*
McCormac, Eugene Irving. *James K. Polk Biography.*
Seller, Charles. *James K. Polk*. 2 volumes.
        Volume 1 - Jacksonian 1795 – 1843.
        Volume 2 - Continentalist 1843 – 1846.

Ronald Reagan
Cannon, Lou. *Ronald Reagan: The Presidential Portfolio.*
Reagan, Nancy. *Ronald Reagan: An American Hero.*
Reagan, Nancy. *A Shining City: The Legacy of Ronald Reagan.*
Signed. First Edition.
Reagan, Ronald. *An American Life.*
Reagan, Ronald. *Speaking My Mind: Selected Speeches.*
        Remembering the Reagans.
Richardson, Alexander. *Too Great for Small Dreams: Daily
        Celebrations of the Legacy of Ronald Reagan.*

Franklin D. Roosevelt
Burns, James MacGregor. *Roosevelt.* 2 volumes.
        Volume 1 - The Lion and the Fox.
        Volume 2 - The Soldier of Freedom.
Churchill, Winston S.; Franklin D. Roosevelt. *Churchill and
        Roosevelt : The Complete Correspondence.*
Lash, Joseph P. *Eleanor and Franklin.* 2 volumes.
Roosevelt, Franklin Delano. *Franklin D. Roosevelt. Selected
        Speeches, Messages, Press Conferences and Letters.*

Roosevelt, Franklin Delano. *A Rendevous With Destiny.*
Schlesinger, Arthur M. *The Coming of the New Deal: the Age of Roosevelt.*

Theodore Roosevelt
Brands, H.W. *Theodore Roosevelt: The Last Romantic.*
Jones, Virgil Carrington. *Roosevelt's Rough Riders.*
McCullough, David. *Mornings on Horseback.*
Pringle, Henry F. *Theodore Roosevelt: A Biography.*
Roosevelt, Theodore. *African Game Trails.*
Roosevelt, Theodore. *The Naval War of 1812.*
Roosevelt, Theodore. *The Theodore Roosevelt Treasury: A Self-Portrait from His Writings.*
Roosevelt, Theodore. *Writings of Theodore Roosevelt.* 3 volumes.
    Volume 1 - An Autobiography.
    Volume 2 - The Rough Riders.
    Volume 3 - The Strenuous Life.

William Taft
Anderson, Donald. *William Taft A Conservative's concept of the Presidency.*
Pringle, Henry F. *Life and Times of William Taft.* 2 volumes.

Zachary Taylor
Bauer, Jack K. *Zachary Taylor: Soldier, Planter, Statesman of the Old Southwest.*
Hamilton, Holman. *Zachary Taylor.* 2 volumes.
    Volume 1 - Soldier of the Republic.
    Volume 2 - Soldier in the White House.

Harry S. Truman
Ferrell, Robert H. *Off the Record the private papers of Harry*

Truman.

McCullough, David. *President Truman Biography.* 2 volumes.

Truman, Harry S. *Truman Speaks.* 4 volumes.

Truman, Margaret. *Harry S. Truman.*

John Tyler

Seger II, Robert. *And Tyler too: A biography of John & Julia Gardiner Tyler.*

Martin Van Buren

Cole, Donald B. *Martin Van Buren and the American Political System.*

Niven, John. *Martin Van Buren: The Romantic Age of American Politics.*

George Washington

Alden, John. *George Washington a Biography.*

Flexner, James. Thomas *George Washington.* 4 volumes.

   Volume 1 - The Forge Experience 1732-1775.

   Volume 2 - In the American Revolution 1775-1783.

   Volume 3 - And the New Nation 1783-1793.

   Volume 4 - Anguish and Farewell 1793-1799.

Freeman, Douglas Southall. *George Washington Biography.*

Padover, Saul K. *The Washington Papers.*

Woodrow Wilson

Heckscher, August. *Woodrow Wilson A Biography.*

Link, Arthur S. *Woodrow Wilson and the Progressive Era 1910-1917.*

Walworth, Arthur. *Woodrow Wilson.* 2 volumes.

   Volume 1 - American Prophet.

   Volume 2 - World Prophet.

Wilson, Woodrow. *Day of Dedication: The Essential Writings and Speeches of Woodrow Wilson.*

Masterpieces of American Literature

This was an early Easton Press series that's no longer in-print.

American Indians Legends.
Bellamy, Edward. *Looking Backward 2000-1887.*
Bierce, Ambrose. *Tales of Soldiers and Civilians.*
Bryant, William Cullen. *Poems of William Cullen Bryant.*
Cable, George Washington. *Old Creole Days.*
Cooper, James Fenimore. *Deerslayer.*
Cooper, James Fenimore. *Pathfinder.*
Cooper, James Fenimore. *Prairie.*
Crane, Stephen. *Maggie.*
Dana, Richard Henry. *Two Years Before the Mast.*
Melville, Herman. *Typee.*
Dickinson, Emily. *Poems of Emily Dickinson.*
Dreiser, Theodore. *American Tragedy.*
Dreiser, Theodore. *Sister Carrie.*
Franklin, Benjamin. *Poor Richard's Almanac.*
Harris, Chandler. *Uncle Remus.*
Harte, Bret. *Tales of the Gold Rush.*
Hawthorne, Nathaniel. *House of Seven Gables.*
Hawthorne, Nathaniel. *Twice-Told Tales.*
Henry, O. *Stories of O. Henry.*
Holmes, Oliver Wendell. *Autocrat at the Breakfast Table.*
Irving, Washington. *Diedrich Knickerbocker's History of New York.*
Irving, Washington. *Sketch Book of Geoffrey Crayon.*
James, Henry. *Daisy Miller.*
James, Henry. *Turn of the Screw.*
James, Henry. *Washington Square.*
Jefferson, Thomas. *Writings of Thomas Jefferson.*
Lewis and Clark: Journals of the Expedition. 2 volumes.

Lincoln, Abraham. *Literary Writings of Abraham Lincoln.*
London, Jack. *Call of the Wild.*
London, Jack. *White Fang.*
Longfellow, Henry Wadsworth. *Poems of Longfellow.*
Melville, Herman. *Billy Budd and Benito Cereno.*
Melville, Herman. *Omoo.*
Parkman, Francis. *Oregon Trail.*
Poe, Edgar Allan. *Arthur Gordon Pym.*
Poe, Edgar Allan. *Complete Poems.*
Sinclair, Upton. *The Jungle.*
Tarkington, Booth. *Monsieur Beaucaire.*
Thoreau, Henry David. *Cape Cod.*
Thoreau, Henry David. *Week on the Concord and Merrimack Rivers.*
Twain, Mark. *Life on the Mississippi.*
Twain, Mark. *Pudd'nhead Wilson.*
Untermeyer, Louis. *Wonderful Adventures of Paul Bunyan.*
Wallace, Lew. *Ben Hur.*
Washington, Booker T. *Up From Slavery.*
Wharton, Edith. *House of Mirth.*
Whittier, John Greenleaf. *Poems of John Greenleaf Whittier.*
Wister, Owen. *Virginian.*

Masterpieces of Fantasy

Yet another Easton Press series that's out-of-print.

Aldiss, Brian. *The Malacia Tapestry.*
Anderson, Poul. *Three Hearts and Three Lions.*
Anthony, Piers. *Spell for Chameleon.*
Beagle, Peter S. *The Last Unicorn.*
Bradley, Marion Zimmer. *Mists of Avalon.* 2 volumes.
Brooks, Terry. *Sword of Shannara.* Signed.
Crowley, John. *Little Big.*
De Camp, L. Sprague. *Complete Enchanter.*
Donaldson, Stephen R. *Lord Foul's Bane.*
Eddings, David. *Pawn of Prophecy.* Signed.
Feist, Raymond E. *Magician: Apprentice.* Signed.
Feist, Raymond E. *Magician: Master.*
Heinlein, Robert A. *Unpleasant Profession of Jonathan Hoag.*
Holdstock, Robert. *Mythago Wood.*
Kay, Guy Gavriel. *Tigana.* Signed.
Kurtz, Katherine. *Deryni Rising.*
Lackey, Mercedes. *Queen's Own.* 2 volumes.
Le Guin, Ursula K. *Wizard of Earthsea.* 2 volumes.
Leiber, Fritz. *Gather, Darkness.*
Llyweln, Morgan. *Lion of Ireland.*
McKillip, Patrica A. *Riddle Master of Hed.*
Moon, Elizabeth. *Sheepfarmer's Daughter*
Norton, Andre. *Witch World.*
Peake, Mervyn. *Gormenghast.* 2 volumes.
Tarr, Judith. *Hound and Falcon.*
Tolkien, J.R. *Fellowship of the Ring.*
Tolkien, J.R. *Return of the King.*
Tolkien, J.R. *The Two Towers.*
Whipple, Lee. *Devil's Day.*

White, T.H. *Once and Future King.*
Williamson, Jack. *Darker Than You Think.*
Zelazny, Roger. *Nine Princes in Amber.*

Masterpieces of Science Fiction

Only a handful of titles from this series are currently in stock at Easton Press.

Abbott, Edwin. *Flatland: A Romance of Many Dimensions.*
Adams, Douglas. *The Hitchhiker's Guide to the Galaxy.*
Aldiss, Brian W. *Helliconia Spring.*
Aldiss, Brian W. *Hothouse.*
Amis, Kingsley. *The Alteration.*
Anderson, Poul. *Tau Zero.*
Anthony, Piers. *Macroscope.*
Asimov, Isaac. *The Foundation Trilogy.* Signed.
Asimov, Isaac. *The Foundation Trilogy.*
Asimov, Isaac. *The Gods Themselves.*
Ballard, J.G. *The Crystal World.*
Bear, Greg. *Blood Music.*
Bear, Greg. *Moving Mars.*
Benfore, Gregory. *Timescape.*
Bester, Alfred. *The Demolished Man.*
Bishop, Michael. *No Enemy But Time.*
Blish, James. *Case of Conscience.*
Bova, Ben. *The Kinsman Saga.*
Bradbury, Ray. *Dandelion Wine.*
Bradbury, Ray. *Fahrenheit 451.*
Bradbury, Ray. *The Martian Chronicles.* Signed.
Brin, David. *The Postman.*
Brin, David. *Startide Rising.*
Brown, Frederic. *What Mad Universe.*
Brunner, John. *Stand on Zanzibar.*
Budrys, Algis. *Rogue Moon.*
Bujold, Lois McMaster. *Falling Free.*
Burgess, Anthony. *A Clockwork Orange.*

Burroughs, Edgar Rice. *A Princess of Mars / At the Earth's Core.*

Burroughs, Edgar Rice. *Tarzan of The Apes.*

Camp, L. Sprague De. *Lest Darkness Fall.*

Camp, L. Sprague de. *Rogue Queen.*

Card, Orson Scott. *Ender's Game.* Signed.

Card, Orson Scott. *Speaker for the Dead.*

Cherryh, C.J. *Downbelow Station.*

Clarke, Arthur C. *Childhood's End.*

Clarke, Arthur C. *Fountains of Paradise.*

Clarke, Arthur C. *Rendezvous with Rama.*

Clarke, Arthur C. *2001: A Space Odyssey.*

Clement, Hal. *Mission of Gravity.*

Clifton, Mark; Frank Riley. *They'd Rather Be Right.*

Delany, Samuel. *Babel-17.*

Delany, Samuel R. *The Einstein Intersection.*

Dick, Philip K. *Do Androids Dream of Electric Sheep?*.

Dick, Philip K. *The Man in the High Castle.*

Dickson, Gordon R. *Dorsai!.*

Disch, Thomas M. *On Wings of Song.*

Doyle, Conan Arthur. *Lost World.*

Doyle, Arthur Conan. *The Poison Belt.*

Effinger, George Alec. *When Gravity Falls.*

Ellison, Harlan. *Deathbird Stories.*

Farmer, Philip Jose. *To Your Scattered Bodies Go.*

Fast, Jonathan. *Mortal Gods.*

Finney, Jack. *Invasion of The Body Snatchers.*

Gibson, William. *Neuromancer.*

Guin, Ursula K. Le. *The Dispossessed.*

Guin, Ursula K. Le. *Left Hand of Darkness.* Signed.

Gunn, James E. *Kampus.*

Gunn, James E. *The Listeners.*

Haggard, H. Rider. *She.*

Haldeman, Joe. *Forever Peace.*

Haldeman, Joe. *Forever War.*

Harness, Charles L. *The Paradox Men.*

Heinlein, Robert A. *Stranger in a Strange Land.*

Herbert, Frank. *Dune.*

Hoyle, Fred. *The Black Cloud.*

Hubbard, L. Ron. *Final Blackout.*

Keyes, Daniel. *Flowers for Algernon.*

King, Stephen. *The Dead Zone.*

Kuttner, Henry. *Fury.*

Leiber, Fritz. *The Big Time.*

Lem, Stanislaw. *The Cyberiad.*

Lem, Stanislaw. *Solaris.*

Levin, Ira. *Rosemary's Baby.*

Lewis, C.S. *Out of The Silent Planet.*

London, Jack. *Before Adam.*

Lovecraft, H.P. *The Dunwich Horror and Others.*

Malzberg, Barry N. *Beyond Apollo.*

Matheson, Richard. *The Shrinking Man.*

McCaffrey, Anne. *Dragonflight.* Signed.

McIntyre, Vonda N. *Dreamsnake.*

McIntyre, Vonda N. *The Moon and the Sun.*

Merritt, A. *The Moon Pool.*

Miller Jr., Walter M. *A Canticle for Leibowitz.*

Moore, Ward. *Bring The Jubilee.*

Morrow, James. *This is the Way the World Ends.*

Niven, Larry; Jerry Pournell. *The Mote in God's Eye.*

Niven, Larry. *Ringworld.*

Orwell, George. *Animal Farm.*

Orwell, George. *Nineteen Eighty Four.*

Panshin, Alexei. *Rite of Passage.*

Pohl, Frederik. *Gateway.* Signed.

Pohl, Frederik. *Jem.*

Pohl, Frederik. *Man Plus.*

Robinson, Kim Stanley. *Green Mars*.

Robinson, Spider; Jeanne Robinson. *Stardance*.

Russ, Joanna. *The Female Man*.

Sargent, Pamela. *Venus of Dreams*.

Sawyer, Robert. *The Terminal Experiment*.

Scarborough, Elizabeth Ann. *The Healer's War*.

Silverberg, Robert. *Dying Inside*. Signed.

Silverberg, Robert. *A Time of Changes*.

Simak, Clifford. *City*.

Simak, Clifford. *Way Station*.

Simmons, Dan. *Hyperion*.

Slonczewski, Joan. *Door Into Ocean*.

Smith, Edward E. *The Skylark of Space*.

Spinrad, Norman. *Bug Jack Barron*.

Stapledon, Olaf. *Odd John*.

Stephenson, Neal. *The Diamond Age*.

Sterling, Bruce. *Islands in the Net*.

Stewart, George R. *Earth Abides*.

Sturgeon, Theodore. *More Than Human*.

Tucker, Wilson. *The Year of The Quiet Sun*.

Vance, Jack. *The Dragon Masters*.

Verne, Jules. *Around the World in 80 Days*.

Verne, Jules. *From the Earth to the Moon*.

Vinge, Joan D. *The Snow Queen*.

Vogt, A.E. Van. *Slan*. Signed.

Vogt, A.E. Van. *The World of A (Null)*.

Vonnegut, Kurt. *The Sirens of Titan*. Signed.

Watson, Ian. *The Embedding*.

Wells, H.G. *The Invisible Man*.

Wells, H.G. *The Island of Dr. Moreau*.

Wells, H.G. *The Time Machine*.

Wells, H.G. *The War of the Worlds*.

Wilhelm, Kate. *Where Late the Sweet Birds Sang*.

Williamson, Jack. *The Humanoids*.
Willis, Connie. *Doomsday Book*.
Wolfe, Gene. *The Claw of the Conciliator*.
Wolfe, Gene. *The Shadow of The Torturer*.
Wolfe, Gene. *The Sword of Lictor*.
Wyndham, John. *The Day of the Triffids*.
 Zamayatin, Yevgeny. *We*.
Zebrowski, George. *Brute Orbits*.
Zebrowski, George. *Macrolife*.
Zelazny, Roger. *Lord of Light*.
Zelazny, Roger. *This Immortal*.

Myths and Legends of the Ancient World

This set is not currently available through Easton Press.

Spencer, Lewis. *Myths and Legends of Ancient Egypt.*
Spencer, Lewis. *Myths and Legends of Babylonia & Assyria.*
Rolleston, T.W. *Celtic Myths and Legends.*
Werner, E.T.C. *Myths and legends of China.*
Graves, Robert. *The Greek Myths.* Volume I.
Graves, Robert. *The Greek Myths.* Volume II.
Noble, Margaret E. *Myths and Legends of Hindus and Buddhists.*
Davis, F. Hadland. *Myths and Legends of Japan.*
Guerber, H.A. *Myths of the Norsemen, from the Eddas of Sagas.*
Spencer, Lewis. *Myths and Legends of the North American Indians.*

Nautical Classics

This set is out-of-stock.

Buckley, Jr., William F. *Airborne: A Sentimental Journey.*
Chichester, Francis. *Gipsy Moth Circles the World.*
Hays, David; Daniel Hays. *My Old Man And The Sea: A Father
     and Son Sail Around Cape Horn.*
London, Jack. *The Cruise Of The Snark.*
Lundy, Derek. *Godforsaken Sea.*
Slocum, Joshua. *Sailing Alone Around the World.*

Nautical Library

This collection was discontinued many years ago.

Berlitz, Charles. *The Bermuda Triangle.*

Buckley Jr., William F. *Atlantic High: A Celebration.*

Buckley Jr., William F. *Racing Through Paradise: A Pacific Passage.*

Byrd, Richard E. *Exploring with Byrd: Episodes from an Adventurous Life.*

Caffrey, Kate. *The Mayflower.*

Chichester, Francis. *Gipsy Moth Circles the World.*

Coles, K. Adlard. *Heavy Weather Sailing.*

Conner, Dennis. *Comeback: My race for the America's Cup.*

Cook, Captain James. *The Explorations of Captain James Cook in the Pacific As Told by Selections of Edwards, Philip. The Last Voyages, Cavendish, Hudson, Ralegh, the Original Narratives.*

Fairfax, John. *Britannia.*

Cook, Captain James. *The Explorations of Captain James Cook in the Pacific As Told by Selections of His Own Journals 1768 to 1779.*

Fiennes, Ranulph. *To the Ends of the Earth: The Transglobe Expedition, The First Pole to Pole Circumnavigation of the Globe.*

Flexner, Thomas. *Steamboats Come True: American Inventors in Action.*

Heyerdahl, Thor. *Kon-Tiki: Across the Pacific By Raft.*

Heyerdahl, Thor. *RA Expeditions.*

Hickey, Des; Gus Smith. *Seven Days to Disaster: The Sinking of the Lusitania.*

Jones, Tristan. *The Incredible Voyage: A Personal Odyssey.*

Lansing, Alfred. *Endurance.*

London, Jack. *The Cruise of the Snark.*

Lucie-Smith, Edward. *Outcasts of the Seas: Pirates and Piracy.*

MacIntyre, Donald. *Jutland.*

Mahan, A.T. *The Influence of Sea Power Upon History 1660 to 1783.*

Marcus, Geoffrey. *The Maiden Voyage.*

Mattingly, Garrett. *The Armada.*

McKay, Richard. *Some Famous Sailing Ships and Their Builder Donald McKay.*

McKee, Alexander. *H.M.S. Bounty.*

McKee, Alexander. *How We Found the Mary Rose.*

Morison, Samuel Eliot. *Admiral of the Ocean Sea: A Life of Christopher Columbus.* 2 volumes.

Morison, Samuel Eliot. *The European Discovery of America: The Northern Voyages A.D. 500 to 1600.*

Morison, Samuel Eliot. *The European Discovery of America: The Southern Voyages A. D. 1492 to 1616.*

Morison, Samuel Eliot. *The Journals and Other Documents on the Life and Voyages of Christopher Columbus.*

Morison, Samuel Eliot. *Old Bruin Commodore Matthew C. Perry 1794 to 1858.*

Moscow, Alvin. *Collision Course: The Andrew Doria and the Stockholm.*

Ohrelius, Bengt. *Vasa: The King's Ship.*

Pierre, Berton. *The Arctic Grail: The Quest for the North West Passage and the Noth Pole 1818 to 1909.*

Pidgeon, Harry. *Around the World Single-Handed.*

Pope, Dudley. *Decision at Trafalgar.*

Potter, E.B. *Nimitz.*

Robinson, Bill. *Legendary Yachts.*

Rodgers, William Ledyard. *Greek and Roman Naval Warfare.*

Rodgers, William Ledyard. *Naval Warfare Under Oars: 4th to 16th Centuries.*

Roth, Hal. *After 50,000 Miles.*

Rousmaniere, John. *Fastnet, Force 10.*

Severin, Tim. *The Brendan Voyage.*

Severin, Tim. *The Sinbad Voyage.*

Slocum, Joshua. *Sailing Alone Around the World.*

Tyler, David Budlong. *Steam Conquers the Atlantic.*

Villiers, Alan. *The Way of the Ship.*

Weems, John Edward. *The Fate of the Maine.*

Whipple, A.B.C. *The Challenge.*

Whipple, A.B.C. *Yankee Whalers in the South Seas.*

White, William Chapman. *Tin Can on a Shingle.*

Williams, Neville. *The Sea Dogs: Privateers, Plunder and Piracy
    in the Elizabethan Age.*

Patrick O'Brian's *Master and Commander*

Currently this set isn't in stock at Easton Press.

Blue at the Mizzen.
Clarissa Oakes.
The Commodore.
Desolation Island.
The Far Side of the World.
The Fortune of War.
HMS Surprise.
The Hundred Days.
The Ionian Mission.
The Letter of Marque.
Master and Commander.
The Mauritius Command.
The Nutmeg Consolation.
Post Captain.
The Reverse of the Medal.
The Surgeon's Mate.
The Thirteen Gun Salute.
Treason's Harbour.
The Wine-Dark Sea.
The Yellow Admiral.

Reader's Choice

Easton Press has only a handful of these titles currently in stock.

Anderson, Sherwood. *Winesburg, Ohio.*
Benchley, Peter. *Jaws.*
Bierce, Ambrose. *The Devil's Dictionary.*
Boulle, Pierre. *The Bridge Over the River Kwai.*
Boulle, Pierre. *Planet of the Apes.*
Buchan, John. *The Thirty-Nine Steps.*
Burroughs, Edgar Rice. *At the Earth's Core.*
Camus, Albert. *The Myth of Sisyphus.*
Camus, Albert. *The Plague.*
Capote, Truman. *Breakfast at Tiffany's.*
Carroll, Lewis. *Through the Looking Glass.*
Chesterton, G.K. *The Innocence of Father Brown.*
Christie, Agatha. *And Then There Were None.*
Clavell, James. *King Rat.*
Conrad, Joseph. *The Secret Agent.*
Conrad, Joseph. *Typhoon and Other Stories.*
Cooper, James, Fenimore. *The Spy.*
Costain, Thomas B. *The Silver Chalice.*
Crichton, Michael. *The Great Train Robbery.*
Defoe, Daniel. *Moll Flanders.*
Dostoevsky, Fyodor Mikhailovich. *Notes From Underground.*
Dumas, Alexandre. *The Man in the Iron Mask.*
Du Maurier, Daphne. *Rebecca.*
Eco, Umberto. *The Name of the Rose.*
Epictetus. *The Art of Living.*
Fast, Howard. *Spartacus.*
Forester, E.M. *The African Queen.*
Gibson, Fred. *Old Yeller.*

Goldman, William. *The Princess Bride*.

Haggard, H. Rider. *She*.

Hardy, Thomas. *Far From the Madding Crowd*.

Hersey, John. *Hiroshima*.

Hesse, Hermann. *Siddhartha*.

Hilton, James. *Goodbye, Mr. Chips*.

Hilton, James. *Lost Horizon*.

Hope, Anthony. *The Prisoner of Zenda*.

I Ching.

Jackson, Shirley. *The Lottery*.

Jefferson, Thomas. *Writings of Thomas Jefferson*.

Jones, James. *From Here to Eternity*.

Kazantzakis, Nikos. *Zorba The Greek*.

Keller, Helen. *The Story of My Life*.

Kennedy, John V. *Profiles in Courage*.

Kipling, Rudyard. *Captains Courageous*.

Knowles, John. *A Separate Peace*.

Lawrence, D.H. *Sons and Lovers*.

London, Jack. *White Fang*.

MacDonald, Betty. *The Egg and I*.

Mason, Alfred Edward Woodley. *The Four Feathers*.

Maugham, Somerset. *The Moon and Sixpence*.

Maugham, Somerset. *The Razor's Edge*.

McCulley, Johnston. *The Mark of Zorro*.

Miller, Arthur. *Death of a Salesman*.

Orwell, George. *Homage to Catalonia*.

Ovid. *The Art of Love*.

Paton, Alan. *Cry, The Beloved Country*.

Rand, Ayn. *The Virtue of Selfishness*.

Sabatini, Rafael. *The Black Swan*.

Scott, Sir Walter. *Rob Roy*.

Smith, Betty. *Tree Grows in Brooklyn*.

Stevenson, Robert Louis. *The Black Arrow*.

Stevenson, Robert Louis. *Kidnapped.*
Straub, Peter. *Ghost Story.*
Verne, Jules. *Around the World in 80 Days.*
Verne, Jules. *Journey to the Center of the Earth.*
Verne, Jules. *Mysterious Island.*
Vonnegut, Kurt. *The Man Without a Country.*
Wells, H.G. *The First Men In the Moon.*
Wouk, Herman. *The Caine Mutiny.*
Wilde, Oscar. *The Importance of Being Earnest.*
Wyss, Johann. *The Swiss Family Robinson.*

Roger Tory Peterson Field Guides

This series was discontinued quite a while ago.

Advanced Birding.
Animal Tracks.
Atlantic Coast Fishes.
Atlantic Seashore.
Atlantic Shells.
Atmosphere.
Beetles.
Birds of Britain & Europe.
Birds of the Caribbean.
Birds of Eastern US. Signed.
Birds of Texas.
Birds of the American West.
Coral Reefs.
Eastern Birds' Nests.
Eastern Butterflies.
Eastern Forests.
Eastern Reptiles & Amphibians.
Eastern Trees.
Edible Wild Plants.
Ferns.
Freshwater Fishes.
Geology.
Hawks.
Hummingbirds.
Insects.
Mammals of Britain & Europe.
Mammals of North America.
Medicinal Plants.
Mexican Birds.
Moths.

Mushrooms.
Northeastern Wildflowers.
Northwestern Forests.
Pacific Coast Fishes.
Pacific Shells.
Pacific States Wildflowers.
Rocks & Minerals.
Rocky Mountain Wildflowers.
Southeastern & Caribbean Seashore.
Southwest & Texas Wildflowers.
Southwestern Forests.
Stars and Planets.
Trees & Shrubs.
Venomous Animals & Poisonous Plants.
Warblers.
Western Birds' Nests.
Western Butterflies.
Western Forests.
Western Reptiles & Amphibians.
Western Trees.

Science Classics

This series is no longer available from Easton Press.

Cohen, I. Bernard. *Birth of New Physics.*
Copernicus. *Revolutionibus.*
Darwin, Charles. *Origin of Species.*
Einstein, Albert. *Meaning of Relativity.*
Feynman, Richard. *Six Easy Pieces.*
Galilei, Galileo. *Dialogues Two Sciences.*
Hawking, Stephen. *Brief History of Time.*
Kepler, Johannes. *Epitome of Copernican Astronomy.*
Kuhn, Thomas. *Structure of Scientific Revolution.*
Lavoisier, Antoine Laurent. *Elements of Chemistry.*
Newton, Isaac. *Principia.*
Sagan, Carl. *Cosmos.*
Singh, Simon. *Fermat's Enigma.*
Thomas, Lewis. *Lives of a Cell.*
Watson, James. *Double Helix.*
Weiner, Jonathan. *Beak of the Finch.*

Signed First Editions

Most of these titles are no longer available through Easton Press with a few exceptions primarily of more recent dates.

Abrams, Elliot. *Undue Process.* Signed. First Edition. 1993

Adler, Mortimer J. *Adler's Philosophical Dictionary.* Signed. First Edition. 1995

Adler, Mortimer J. *The Four Dimensions of Philosophy.* Signed. First Edition. 1993

Albright, Madeleine. *Madame Secretary.* Signed. First Edition. 2003

Albright, Madeleine. *Memo to the President Elect.* Signed. First Edition. 2008

Albright, Madeleine. *The Mighty and the Almighty.* Signed. First Edition. 2006

Albright, Madeleine. *Prague Winter.* Signed. First Edition. 2012

Alda, Alan. *Never Have Your Dog Stuffed.* Signed. First Edition. 2005

Alexander, Jane. *Command Performance.* Signed. First Edition. 2000

Ambrose, Stephen E. *Citizen Soldiers.* Signed. First Edition. 1997

Ambrose, Stephen E. *Nixon: Ruin and Recovery.* Signed. First Edition. 1991

Ambrose, Stephen E. *Nothing Like It in the World.* Signed. First Edition. 2000

Angelou, Maya. *Celebrations.* Signed. First Edition. 2006

Archer, Jeffrey. *Kane & Abel.* Signed. First Edition. 2013

Arens, Moshe. *Broken Covenant.* Signed. First Edition. 1995

Arnett, Peter. *Live from the Battle Field.* Signed. First Edition. 1994

Ashcroft, John. *Never Again.* Signed. First Edition. 2007

Ashrawi, Hanan. *This Side of Peace.* Signed. First Edition. 1995

Atkinson, Rick. *The Long Gray Line.* Signed. 1989

Auletta, Ken. *Three Blind Mice.* Signed. First Edition. 1991

Bacall, Lauren. *By Myself and Then Some.* Signed. First Edition. 2005

Baker, James. *The Politics of Diplomacy.* Signed. First Edition. 1995

Baker, James. *Work Hard, Study and Keep Out of Politics.* Signed. First Edition. 2007

Barenboim, Daniel. *A Life in Music.* Signed. First Edition. 1992

Barry, Dave. *Dave Barry's History of the Millenium (So Far).* Signed. First Edition. 2007

Barry, Dave. *I'll Mature When I'm Dead.* Signed. First Edition. 2010

Barry, Dave. *Insane City.* Signed. First Edition. 2013

Belafonte, Harry. *My Song.* Signed. First Edition. 2011

Bennett, William. *The Book of Virtues.* Signed. First Edition. 1993

Bennett, William. *The Moral Compass.* Signed. First Edition. 1995

Bernstein, Carl. *Loyalties.* Signed. First Edition. 1989

Blum, Howard. *Out There.* Signed. First Edition. 1990

Bocelli, Andrea. *The Music of Silence.* Signed. First Edition. 2001

Boorstin, Daniel J. *Cleopatra's Nose.* Signed. First Edition. 1995

Boutros-Ghali, Boutros. *Egypt's Road to Jerusalem.* Signed. First Edition. 1997

Bradbury, Ray. *Bradbury Stories.* Signed. First Edition. 2003

Bradlee, Benjamin C. *A Good Life.* Signed. First Edition. 1995

Bradley, Bill. *America's Choice.* Signed. First Edition. 2006

Bradley, Bill. *The New American Story.* Signed. First Edition. 2007

Bradley, Bill. *Time Present, Time Past: A Memoir.* Signed. First

Edition. 1995

Bradley, James. *Flags of our Fathers.* Signed. First Edition. 2007

Branch, Taylor. *The Clinton Tapes.* Signed. First Edition. 2009

Bremer, L. Paul. *My Year in Iraq.* Signed. First Edition. 2006

Breslin, Jimmy. *I Don't Want to Go to Jail.* Signed. First Edition. 2001

Brinkley, Douglas. *The Wilderness Warrior.* Signed. First Edition. 2009

Brokaw, Tom. *A Long Way From Home.* Signed. First Edition. 2002

Brokaw, Tom. *Boom: Voices of the Sixties Personal Reflections on the '60s and Today.* Signed. First Edition. 2008

Brown, Scott. *Against All Odds.* Signed. First Edition. 2011

Brzezinski, Zbigniew. *The Grand Chessboard.* Signed. First Edition. 1997

Brzezinski, Zbigniew. *Out of Control.* Signed. First Edition. 1993

Buchwald, Art. *I'll Always Have Paris.* Signed. First Edition. 1996

Buchwald, Art. *We'll Laugh Again.* Signed. First Edition. 2002

Buckley Jr., William F. *The Redhunter.* Signed. First Edition. 1999

Buckley Jr., William F. *The Right Word.* Signed. First Edition. 1996

Buckley Jr., William F. *Windfall.* Signed. First Edition. 1992

Burns, James McGregor. *Crosswinds of Freedom.* Signed. First Edition. 1989

Bush, Barbara. *Barbara Bush: Autobiography.* Signed. First Edition. 1994

Bush, Barbara. *Reflections: Life After the White House.* Signed. First Edition. 2003

Bush, President George H.W. *All The Best: Autobiography.* Signed. First Edition. 1999

Bush, President George W. *A Charge to Keep.* Signed. First

Edition. 1999

Bush, Jeb. *Immigration Wars.* Signed. First Edition. 2013

Carlin, George. *Brain Droppings.* Signed. First Edition. 1997

Carter, President Jimmy. *An Hour Before Daylight: Memories of a Rural Boyhood.* Signed. First Edition. 2001

Carter, President Jimmy. *Turning Point.* Signed. First Edition. 1993

Carville, James; Mary Matalin. *All's Fair: Love, War and Running for President.* Signed. First Edition. 1994

Carville, James; Paul Begala. *Take It Back.* Signed. First Edition. 2005

Castaneda, Carlos. *The Art of Dreaming.* Signed. First Edition. 1993

Chancellor, John. *Peril and Promise.* Signed. First Edition. 1990

Cheney, Dick. *In My Time.* Signed. First Edition. 2011

Churchill, Winston S. *Never Give In.* Signed. First Edition. 2003

Collins, Judy. *Over The Rainbow.* Signed. First Edition. 2012

Collins, Judy. *Singing Lessons.* Signed. First Edition. 1998

Cosby, Bill. *Friends of a Feather.* Signed. First Edition. 2003

Cosby, Bill. *It's All Relative.* Signed. First Edition. 2000

Cosby, Bill. *Love and Marriage.* Signed. First Edition. 1989

Cosell, Howard. *What's Wrong with Sports.* Signed. First Edition. 1991

Crawford, Craig; Helen Thomas. *Listen Up, Mr. President.* Signed. First Edition. 2010

Cronkite, Walter. *Around America.* Signed. First Edition. 2001

Curtis, Tony. *American Prince.* Signed. First Edition. 2009

D'Amato, Alfonse. *Power, Pasta and Politics.* Signed. First Edition. 1995

Danforth, John. *Faith and Politics.* Signed. First Edition. 2006

Danforth, John. *Resurrection.* Signed. First Edition. 1994

Dangerfield, Rodney. *It's Not Easy Being Me.* Signed. First Edition. 2004

Daniels, Mitch. *Keeping The Republic.* Signed. First Edition. 2011

David, Kenneth C. *A Nation Rising.* Signed. First Edition. 2010

Davis, Clive. *The Soundtrack of My Life.* Signed. First Edition. 2012

Delay, Tom. *No Retreat, No Surrender.* Signed. First Edition. 2007

Dench, Judi. *And Furthermore.* Signed. First Edition. 2011

Dershowitz, Alan. *Just Revenge.* Signed. First Edition. 1999

Dershowitz, Alan. *Taking The Stand.* Signed. First Edition. 2014

Dillard, Annie. *For the Time Being.* Signed. First Edition. 1999

Doctorow, E.L. *Homer and Langley.* Signed. First Edition. 2009

Dole, Bob. *One Soldier's Story.* Signed. First Edition. 2005

Dole, Bob. *Great Political Wit.* Signed. First Edition. 1998

Dole, Bob. *Great Presidential Wit.* Signed. First Edition. 2001

Douglas, Kirk. *Climbing the Mountain.* Signed. First Edition. 1997

Douglas, Kirk. *I Am Spartacus.* Signed. First Edition. 2012

Dowd, Maureen. *Are Men Necessary?.* Signed. First Edition. 2005

Downs, Hugh. *My America: What My Country Means to Me.* Signed. First Edition. 2002

Dukakis, Olympia. *Ask Me Again Tomorrow.* Signed. First Edition. 2003

Dunaway, Faye. *Looking for Gatsby.* Signed. First Edition. 1995

Ebadi, Shirin. *Iran Awakening.* Signed. First Edition. 2006

Ebert, Roger. *The Great Movies.* Signed. First Edition. 2002

Eden, Barbara; Wendy Leigh. *Jeannie Out of The Bottle.* Signed. First Edition. 2011

Eisenhower, John S.D. *General Ike.* Signed. First Edition. 2003

Fleischer, Ari. *Taking Heat.* Signed. First Edition. 2005

Fonda, Peter. *Don't Tell Dad.* Signed. First Edition. 1998

Ford Jr., Harold. *More Davids Than Goliath.* Signed. First Edition.

2010

Foreman, George. *By George: Autobiography.* Signed. First Edition. 1995

Forstchen, William. *Gettysburg.* Signed. First Edition. 2003

Frankel, Max. *The Times of My Life and My Life With the Times.* Signed. First Edition. 1999

Franks, Tommy. *American Soldier.* Signed. First Edition. 2004

Fraser, Antonia. *The Wives of Henry VIII.* Signed. First Edition. 1992

Friedkin, William. *The Friedkin Connection.* Signed. First Edition. 2013

Friedman, Thomas L. *Hot, Flat And Crowded.* Signed. First Edition. 2008

Friedman, Thomas L.; Michael Mandelbaum *That Used To Be Us.* Signed. First Edition. 2011

Gabaldon, Diana. *Seven Stones to Stand or Fall.* Signed. First Edition.

Galbraith, John Kenneth. *The Economics of Innocent Fraud.* Signed. First Edition. 2004

Galbraith, John Kenneth. *Name Dropping: From FDR On.* Signed. First Edition. 1999

Gergen, David. *Eyewitness to Power.* Signed. First Edition. 2000

Gibson, Bob; Lonnie Wheeler. *Stranger to the Game.* Signed. First Edition. 1994

Gifford, Frank. *The Glory Game.* Signed. First Edition. 2009

Gingrich, Newt. *To Renew America.* Signed. First Edition. 1995

Goodall, Jane. *Reason for Hope.* Signed. First Edition. 1999

Goodwin, Doris Kearns. *The Bully Pulpit.* Signed. First Edition. 2014

Goodwin, Doris Kearns. *Team of Rivals.* Signed. First Edition. 2005

Gould, Stephen Jay. *Bully for Brontosaurus.* Signed. First Edition. 1991

Gould, Stephen. Jay *Lying Stones of Marrakech.* Signed. First Edition. 2000

Gooden, Dwight. *Heat.* Signed. First Edition. 1999

Grodin, Charles. *How I Got to Be Whoever it is I am.* Signed. First Edition. 2009

Hagel, Chuck. *America: Our Next Chapter.* Signed. First Edition. 2008

Hagman, Larry. *Hello Darlin.* Signed. First Edition. 2001

Haig, Alexander. *Inner Circles.* Signed. First Edition. 1992

Halberstam, David. *The Next Century.* Signed. First Edition. 1991

Halberstam, David. *War in a Time of Peace.* Signed. First Edition. 2001

Hawn, Goldie. *A Lotus Grows in the Mud.* Signed. First Edition. 2005

Hayes, Helen. *My Life in Three Acts.* Signed. First Edition. 1990

Herblock: A Cartoonist's Life. Signed. First Edition. 1993

Hersey, John. *Life-Sketches.* Signed. First Edition. 1989

Herzog, Whitey. *You're Missing a Great Game.* Signed. First Edition. 1999

Heston, Charleton. *Beijing Diary.* Signed. First Edition. 1990

Heston, Charleston. *In the Arena.* Signed. First Edition. 1995

Hornung, Paul. *Golden Boy.* Signed. First Edition. 2004

Hotchner, A.E. *Blown Away.* Signed. First Edition. 1990

Huston, Smith. *The World's Religions.* Signed. First Edition. 2009

Hutchison, Kay Bailey. *American Heroines.* Signed. First Edition. 2004

Hutchison, Kay Bailey. *Leading Ladies.* Signed. First Edition. 2007

Jackson, Jermaine. *You Are Not Alone.* Signed. First Edition. 2011

Jeffords, James M. *An Independent Man.* Signed. First Edition. 2003

Jennings, Waylon. *Waylon: Autobiography.* Signed. First Edition. 1996

Johnson, Haynes. *Divided We Fall.* Signed. First Edition. 1994

Jones, George. *George Jones: I Lived to Tell It All.* Signed. First Edition. 1996

Jones, James Earl. *Voices and Silences.* Signed. First Edition. 1993

Jong, Erica. *Fanny.* Signed. First Edition. 2009

Jong, Erica. *Fear of 50.* Signed. First Edition. 1994

Kampelman, Max M. *Entering New Worlds.* Signed. First Edition. 1991

Karpov, Anatoly. *Karpov on Karpov.* Signed. First Edition. 1991

Kasparov, Garry. *How Life Imitates Chess.* Signed. First Edition. 2007

Keillor, Garrison. *Lake Wobegon: Summer 56.* Signed. First Edition. 2001

Keneally, Thomas. *American Scoundrel.* Signed. First Edition. 2002

Kennedy, Edward. *America Back on Track.* Signed. First Edition. 2006

Kennedy, William. *Riding the Yellow Trolley Car.* Signed. First Edition. 1992

Kerrey, Bob. *When I Was a Young Man.* Signed. First Edition. 2002

Kerry, John. *A Call to Service.* Signed. First Edition. 2003

Kerry, John. *The New War.* Signed. First Edition. 1997

King, Alan. *Name-Dropping.* Signed. First Edition. 1996

King, B.B. *Blues All Around Me.* Signed. First Edition. 1996

King, Larry. *Anything Goes! .* Signed. First Edition. 2000

King, Larry. *Future Talk.* Signed. First Edition. 1998

King, Larry. *On the Line.* Signed. First Edition. 1993

King, Larry. *Tell Me More.* Signed. First Edition. 1990

Kluger, Jeff; James Lovell. *Lost Moon.* Signed. First Edition.

1994

Koch, Edward; John Cardinal O'Connor. *His Eminence and Hizzoner.* Signed. First Edition. 1989

Kramer, Stanley. *A Mad, Mad, Mad, Mad World.* Signed. First Edition. 1997

Kuralt, Charles. *Life on the Road.* Signed. First Edition. 1990

Lang, Michael. *The Road to Woodstock.* Signed. First Edition. 2009

Leakey, Richard; Roger Lewin. *Origins Reconsidered.* Signed. First Edition. 1992

Le Carre, John. *A Delicate Truth.* Signed. First Edition. 2013

Lehrer, Jim. *A Bus of My Own.* Signed. First Edition. 1992

Lehrer, Jim. *Special Prisoner.* Signed. First Edition. 2000

Leno, Jay. *Leading With My Chin.* Signed. First Edition. 1996

Lewis, Jerry; James Kaplan. *Dean and Me: A Love Story.* Signed. First Edition. 2005

Lieberman, Joseph; Hadassah Lieberman. *An Amazing Adventure.* Signed. First Edition. 2003

Lieberman, Joe. *In Praise of Public Life.* Signed. First Edition. 2000

Lincoln, W. Bruce. *Red Victory.* Signed. First Edition. 1989

Lott, Trent. *Herding Cats.* Signed. First Edition. 2005

Lupone, Patti. *Patti Lupone: A Memoir.* Signed. First Edition. 2010

Lynn, Loretta. *Still Woman Enough.* Signed. First Edition. 2002

Mackay, Harvey. *Beware the Naked Man Who Offers You His Shirt.* Signed. First Edition. 1990

Mailer, Norman. *The Castle In The Forest.* Signed. First Edition. 2007

Malden, Karl. *When Do I Start?.* Signed. First Edition. 1997

Marsalis, Wynton. *Moving to Higher Ground.* Signed. First Edition. 2004

Maraniss, David. *Barack Obama: The Story.* Signed. First Edition.

2013

Martin, Steve. *The Pleasure of My Company.* Signed. First Edition. 2003

Matthiessen, Peter. *Lost Man's River.* Signed. First Edition. 1997

McCain, John. *Why Courage Matters.* Signed. First Edition. 2004

McCain, John. *Worth Fighting For: A Memoir.* Signed. First Edition. 2002

McChrystal, Stanley. *My Share of The Task.* Signed. First Edition. 2013

McCourt, Frank. *'Tis: A Memoir.* Signed. First Edition. 1999

McKay, Jim. *The Real McKay.* Signed. First Edition. 1998

McNamara, Robert. *In Retrospect: The Tragedy and Lessons of Vietnam.* Signed. First Edition. 1995

Moore, Thomas. *The Re-Enchantment of Everyday Life.* Signed. First Edition. 1996

Moyers, Bill. *Healing and the Mind.* Signed. First Edition. 1993

Naisbitt, John. *Global Paradox.* Signed. First Edition. 1994

Newhart, Bob. *I Shouldn't Even Be Doing This.* Signed. First Edition. 2006

Newman, Paul; A.E. Hotchner. *Shameless Exploitation.* Signed. First Edition. 2003

Noonan, Peggy. *Life, Liberty and the Pursuit of Happiness.* Signed. First Edition. 1994

Oates, Joyce Carol. *My Heart Laid Bare.* Signed. First Edition. 1998

Oates, Joyce Carol. *A Widow's Story.* Signed. First Edition. 2011

Obama, George Hussein. *Homeland.* Signed. First Edition. 2010

O'Connor, Sandra Day. *The Majesty of the Law.* Signed. First Edition. 2003

O'Connor, Sandra Day. *Out of Order.* Signed. First Edition. 2013

O'Neal, Shaquille. *Shaq Uncut.* Signed. First Edition. 2011

O'Neal, Tatum. *A Paper Life.* Signed. First Edition. 2004

O'Neill, Buck. *I Was Right on Time.* Signed. First Edition. 1996

Osgood, Charles. *Funny Letters From Famous People.* Signed. First Edition. 2003

Pataki, George. *Pataki: An Autobiography.* Signed. First Edition. 1998

Pauley, Jane. *Your Life Calling.* Signed. First Edition. 2014

Peck, M. Scott. *Further Along the Road.* Signed. First Edition. 1993

Peck, M. Scott. *In Heaven As on Earth.* Signed. First Edition. 1996

Peres, Shimon. *The New Middle East.* Signed. First Edition. 1994

Philbin, Regis. *How I Got This Way.* Signed. First Edition. 2011

Piazza, Mike. *Long Shot.* Signed. First Edition. 2013

Pickens, T. Boone. *The First Billion is the Hardest.* Signed. First Edition. 2008

Podhoretz, Norman. *Ex-Friends.* Signed. First Edition. 1999

Poitier, Sidney. *Life Beyond Measure.* Signed. First Edition. 2008

Powell, Colin. *It Worked For Me.* Signed. First Edition. 2012

Quayle, Dan; Diane Medved. *The American Family.* Signed. First Edition. 1996

Quayle, Dan. *Worth Fighting For.* Signed. First Edition. 1999

Quinn, Anthony. *One Man Tango.* Signed. First Edition. 1995

Rather, Dan. *The American Dream.* Signed. First Edition. 2001

Rather, Dan. *The Camera Never Blinks.* Signed. First Edition. 1994

Rather, Dan. *Deadlines and Datelines.* Signed. First Edition. 1999

Rather, Dan. *Rather Outspoken.* Signed. First Edition. 2013

Reagan, Nancy. *A Shining City: Ronald Reagan.* Signed. First Edition. 1998

Redstone, Sumner. *A Passion to Win.* Signed. First Edition. 2001

Reich, Robert B. *Locked in the Cabinet.* Signed. First Edition. 1997

Reiner, Carl. *NNNNN.* Signed. First Edition. 2006

Reston, James. *Collision at Home Plate.* Signed. First Edition. 1991

Rice, Condoleezza. *Extraordinary, Ordinary People.* Signed. First Edition. 2011

Rice, Condoleezza. *No Higher Honor.* Signed. First Edition. 2012

Rivers, Joan. *Bouncing Back.* Signed. First Edition. 1997

Roberts, Cokie. *Founding Mothers.* Signed. First Edition. 2004

Roberts, Cokie. *Ladies of Liberty: The Women who Shaped our Nation.* Signed. First Edition. 2008

Rockefeller, David. *Memoirs of David Rockefeller.* Signed. First Edition. 2002

Rogers, Ginger. *Ginger.* Signed. First Edition. 1991

Roker, Al. *Don't Make Me Stop the Car!.* Signed. First Edition. 2000

Rooney, Andrew A. *Not That You Asked.* Signed. First Edition. 1989

Rubio, Marco. *An American Son.* Signed. First Edition. 2012

Rumsfeld, Donald. *Known and Unknown.* Signed. First Edition. 2011

Rushdie, Salman. *The Enchantress Of Florence.* Signed. First Edition. 2008

Russell, Bill. *Red and Me, My Coach, My Life Long Friend.* Signed. First Edition. 2009

Russert, Tim. *Big Russ and Me.* Signed. First Edition. 2004

Russert, Tim. *Wisdom of Our Fathers.* Signed. First Edition. 2006

Sack, Oliver. *Hallucinations.* Signed. First Edition. 2012

Safire, William. *The First Dissident.* Signed. First Edition. 1992

Schieffer, Bob. *This Just In.* Signed. First Edition. 2003

Schlesinger, Arthur M. *A Life in the 20th Century.* Signed. First Edition. 2000

Schonberg, Harold C. *Horowitz: His Life and Music.* Signed. First Edition. 1992

Schorr, Daniel. *Come to Think of It.* Signed. First Edition. 2008

Schwarzenegger, Arnold. *Total Recall.* Signed. First Edition. 2013

Scribner Jr., Charles. *In the Company of Writers: A Life in Publishing.* Signed. First Edition. 1990

Shatner, William. *Get a Life.* Signed. First Edition. 1999

Shepherd, Cybill. *Cybill Disobedience.* Signed. First Edition. 2000

Simon, Paul. P*aul Simon: Autobiography.* Signed. First Edition. 1998

Sinatra, Barbara. *Lady Blue Eyes.* Signed. First Edition. 2010

Smiley, Jane. *A Thousand Acres.* Signed. First Edition. 2008

Smith, Dennis. *A Decade of Hope.* Signed. First Edition. 2011

Smith, Hedrick. *The New Russians.* Signed. First Edition. 1990

Sorensen, Ted. *Counselor: A Life at the Edge of History.* Signed. First Edition. 2008

Sorensen, Theodore C. *Why I Am a Democrat.* Signed. First Edition. 1996

Stahl, Lesley. *Reporting Live.* Signed. First Edition. 1999

Stephanopoulos, George. *All Too Human.* Signed. First Edition. 1999

Stern, Isaac; Chaim Potok. *My First 79 Years.* Signed. First Edition. 1999

Stockett, Kathryn. *The Help.* Signed. First Edition. 2012

Stiller, Jerry. *Married to Laughter.* Signed. First Edition. 2000

Summerall, Pat. *Giants.* Signed. First Edition. 2010

Tan, Amy. *Saving Fish From Drowning.* Signed. First Edition. 2005

Teller, Edward. *Memoirs.* Signed. First Edition. 2001

Tenet, George. *At the Center of the Storm.* Signed. First Edition. 2007

Tharp, Twyla. *Push Come to Shove.* Signed. First Edition. 1992

Theroux, Paul. *The Happy Isles of Oceania.* Signed. First Edition. 1992

Thomas, Clarence. *My Grandfather's Son.* Signed. First Edition. 2007

Thomas, Helen. *Front Row at the White House.* Signed. First Edition. 1999

Thompson, Fred. *Teaching The Pig To Dance.* Signed. First Edition. 2010

Trillin, Calvin. *Messages from My Father.* Signed. First Edition. 1996

Turner, Ted. *Call Me Ted.* Signed. First Edition. 2008

Tutu, Desmond. *No Future Without Forgiveness.* Signed. First Edition. 2009

Tutu, Desmond. *God Has a Dream.* Signed. First Edition. 2004

Updike, John. *Bech At Bay.* Signed. First Edition. 1998

Updike, John. *Licks of Love.* Signed. First Edition. 2000

Updike, John. *Self-Consciousness.* Signed. First Edition. 1989

Vidal, Gore. *The Golden Age.* Signed. First Edition. 2000

Vincent, Fay. *The Only Game in Town.* Signed. First Edition. 2006

Vonnegut, Kurt. *Bagombo Snuff Box.* Signed. First Edition. 1999

Vonnegut, Kurt. *Fates Worse Than Death.* Signed. First Edition. 1991

Vonnegut, Kurt. *Look at the Birdie.* Signed. First Edition. 2011

Vonnegut, Kurt. *Timequake.* Signed. First Edition. 1997

Vonnegut, Kurt. *While Mortals Sleep.* Signed. First Edition. 2010

Wagner, Robert. *Pieces of my Heart: A Life.* Signed. First Edition. 2009

Waite, Terry. *Taken on Trust.* Signed. First Edition. 1993

Walton, Bill. *Back from the Dead.* Signed. First Edition. 2015.

Ward, Geoffrey C. *American Originals.* Signed. First Edition.

1991

Wasserstein, Wendy. *Bachelor Girls.* Signed. First Edition. 1990

Watson, James D. *Avoid Boring People: Lessons from a Life in Science.* Signed. First Edition. 2007

Watson, James D. *Genes, Girls and Gamow, After the Double Helix.* Signed. First Edition. 2002

Weinberger, Caspar. W. *Fighting for Peace.* Signed. First Edition. 1990

Welch, Jack; Suzy Welch. *Winning: The Ultimate Business How-To Book.* Signed. First Edition. 2005

Welch, Raquel. *Beyond The Cleavage.* Signed. First Edition. 2010

West, Jerry. *West By West.* Signed. First Edition. 2011

Whitehead, Colson. *The Underground Railroad.* Signed. 2017

Wiesel, Elie. *Hostage.* Signed. First Edition. 2012

Wiesel, Elie. *The Judges.* Signed. First Edition.

Wiesel, Elie. *Sages and Dreamers.* Signed. First Edition. 1991

Wiesel, Elie. *The Sonderberg Case.* Signed. First Edition. 2010

Weiss, Helga. *Helga's Diary.* Signed. First Edition. 2014

Wilder, Gene. *Kiss Me Like a Stranger* First Edition. 2005

Will, George F. *Leveling Wind.* Signed. First Edition. 1994

Will, George F. *Men at Work.* Signed. First Edition. 1990

Wills, Garry. *Bomb Power.* Signed. First Edition. 2009

Wills, Garry. *Certain Trumpets.* Signed. First Edition. 1994

Wills, Garry. *Under God: Religion and American Politics.* Signed. First Edition. 1990

Wood, Gordon S. *The Idea of America.* Signed. First Edition. 2011

Woodward, Bob. *Maestro.* Signed. First Edition. 2000

Woodward, Bob. *Obama's Wars.* Signed. First Edition. 2010

Young, Andrew. *An Easy Burden.* Signed. First Edition. 1996

Signed First Editions of Science Fiction

Nearly all of these titles are sold out with the exception of a few more recent titles.

Aaron, Shale. *Virtual Death.* Signed. First Edition. 1995

Adams, Douglas. *Mostly Harmless.* Signed. First Edition. 1992

Aldiss, Brian W. *Dracula Unbound.* Signed. First Edition. 1991

Aldiss, Brian W. *Harm.* Signed. First Edition. 2007

Aldiss, Brian W. *Somewhere East of Life.* Signed. First Edition. 1994

Anderson, Kevin J. *Climbing Olympus.* Signed. First Edition. 1994

Anderson, Poul. *The Boat of a Million Years.* Signed. First Edition. 1989

Asaro, Catherine. *Alpha.* Signed. First Edition. 2006

Asaro, Catherine. *Diamond Star.* Signed. First Edition. 2009

Asimov, Isaac. *Prelude To Foundation.* Signed. First Edition. 1988

Attanasio, A.A. *The Last Legends of Earth.* Signed. First Edition. 1989

Attanasio, A.A. *Solis.* Signed. First Edition. 1994

Banks, Iain M. *Matter.* Signed. First Edition. 2008

Barnes, John. *Directive 51.* Signed. First Edition. 2010

Baxter, Stephen. *Emperor.* Signed. First Edition. 2007

Baxter, Stephen. *Evolution.* Signed. First Edition. 2003

Baxter, Stephen. *Silverhair.* Signed. First Edition. 1999

Bear, Greg. *Anvil of Stars.* Signed. First Edition. 1992

Bear, Greg. *Darwin's Radio.* Signed. First Edition. 1999

Bear, Greg. *Dead Lines.* Signed. First Edition. 2004

Bear, Greg. *Foundations and Chaos.* Signed. First Edition. 1998

Bear, Greg. *Mariposa.* Signed. First Edition. 2009

Bear, Greg. *Quantico.* Signed. First Edition. 2006

Bear, Greg. *Queen of Angels.* Signed. First Edition. 1990

Bear, Greg. *Vitals.* Signed. First Edition. 2001

Benford, Gregory. *Beyond Infinity.* Signed. First Edition. 2004

Benford, Gregory. *Cosm.* Signed. First Edition. 1998

Benford, Gregory. *Foundation's Fear.* Signed. First Edition. 1997

Benford, Gregory. *Furious Gulf.* Signed. First Edition. 1994

Benford, Gregory. *The Martian Race.* Signed. First Edition. 1999

Benford, Gregory. *Matter's End.* Signed. First Edition. 1994

Benford, Gregory. *Sailing Bright Eternity.* Signed. First Edition. 1995

Benford, Gregory. *The Sunborn.* Signed. First Edition. 2005

Blaylock, James P. *All the Bells on Earth.* Signed. First Edition. 1995

Blaylock, James P. *The Paper Grail.* Signed. First Edition. 1991

Bova, Ben. *Brothers.* Signed. First Edition. 1996

Bova, Ben; Bill Pogue. *Trikon Deception.* Signed. First Edition. 1992

Bova, Ben. *The Immortality Factor.* Signed. First Edition. 2009

Bova, Ben. *Jupiter.* Signed. First Edition. 2001

Bova, Ben. *Mercury.* Signed. First Edition. 2005

Bova, Ben. *Moonrise.* Signed. First Edition. 1996

Bova, Ben. *Moonwar.* Signed. First Edition. 1998

Bova, Ben. *Return to Mars.* Signed. First Edition. 1999

Bova, Ben. *Saturn.* Signed. First Edition. 2003

Bova, Ben. *Venus.* Signed. First Edition. 2000

Bova, Ben. *Voyagers III: Star Brothers.* Signed. First Edition. 1990

Bradbury, Ray. *From the Dust Returned.* Signed. First Edition. 2001

Bradbury, Ray. *Leviathan 99.* Signed. First Edition. 2007

Bradbury, Ray. *Short Stories.* Signed. First Edition. 2003

Brin, David. *Brightness Reef.* Signed. First Edition. 1995

Brin, David. *Foundation's Triumph.* Signed. First Edition. 1999

Brin, David. *Glory Season.* Signed. First Edition. 1993

Brin, David. *Heaven's Reach.* Signed. First Edition. 1998

Brin, David. *Infinity's Shore.* Signed. First Edition. 1996

Brunner, John. *A Maze of Stars.* Signed. First Edition. 1991

Bujold, Lois McMaster. *Barrayar.* Signed. First Edition. 1991

Bujold, Lois McMaster. *Borders of Infinity.* Signed. First Edition. 1989

Bujold, Lois McMaster. *Cetaganda.* Signed. First Edition. 1996

Bujold, Lois McMaster. *A Civil Campaign.* Signed. First Edition. 1999

Bujold, Lois McMaster. *Diplomatic Immunity.* Signed. First Edition. 2002

Bujold, Lois McMaster. *Komarr.* Signed. First Edition. 1998

Bujold, Lois McMaster. *Mirror Dance.* Signed. First Edition. 1994

Bujold, Lois McMaster. *The Vor Game.* Signed. First Edition. 1990

Camp, L. Sprague de. *The Honorable Barbarian.* Signed. First Edition. 1989

Card, Orson Scott. *Maps in a Mirror.* Signed. First Edition. 1990

Chabon, Michael. *The Yiddish Policemen's Union.* Signed. First Edition. 2007

Cherryh, C.J. *Chernevog.* Signed. First Edition. 1990

Cherryh, C.J. *Cloud's Rider.* Signed. First Edition. 1996

Cherryh, C.J. *Conspirator.* Signed. First Edition. 2009

Cherryh, C.J. *Heavy Time.* Signed. First Edition. 1991

Cherryh, C.J. *Rider at the Gate.* Signed. First Edition. 1995

Cherryh, C.J. *Rusalka.* Signed. First Edition. 1989

Clarke, Arthur C.; Frederik Pohl. *The Last Theorem.* Signed. First Edition. 2008

Crowley, John. *Daemonomania.* Signed. First Edition. 2000

Crowley, John. *Love and Sleep.* Signed. First Edition. 1994

Dann, Jack. *The Memory Cathedral.* Signed. First Edition. 1995

Denton, Bradley. *Buddy Holly is Alive and Well on Ganymede.* Signed. First Edition. 1991

Dickson, Gordon. *Wolf and Iron.* Signed. First Edition. 1989

Dietz, William C. *At Empire's Edge.* Signed. First Edition. 2009

Doctorow, Cory. *Overclocked.* Signed. First Edition. 2007

Drake, David. *When The Tide Rises.* Signed. First Edition. 2008

Effinger, George Alec. *The Exile Kiss.* Signed. First Edition. 1991

Ellison, Harlan. *Angry Candy.* Signed. First Edition. 1988

Flynn, Michael; Larry Niven; Jerry Pournelle. *Fallen Angels.* Signed. First Edition. 1991

Ford, John M. *Growing Up Weightless.* Signed. First Edition. 1993

Forward, Robert L. *Martian Rainbow.* Signed. First Edition. 1991

Foster, Alan Dean. *Call To Arms.* Signed. First Edition. 1991

Foster, Alan Dean. *Dirge.* Signed. First Edition. 2000

Foster, Alan Dean. *The Mocking Program.* Signed. First Edition. 2002

Foster, Alan Dean. *Sagramanda.* Signed. First Edition. 2006

Gardner, James Alan. *Trapped.* Signed. First Edition. 2002

Guin, Ursula K. Le. *A Fisherman of the Island Sea.* Signed. First Edition. 1995

Guin, Ursula K. Le. *Four Ways to Forgiveness.* Signed. First Edition. 1995

Guin, Ursula K. Le. *The Telling.* Signed. First Edition. 2000

Gunn, David. *Death's Head Maximum Offense.* Signed. First Edition. 2008

Gunn, James. *Gift From The Stars.* Signed. First Edition. 2005

Gunn, James. *Millennium Blues.* Signed. First Edition. 2001

Haldeman, Joe W. *The Accidental Time Machine.* Signed. First Edition. 2007

Haldeman, Joe W. *Buying Time.* Signed. First Edition. 1989

Haldeman, Joe W. *Camouflage.* Signed. First Edition. 2004

Haldeman, Joe W. *The Coming.* Signed. First Edition. 2000

Haldeman, Joe W. *The Guardian.* Signed. First Edition. 2002

Haldeman, Joe W. *Old Twentieth.* Signed. First Edition. 2005

Haldeman, Joe W. *Starbound.* Signed. First Edition. 2010

Hamilton, Peter. *The Dreaming Void.* Signed. First Edition. 2008

Hamilton, Peter. *Fallen Dragon.* Signed. First Edition. 2002

Hamilton, Peter. *Judas Unchained.* Signed. First Edition. 2006

Hamilton, Peter. *Pandora's Star.* Signed. First Edition. 2004

Harrison, John M. *Nova Swing.* Signed. First Edition. 2007

Harrison, Harry. *Stars and Stripes Forever.* Signed. First Edition. 1998

Heinlein, Robert A. *Starship Troopers.* Signed. First Edition. 2008

Hendrix, Howard. *Empty Cities of the Full Moon.* Signed. First Edition. 2001

Hogan, James P. *The Anguished Dawn.* Signed. First Edition. 2003

Hogan, James P. *The Legend that was Earth.* Signed. First Edition. 2000

Jablokov, Alexander. *DeepDrive.* Signed. First Edition. 1998

Jeter, K.W. *Blade Runner 2.* Signed. First Edition. 1995

Keyes, J. Gregory. *The Briar King.* Signed. First Edition. 2003

Kress, Nancy. *Beggars In Spain.* Signed. First Edition. 1993

Lee, Gantry. *The Tranquility Wars.* Signed. First Edition. 2000

Lindshold, Jane; Roger Zelazny. *DonnerJack.* Signed. First Edition. 1997

May, Julian. *Jack the Bodiless.* Signed. First Edition. 1991

McAuley, Paul. *White Devils.* Signed. First Edition. 2004

McCaffrey, Anne. *The Chronicles of Pern.* Signed. First Edition. 1994

McCaffrey, Anne. *Dragons Fire.* Signed. First Edition. 2006

McCaffrey, Anne. *Dragonsdawn.* Signed. First Edition. 1988

McCaffrey, Anne. *Dragonseye.* Signed. First Edition. 1997

McCaffrey, Anne. *Nimisha's Ship.* Signed. First Edition. 1999

McCaffrey, Anne. *Pegasus in Flight.* Signed. First Edition. 1990

McCaffrey, Anne. *Pegasus in Space.* Signed. First Edition. 2000

McCaffrey, Anne. *The Skies of Pern.* Signed. First Edition. 2001

McCarthy, Wil. *The Collapsium.* Signed. First Edition. 2000

McDevitt, Jack. *Ancient Shores.* Signed. First Edition. 1996

McDevitt, Jack. *Cauldron.* Signed. First Edition. 2007

McDevitt, Jack. *The Engines of God.* Signed. First Edition. 1994

McDevitt, Jack. *Eternity Road.* Signed. First Edition. 1997

McDevitt, Jack. *Infinity Beach.* Signed. First Edition. 2000

McDevitt, Jack. *Odyssey.* Signed. First Edition. 2006

McDevitt, Jack. *Omega.* Signed. First Edition. 2003

McDevitt, Jack. *Polaris*. Signed. First Edition. 2004

McDevitt, Jack. *Seeker.* Signed. First Edition. 2005

McDevitt, Jack. *Time Travelers Never Die.* Signed. First Edition.
2009

McDonald, Ian. *Evolution's Shore.* Signed. First Edition. 1995

McDonald, Ian. *Terminal Cafe.* Signed. First Edition. 1994

McIntyre, Vonda N. *Starfarers.* Signed. First Edition. 1989

McIntyre, Vonda N. *Transition.* Signed. First Edition. 1990

Metzger, Robert A. *Cusp.* Signed. First Edition. 2005

Mieville, China. *The Scar.* Signed. First Edition. 2002

Mitchell, Syne. *The Changeling Plague.* Signed. First Edition.
2003

Moon, Elizabeth. *Marque and Reprisal.* Signed. First Edition.
2004

Moon, Elizabeth. *Once A Hero.* Signed. First Edition. 1997

Moon, Elizbeth. *Rules of Engagement.* Signed. First Edition.
1998

Moon, Elizabeth. *The Speed of Dark.* Signed. First Edition. 2003

Morgan, Richard. *Broken Angels.* Signed. First Edition. 2004

Morgan, Richard. *Market Forces.* Signed. First Edition. 2005

Morgan, Richard. *Thirteen.* Signed. First Edition. 2007

Morrow, James. *The Philosopher's Apprentice.* Signed. First Edition. 2008

Morrow, James. *Towing Jehovah.* Signed. First Edition. 1994

Mosley, Walter. *Futureland.* Signed. First Edition. 2001

Mosley, Walter. *The Wave.* Signed. First Edition. 2006

Niven, Larry. *Destiny's Road.* Signed. First Edition. 1997

Norton, Andre. *Brother to Shadows.* Signed. First Edition. 1993

Norton, Andre. *Wizard's Worlds.* Signed. First Edition. 1989

Pellegrino, Charles. *Dust.* Signed. First Edition. 1998

Pellegrino, Charles. *Flying to Valhalla.* Signed. First Edition. 1993

Pellegrino, Charles; George Zebrowski. *The Killing Star.* Signed. First Edition. 1995

Pohl, Frederik. *The Day The Martians Came.* Signed. First Edition. 1988

Pohl, Frederik. *The Gateway Trip.* Signed. First Edition. 1990

Pohl, Frederik. *Homegoing.* Signed. First Edition. 1989

Resnick, Mike. *The Outpost.* Signed. First Edition. 2001

Resnick, Mike. *Purgatory.* Signed. First Edition. 1993

Resnick, Mike. *The Return of Santiago.* Signed. First Edition. 2003

Resnick, Mike. *Second Contact.* Signed. First Edition. 1990

Resnick, Mike. *Starship Flagship.* Signed. First Edition. 2009

Resnick, Mike. *Starship Mercenary.* Signed. First Edition. 2007

Resnick, Mike. *Starship Mutiny.* Signed. First Edition. 2005

Resnick, Mike. *Starship Pirate.* Signed. First Edition. 2006

Reynolds, Alastair. *Century Rain.* Signed. First Edition. 2005

Reynolds, Alastair. *The Prefect.* Signed. First Edition. 2008

Reynolds, Alastair. *Pushing Ice.* Signed. First Edition. 2006

Ringo, John. *The Last Centurion.* Signed. First Edition. 2008

Robinson, Jeanne. *Starmind.* Signed. First Edition. 1995

Robinson, Kim Stanley. *Antarctica.* Signed. First Edition. 1998

Robinson, Kim Stanley. *Blue Mars.* Signed. First Edition. 1996

Robinson, Kim Stanley. *Escape from Kathmandu.* Signed. First Edition. 1989

Robinson, Kim Stanley. *Fifty Degrees Below.* Signed. First Edition. 2005

Robinson, Kim Stanley. *Forty Signs of Rain.* Signed. First Edition. 2004

Robinson, Kim Stanley. *Pacific Edge.* Signed. First Edition. 1990

Robinson, Kim Stanley. *Red Mars.* Signed. First Edition. 1993

Robinson, Kim Stanley. *Sixty Days and Counting.* Signed. First Edition. 2007

Robinson, Kim Stanley. *The Years of Rice and Salt.* Signed. First Edition. 2001

Robinson, Spider. *Callahans Con.* Signed. First Edition. 2003

Robinson, Spider. *Callahan's Key.* Signed. First Edition. 2000

Robinson, Spider. *Lifehouse.* Signed. First Edition. 1997

Robinson, Spider; Jeanne Robinson. *Starseed.* Signed. First Edition. 1991

Robinson, Spider. *Very Bad Deaths.* Signed. First Edition. 2004

Robinson, Spider. *Very Hard Choices.* Signed. First Edition. 2008

Sargent, Pamela. *Child of Venus.* Signed. First Edition. 2001

Sargent, Pamela. *Thumbprints.* Signed. First Edition. 2004

Sawyer, Robert J. *Illegal Alien.* Signed. First Edition. 1997

Sawyer, Robert J. *WWW: Wake.* Signed. First Edition. 2009

Sawyer, Robert J. *WWW: Watch.* Signed. First Edition. 2010

Sheffield, Charles. *Aftermath.* Signed. First Edition. 1998

Sheffield, Charles. *Brother to Dragons.* Signed. First Edition. 1992

Sheffield, Charles. *Divergence.* Signed. First Edition. 1991

Sheffield, Charles. *Tomorrow and Tomorrow.* Signed. First

Edition. 1997

Silverberg, Robert. *The Alien Years.* Signed. First Edition. 1998

Silverberg, Robert. *Hot Sky at Midnight.* Signed. First Edition. 1994

Silverberg, Robert. *Kingdoms of Wall.* Signed. First Edition. 1993

Silverberg, Robert. *The Longest Way Home.* Signed. First Edition. 2002

Silverberg, Robert. *Starborne.* Signed. First Edition. 1996

Silverberg, Robert. *The Mountains of Majipoor.* Signed. First Edition. 1995

Silverberg, Robert. *To The Land of The Living.* Signed. First Edition. 1990

Simmons, Dan. *The Crook Factory.* Signed. First Edition. 1999

Simmons, Dan. *The Rise of Endymion.* Signed. First Edition. 1997

Slonczewski, Joan. *Daughter of Elysium.* Signed. First Edition. 1993

Steele, Allen. *Chronospace.* Signed. First Edition. 2001

Steele, Allen. *Coyote.* Signed. First Edition. 2002

Steele, Allen. *Coyote Destiny.* Signed. First Edition. 2010

Steele, Allen. *Coyote Frontier.* Signed. First Edition. 2005

Steele, Allen. *Coyote Rising.* Signed. First Edition. 2004

Steele, Allen. *Galaxy Blues.* Signed. First Edition. 2008

Steele, Allen. *Spindrift.* Signed. First Edition. 2007

Sterling, Bruce. *Distraction.* Signed. First Edition. 1998

Sterling, Bruce. *Heavy Weather.* Signed. First Edition. 1994

Sterling, Bruce. *Holy Fire.* Signed. First Edition. 1996

Stross, Charles. *Glasshouse.* Signed. First Edition. 2006

Stross, Charles. *Halting State.* Signed. First Edition. 2007

Swanwick, Michael. *The Iron Dragon's Daughter.* Signed. First Edition. 1994

Swanwick, Michael. *Stations of The Tide.* Signed. First Edition.

1991

Tepper, Sheri S. *The Companions.* Signed. First Edition. 2003

Tepper, Sheri S. *The Fresco.* Signed. First Edition. 2000

Tepper, Sheri, S. *A Plague of Angels.* Signed. First Edition. 1993

Tepper, Sheri S. *Shadows's End.* Signed. First Edition. 1994

Tepper, Sheri S. *Singer From The Sea.* Signed. First Edition. 1999

Tepper, Sheri S. *Six Moon Dance.* Signed. First Edition. 1998

Traviss, Karen. *City of Pearl.* Signed. First Edition. 2004

Traviss, Karen. *Matriarch.* Signed. First Edition. 2006

Turtledove, Harry. *Counting Up, Counting Down.* Signed. First Edition. 2002

Turtledove, Harry. *Earthgrip.* Signed. First Edition. 1991

Turtledove, Harry. *How Few Remain.* Signed. First Edition. 1997

Turtledove, Harry. *The Man With the Iron Heart.* Signed. First Edition. 2008

Varley, John. *Mammoth.* Signed. First Edition. 2005

Varley, John. *Red Thunder.* Signed. First Edition. 2003

Varley, John. *Steel Beach.* 1992

Vinge, Joan D. *Dreamfall.* Signed. First Edition. 1996

Vinge, Vernor. *A Fire Upon The Deep.* Signed. First Edition. 1992

Vinge, Joan D. *The Summer Queen.* Signed. First Edition. 1991

Watson, Ian. *Mockymen.* Signed. First Edition. 2003

Webber, David. *Empire from the Ashes.* 2003

Williamson, Jack. *Beachhead.* Signed. First Edition. 1992

Williamson, Jack. *Mazeway.* Signed. First Edition. 1990

Williamson, Jack. *The Stonehenge Gate.* Signed. First Edition. 2005

Williamson, Michael Z. *Contact with Chaos.* Signed. First Edition. 2009

Williams, Walter Jon. *Metropolitan.* Signed. First Edition. 1995

Williams, Walter Jon. *The Rift.* Signed. First Edition. 1999

Willis, Connie. *To Say Nothing of the Dog.* Signed. First Edition. 1997

Wilson, F. Paul. *Dydeetown World.* Signed. First Edition. 1989

Wilson, Robert Charles. *Julian Comstock.* Signed. First Edition. 2009

Wolfe, Gene. *Endangered Species.* Signed. First Edition. 1989

Womack, Jack. *Elvissey.* Signed. First Edition. 1993

Zebrowski, George. *Black Pockets.* Signed. First Edition. 2006

Zebrowski, George. *Cave of Stars.* Signed. First Edition. 1999

Zebrowski, George. *Empties.* Signed. First Edition. 2009

Zebrowski, George. *Stranger Suns.* Signed. First Edition. 1991

Zebrowski, George. *Swift Thoughts.* Signed. First Edition. 2002

Zelazny, Roger. *A Night in the Lonesome October.* Signed. First Edition. 1993

Zettel, Sarah. *Kingdom of Cages.* Signed. First Edition. 2001

Zettel, Sarah. *The Quiet Invasion.* Signed. First Edition. 2000

Signed Modern Classics & Misc. Editions

Most of these titles are out-of-stock though quite a few are still available.

Adichie, Chimamanda Ngozi. *Americanah.* Signed.
Albee, Edward. *Who's Afraid of Virginia Woolf?.* Signed.
Albom, Mitch *The Five People You Meet in Heaven* (Part of set). Signed.
Allende, Isabel. *The House of the Spirits.* Signed.
Allsburg, Chris Van. *Jumanji.* Signed.
Allsburg, Chris Van. *The Polar Express.* Signed.
Al-Sharif, Manal. *Daring to Drive.* Signed.
Amis, Martin. *Time's Arrow.* Signed.
Angelou, Maya. *I Know Why the Caged Bird Sings.* Signed.
Atkinson, Rick. *The Liberation Trilogy.* Signed.
Atwood, Margaret. *The Blind Assassin.* Signed.
Auel, Jean M. *Clan of the Cave Bear.* Signed.
Babbitt, Natalie. *Tuck Everlasting.* Signed.
Bacigalupi, Paolo. *The Windup Girl.* Signed.
Barnes, Julian. *The Noise of Time.* Signed.
Barnes, Julian. *The Sense of an Ending.* Signed.
Barry, Dave. *Insane City.* Signed.
Bennett, William J. *America: The Last Best Hope.* Signed. 2 volumes.
Berendt, John. *Midnight in the Garden of Good and Evil.* Signed.
Berger, Thomas. *Little Big Man.* Signed.
Boyle, T. Coraghessan. *World's End.* Signed.
Bradbury, Ray. *Fahrenheit 451.* Signed.
Breyer, Stephen. *Active Liberty.* Signed.
Brooks, David. *The Road to Character.* Signed.
Brown, Rita Mae. *Rubyfruit Jungle.* Signed.
Burke, James Lee. *The Tin Roof Blowdown.* Signed.

Byatt, A.S. *Possession.* Signed.

Carpenter, Scott *For Spacious Skies.* Signed.

Carr, Caleb. *The Alienist.* Signed.

Carter, Jimmy *We Can Have Peace In the Holy Land.* Signed.

Chevalier, Tracy. *Girl With the Pearl Earring.* Signed.

Choi, Susan *A Person of Interest.* Signed.

Cleave, Chris. *Little Bee.* Signed.

Cook, Robin. *Coma.* Signed.

Cooper, Susan *Dark is Rising* (From trilogy). Signed.

Cornwell, Bernard *Sharpe's Tiger* (part of trilogy). Signed.

Crichton, Michael. *The Andromeda Strain.* Signed.

Daniels, Mitch. *Keeping the Republic.* Signed.

Davis, Jim *Garfield's Sunday Finest.* Signed.

Davis, Kenneth. *A Nation Rising.* Signed.

DePaola, Tomie. *Strega Nona.* Signed.

Desai, Kiran. *The Inheritance of Loss.* Signed.

Didion, Joan. *A Book of Common Prayer.* Signed.

Dillard, Annie. *Pilgrim at Tinker Creek.* Signed.

Doctorow, E.L. *Homer & Langley.* Signed.

Doctorow, E.L. *Ragtime.* Signed.

Doyle, Roddy. *Paddy Clarke Ha Ha Ha.* Signed.

Esquivel, Laura. *Like Water for Chocolate.* Signed.

Eugenides, Jeffrey. *Middlesex.* Signed.

Fanagan, Richard. *The Narrow Road to the Deep North.* Signed.

Ford, President Gerald R. *Humor and the Presidency.* Signed.

Ford, Harold *More Davids than Goliaths.* Signed.

Ford, Richard *Independence Day.* Signed.

Fowles, John. *The French Lieutenant's Woman.* Signed.

Franzen, Jonathan. *The Corrections.* Signed.

Frayn, Michael. *Spies.* Signed.

Frazier, Charles. *Cold Mountain.* Signed.

Frazier, Walt *The Game Within the Game.* Signed.

Gabaldon, Diana. *Outlander.* Signed.

Gaiman, Neil. *American Gods.* Signed.

Gaiman, Neil. *The Ocean at the End of the Lane.* Signed.

Gaines, Ernest. J. *A Lesson Before Dying.* Signed.

Gates Jr., Henry Louis. *And Still I Rise: Black America Since MLK.* Signed.

Gingrich, Newt; Jackie Gingrich *The Essential American.* Signed.

Golden, Arthur. *Memoirs of a Geisha.* Signed.

Goodall, Jane *50 Years at Gombe.* Signed.

Grady, James. *Six Days of the Condor.* Signed.

Greenspan, Alan *The Map and The Territory.* Signed.

Gregory, Philippa. *The Other Boleyn Girl.* Signed.

Groom, Winston. *Forrest Gump.* Signed.

Gustafson, Scott *Bedtime Stories.* Signed.

Gustafson, Scott. *Classic Storybook Fables.* Signed.

Halberstam, David. *The Best and the Brightest.* Signed.

Harbach, Chad. *The Art of Fielding.* Signed.

Harding, Paul *Tinkers.* Signed.

Harrer, Heinrich. *Seven Years in Tibet.* Signed.

Harris, Mark. *Bang the Drum Slowly.* Signed.

Hart, Gary. *The Republic of Conscience.* Signed.

Helprin, Mark. *A Winters Tale.* Signed.

Hijuelos, Oscar. *The Mambo Kings Play Songs of Love.* Signed.

Hill, Christopher *Outpost.* Signed.

Hill, Clint *Five Days in November.* Signed.

Hornby, Nick. *High Fidelity.* Signed.

Horowitz, Anthony. *Trigger Mortis.* Signed.

Ingpen, Robert. *A Christmas Carol.* Signed.

Isaacson, Walter *Einstein His Life and Universe.* Signed.

Jakes, John *North and South* (Part of trilogy). Signed.

James, Marlon. *A Brief History of Seven Killings.* Signed.

James, P.D. *Cover Her Face.* Signed.

Jeffords, Jim. *An Independent Man.* Signed.

Jindal, Bobby. *American Will.* Signed.

Johnson, Denis. *Tree of Smoke.* Signed.

Jones, Edward P. *The Known World.* Signed.

Jong, Erica. *Fear of Flying.* Signed.

Kahn, Roger. *The Boys of Summer.* Signed.

Kaku, Michio. *The Future of the Mind.* Signed.

Kean, Thomas H.; Lee H. Hamilton. *Without Precedent.* Signed.

Keillor, Garrison. *Lake Wobegon Days.* Signed.

Keneally, Thomas. *Schindler's List.* Signed.

Kennedy, William. *Ironweed.* Signed.

Kerman, Piper. *Orange is The New Black.* Signed.

Kesey, Ken. *One Flew Over the Cuckoo's Nest.* Signed.

Keyes, Daneil. *Flowers for Algernon.* Signed.

Kinney, Jeff. *Diary of a Wimpy Kid.* Signed.

Kinsella, W.P. *Shoeless Joe.* Signed.

Kline, Christina Baker. *Orphan Train.* Signed.

Knight, Michelle. *Finding Me.* Signed.

Kushner, Tony. *Angels in America.* Signed.

Lahiri, Jhumpa. *Interpreter of Maladies.* Signed.

Lawrence, Jerome. *Inherit the Wind.* Signed.

Lethem, Jonathan. *Motherless Brooklyn.* Signed.

Lowry, Lois. *The Giver.* Signed.

Martel, Yann. *Life of Pi.* Signed.

Mason, Bobblie Ann. *In Country.* Signed.

Matthiessen, Peter. *At Play in the Fields of the Lord.* Signed.

Matthiessen, Peter. *The Snow Leopard.* Signed.

Maupin, Armistead. *Tales of the City.* Signed.

McCourt, Frank. *Angela's Ashes.* Signed.

McCullough, Colleen. *The Thorn Birds.* Signed.

McInerney, Jay. *Bright Lights, Big City.* Signed.

Mehta, Ved. *The Ledge Between the Streams.* Signed.

Mieville, China. *The City & The City.* Signed.

Miller, Arthur. *Death of a Salesman.* Signed.

Mitchell, David. *The Bone Clocks.* Signed.

Mitchell, David *Cloud Atlas.* Signed.

Mitchell, Edgar *The Way of the Explorer.* Signed.

Moody, Rick. *The Ice Storm.* Signed.

Mortimer, John. *Rumpole of the Bailey.* Signed.

Mosley, Walter. *Devil in a Blue Dress.* Signed.

Mukherjee, Siddhartha. *The Emperor of All Maladies.* Signed.

Naipaul, V. S. *A Bend in the River.* Signed.

Nguyen, Viet Thanh. *The Sympathizer.* Signed.

North, Oliver *War Stories.* Signed.

Nye, Bill. *Unstoppable.* Signed.

Palahniuk, Chuck. *Fight Club.* Signed.

Pearce, Donn. *Cool Hand Luke.* Signed.

Pepin, Jacques. *New Complete Techniques.* Signed.

Pinter, Harold. The Homecoming. Signed.

Oates, Joyce Carol. *The Man Without a Shadow.* Signed.

Oates, Joyce Carol. *Them.* Signed.

Obama, George. *Homeland.* Signed.

O'Barr, James. *The Crow.* Signed.

O'Brien, Tim. *Going After Cacciato.* Signed.

O'Connor, Sandra Day; H. Alan Day *Lazy B.* Signed.

Ondaatje, Michael. *The English Patient.* Signed.

Palahniuk, Chuck. *Beautiful You.* Signed.

Palahniuk, Chuck. *Make Something Up.* Signed.

Palahniuk, Chuck. *Survivor.* Signed.

Panetta, Leon. *Worthy Fights.* Signed.

Patchett, Ann *Bel Canto.* Signed.

Paterson, Katherine. *Bridge to Terabithia.* Signed.

Paul, Ron *The School Revolution.* Signed.

Pirsig, Robert. *Zen and the Art of Motorcycle Maintenance.* Signed.

Potok, Chaim. *The Chosen.* Signed.

Price, Richard. *Clockers.* Signed.

Proulx, E. Annie. *The Shipping News.* Signed.

Rather, Dan. *Rather Outspoken.* Signed.

Rawicz, Slavomir. *The Long Walk.* Signed.

Read, Piers Paul. *Alive.* Signed.

Robbins, Tom. *Even Cowgirls Get the Blues.* Signed.

Robinson, Jackie *An Intimate Portrait.* Signed.

Robinson, Marilynne *Housekeeping.* Signed.

Roker, Al. *Storm of the Century.* Signed.

Rooney, Andrew *My 75 Years with the Pittsburgh Steelers and the NFL.* Signed.

Roth, Veronica *Divergent* (Sold as trilogy). Signed.

Russo, Richard. *Empire Falls.* Signed.

Sachar, Louis. *Holes.* Signed.

Sawyer, Robert J. *Flash Forward.* Signed.

Schulberg, Budd. *What Makes Sammy Run.* Signed.

Segal, Erich. *Love Story.* Signed.

Setterfield, Diane. *The Thirteenth Tale.* Signed.

Shaffer, Peter. *Amadeus.* Signed.

Short, Martin *I Must Say.* Signed.

Smiley, Jane. *A Thousand Acres.* Signed.

Smith, Zadie. *White Teeth.* Signed.

Smoot, George. *Wrinkles in Time.* Signed.

Spark, Muriel. *The Prime of Miss Jean Brodie.* Signed.

Spillane, Mickey. *I the Jury.* Signed.

Stillitoe, Alan. *Loneliness of the Long Distance Runner.* Signed.

Styron, William. *The Confessions of Nat Turner.* Signed.

Styron, William. *Sophie's Choice.* Signed.

Tan, Amy. *The Joy Luck Club.* Signed.

Tan, Amy. *The Valley of Amazement.* Signed.

Tartt, Donna. *The Secret History.* Signed.

Terpning, Howard *Tribute to the Plains People.* Signed.

Thompson, Hunter S. *Fear and Loathing in Las Vegas.* Signed.

Toibin, Colm. *Brooklyn.* Signed.

Turow, Scott *One L.* Signed.

Tutu, Desmond; Mpho Tutu *Made for Goodness.* Signed.
Tyler, Anne. *The Accidental Tourist.* Signed.
Updike, John. *Rabbit Run.* Signed.
Uris, Leon. *Exodus.* Signed.
Uris, Leon. *Trinity.* Signed.
Vidal, Gore. *Burr.* Signed.
Vonnegut, Kurt. *Slaughterhouse Five.* Signed.
Walton, Bill. *Back from the Dead.* Signed.
Webb, Charles. *The Graduate.* Signed.
Wiesberger, Lauren. *The Devil Wears Prada.* Signed.
Wells, Rosemary; Iona Opie. *My Very First Mother Goose.*
      Signed.
Welsh, Irvine. *Trainspotting.* Signed.
Whitehead, Colson. *The Underground Railroad.* Signed.
Wilson, Edward O. *The Origins of Creativity.* Signed.
Yunus, Muhammad. *Banker To The Poor.* Signed.
Xingjian, Gao. *Soul Mountain.* Signed.
Zraly, Kevin *Windows on the World Complete Wine Course.*
      Signed.

STAND ALONE AND SMALL SETS

Most of these titles are in stock at the time of printing this book. This list is far from exhaustive of all of Easton Press' past small sets and stand alone titles.

Ailsby, Christopher. *The Third Reich Day by Day.*
Alcoholics Annonymous.
Alcott, Louisa M. *Little Women.*
Alexander Hamilton: A Founding Father's Visionary Genius-and His Fate.
Ambrose, Stephen E. *D-Day.*
Architecture of the Future.
Arnold Palmer: 1929-2016.
Art That Changed the World.
Austen, Jane. *In Her Own Hand.* 3 volumes.
Austen, Jane. *The Novels.* 6 volumes.
Base, Graham. *Animalia.*
Bassham, Gregory. *The Philosophy Book.*
Baum, L. Frank. *The Life and Adventures of Santa Claus.*
Baum, L. Frank. *The Wonderful Wizard of Oz.*
    The Beauty and the Beast: The Story of Belle.
Believe It! Chicago Cubs World Series Champions.
Bergoglio, Jorge Mario. *Pope Francis: Thoughts and Words for the Soul.*
Big Papi: The Legend and Legacy of David Ortiz.
Blehm, Eric. *Legend.*
Bray, Adam; Cole Horton. *Star Wars: The Visual Encyclopedia.*
Brett, Jan. *The Twelve Days of Christmas.*
Brotherton, Theodore. *We the People: The Declaration of Independence & The Constitution of the United States.*
Buchan, John. *The 39 Steps.*
Burdick, Eugene; William J. Lederer. *The Ugly American.*

Burnett, Frances Hodgson. *The Secret Garden Set.*

Carroll, Lewis. *Alice's Adventures in Wonderland.*

Charters of Freedom: Democracy's Founding Documents.

Collins, Father Michael. *Pope Francis: A Photographic Portrait of the People's Pope.*

Commanders: History's Greatest Military Leaders.

The Complete Kurz & Allison Civil War Art Print Portfolio.

Connell, Richard. *The Most Dangerous Game.*

Cooper, James Fenimore. *The Leatherstocking Tales.* 5 volumes.

Copernicus, Nicolaus. *Revolutionibus.*

Croffutt's New Overland Tourist. Illustrated.

Dalrymple, William. *Return of a King: The Battle for Afghanistan, 1839-42.*

David Bowie: His Life on Earth: 1947-2016.

David and NeoClassicism.

The Dead Sea Scrolls.

Derham, William. *Lost Ireland.*

Dickens, Charles. *The Complete Christmas Novels.*

Disney. *Beauty and the Beast: The Story of Belle.*

Disney. *Mickey and Minnie Storybook Collection.*

The Doctors Book of Home Remedies.

Dougherty, Martin J. *King Arthur and The Knights of the Round Table*

Doyle, Arthur Conan. *The Complete Sherlock Holmes.* 3 volumes.

Duncan-Clark, S.J. *Pictorial History of the World War.*

Duyckinck, Evert A. *The War for the Union.*

Eckstut. *The Secret Language of Color.*

Edsel, Robert. *Monuments Men.*

The Enduring Power of To Kill a Mockingbird.

Everett, Susanne. *The History of Slavery: The Illustrated History of the Monstrous Evil.*

Felix, Antonia. *Michelle Obama: A Photographic Journey.*

Fischer, Stefan. *Hieronymus Bosch.*

Fisk, Wilbur. *Hard Marching Every Day.*

Fonstad, K.W. *The Atlas of the Middle-Earth.*

Francis, Pope. *The Joy of the Gospel.*

Freedman, Lew. *Chicago's Big Teams: Great Moments of the Cubs, Bears, White Sox, Blackhawks, and Bulls.*

Garfield, Ken. *Billy Graham: A Life in Pictures.*

Gates, Robert M. *Duty.*

Gene Wilder: 1933-2016.

Goldman, William. *The Princess Bride.*

Golembesky, Michael. *Level Zero Heroes.*

Gray, Thomas R. *The Confessions of Nat Turner.*

Greenberg, Amy S. *A Wicked War.*

Grey, Zane. *The Lone Star Ranger.*

Handel, George Frideric. *Messiah.*

Harry Potter: 20 Years of Magic.

Hawaii at War.

Hawthorne, Nathaniel. *The Blithedale Romance.*

Herbert, Frank. *Dune Chronicles.* 6 volumes.

Hill, Clint. *Five Days in November.*

The Holy Bible.

Holzer, Harold. *The New York Times Complete Civil War 1861 – 1865.*

Hubbard, Ben. *Gladiator: Fighting for Life, Glory and Freedom.*

Hubbard, Elbert. *A Message to Garcia and Thirteen Other Things.*

The Illustrated Book of Genesis.

Jaffe, Deborah. *Victoria: A Celebration of a Queen and Her Glorious Reign.*

Jefferson, Thomas. *The Quotations of Thomas Jefferson.*

John Glenn: A Hero's Life 1921-2016.

Katcher, Phillip. *Flags of the Civil War.*

Kempis, Thomas A. *The Imitation of Christ.*

Kipling, Rudyard. *Just So Stories.*

Knauer, Kelly. *Nelson Mandela: A Hero's Journey.*

Kohli, M.S. *Spies in the Himalayas.*

Lacey, James. *The First Clash.*

Lang, Andrew. *Tales of Troy and Greece.*

Larson, Erik. *Dead Wake.*

Lee, Harper. *Go Set a Watchman.*

Leslie, Frank. *The Soldier in Our Civil War.*

London, Jack. *To Build a Fire.*

Lovecraft, H.P. *The Complete Fiction of H.P. Lovecraft.*

Lovett, Charlie. *The Bookman's Tale.*

Mackin, Elton E. *Suddenly We Didn't Want to Die/Memoirs of a World War I Marine.*

Madden, Thomas. *Crusades: The Illustrated History.*

Marshall, George C.; H.H. Arnold; Ernest J. King. *The War Reports.* 3 volumes.

McNab, Chris. *Native American Warriors: 1500-1890 CE.*

McPherson, James M. *For Cause and Comrades.*

Merriam-Webster's Visual Dictionary.

Michelangelo. *Michelangelo's Notebooks.*

Mosby, John Singleton. *Mosby's War Reminiscences.*

Moser, Barry. The Holy Bible.

Myths and Legends of China.

The New Testament WWII Issue

Northup, Solomon. *Twelve Years a Slave.*

Obama, Michelle. *The World as it Should Be.*

One Nation: America Remembers September 11, 2001.

Owen, Nicholas. *Diana: The People's Princess.*

Potter, Beatrix. The Complete Tales.

Preston, Paul. *The Spanish Civil War.*

Price, Bill, *The History of Chess in Fifty Moves.*

Pyle, Howard. *Howard Pyle's Book of Pirates.*

Reischel, Rob. *Aaron Rodgers: Titletown MVP.*

Reiss, Tom. *The Black Count.*

Rembrandt Family Bible.

Revenson, Jody. *Harry Potter: The Character Vault.*

Rey, Margret & H.A. *Merry Christmas, Curious George.*

Rhys, Jean. *The Wide Sargasso Sea.*

Riis, Jacob. *How the Other Half Lives.*

Roberts, Chris. *Michael Jackson: The King of Pop.*

Robert's Rules of Order.

Schulz, Charles. *Happiness is a Warm Puppy.*

Shirer, William L. *The Rise and Fall of the Third Reich.*

Smith, Graham. *Civil War Weapons.*

Smithsonian Atlas of Space Exploration.

Smithsonian Timelines of History.

Sontag, Sherry; Christopher Drew. *Blind Man's Bluff.*

Stern, Philip Van Doren. *The Greatest Gift.*

Strassler, Robert B. *The Landmark Herodotus. The Landmark Thucydides.* 2 volumes.

Submarines: WWI to the Present.

Sullivan, Robert. *Secrets of the Vatican: Inside the Realm of Awe and Intrigue.*

Super Bowl Gold: 50 Years of the Big Game.

Swarthout, Glendon, *The Shootist.*

This is the Day the Lord Has Made.

Tolkien, J.R.R. *Beren and Luthien.*

Tolkien, J.R.R. *Classics.* 5 volumes.

Tolkien, J.R.R. *History of the Lord of the Rings.* 4 volumes.

Tom Petty: The Ultimate Guide to His Music & Legend.

Tranquillus, C. Sustonius. *The Lives of the First Twelve Caesars.*

Truth, Sojourner. *Narrative of Sojourner Truth.*

Twain, Mark. *Mark Twain's Speeches.*

Van Gogh.

Vietnam Combat Classics. 6 volumes.

The Vietnam War: 50 Years Ago-Two Countries Torn Apart.

Vishniac, Roman. *The Vanished World.*

Walpole, Horace. *The Castle of Otranto.*
War Comes to the U.S.-Dec. 7, 1941: The First 30 Hours.
White, Ryan. *Springstein: Album by Album.*
Wiest, Andrew. *The Boys of '67.*
Winchester, Jim. *Modern Military Aircraft: The Aviation Factfile.*
The Wizard of Oz: 75 Years Along the Yellow Brick Road.
World War II: Dunkirk.
Wright, Nicky *The Classic Era of American Comics.*
Zamperini, Louis; David Rensin. *Devil at My Heels.*

Note to Readers

If you know of an out-of-print Easton Press title that wasn't included in this guide, please let me know for inclusion in the 2nd Edition of *Collector's Guide to Easton Press Books*. Send titles to: info@greengrovepress.com

If you'd like to be notified when the second edition comes out, email info@greengrovepress.com with 'Notify Me' in the subject line.

Note to Booksellers

Do you stock Easton Press titles? If so, get your store listed in the next edition of *Collector's Guide to Easton Press Books: A Compendium.* Just email info@greengrovepress.com with 'How do I get my store listed in the Easton Press guide' in the subject line.

Milton Keynes UK
Ingram Content Group UK Ltd.
UKHW021350020424
440487UK00009B/924